Tne

The Beatitude of Truth

Reflections of a Lifetime

DONALD NICHOLL

Edited by Adrian Hastings

DARTON · LONGMAN + TODD

First published in 1997 by
Darton, Longman and Todd Ltd
1 Spencer Court
140–142 Wandsworth High Street
London SW18 4JJ

Reprinted 1997

ISBN 0–232–52216–2

A catalogue record for this book is available from the British Library

Cover illustration: *The Wandering Scholar*
by Anthony Bolton.

Phototypeset by Intype London Ltd
Printed and bound in Great Britain
by Page Bros, Norwich

For

NADIR DINSHAW

faithful companion

Contents

Acknowledgements

Chapter 1 first appeared in the *University of Leeds Review* for 1988; Chapter 2 in *The Month* (November 1959); Chapter 3 in *Christian* (November 1978); Chapter 4 in the *Year Book of the Ecumenical Institute*, Tantur, Jerusalem, 1981–2; and Chapter 5 in *Katallegete* (Fall 1989). Chapter 6 was published separately as the Inaugural John M. Todd Memorial Lecture, by St Andrew's Press, Wells. Chapter 7 was in *The Life of the Spirit* (March 1951); Chapter 8 in *New Blackfriars* (October 1969). Chapters 9–12 all first appeared in the *Tablet* (19–26 December 1987; 13 June 1992; 3 July 1993; 8 January 1994). Chapter 13 was published by the William James Society, Santa Cruz, California, in 1975. Chapter 14 appeared in *Christian* (Epiphany 1980); Chapter 15 in *Dialogue*, Sri Lanka (December–January 1985–6). Chapter 16 was written as the Foreword to James Stuart's *Abhishiktananda: His Life Told through his Letters*, ISPCK, Delhi, 1989; while Chapter 17 is reprinted from *Shabda Shakti Sangam*, edited by Vandana Mataji, Bangalore, 1995.

Preface

It was when my husband was teaching at the University of California in Santa Cruz in the late 1970s that a group of his students first put forward the idea of collecting some of his articles, talks and broadcasts and producing them in book form. This they did, but unfortunately never managed to get the book published. However, I would like to thank Gildas Hamel, Peter Kirkup and Douglas Burton-Christie for their original initiative and efforts.

More recently, several friends in this country made a similar suggestion and this met with the approval of Professor Adrian Hastings and David Moloney, commissioning editor at Darton, Longman & Todd, who discussed it while preparing Donald's book *Triumphs of the Spirit in Russia* for publication. Adrian generously agreed to edit such a book, adding several more items and omitting some of the earlier ones. *The Beatitude of Truth* is the result. Thanks are due to Barbara Hastings for reading through the proofs.

I am most grateful to David Moloney for the sympathetic understanding he has shown both to Donald and myself during Donald's terminal illness. Above all, I wish to thank Adrian, whose intimate friendship stretches back over 50 years, and Nadir Dinshaw, a more recent friend, to whom this book is dedicated.

DOROTHY NICHOLL

Introduction

It was at Oxford in the autumn term of 1946 that Donald and I first met and fell, almost instantly, in love. Fifty years of friendship have followed. I was a young 17-year-old straight from school, and he a demobbed trooper who had been carried by the fortunes of war across half of Asia. When we first met he had only just become a Catholic, and I was privileged, a few months later, to be his sponsor at his confirmation. Apart from that formal role, exercised one Sunday in Blackfriars Church, I was very much the younger brother, privileged to re-discover the world through the eyes of someone whose knowledge, penetration of vision and breadth of personal experience already seemed exceptional. He lent me his books. He suggested my reading for the long vacation. He read my essays. He took me to stay at his home in Halifax and to walk together across his beloved Yorkshire.

Between then and now, Donald and I have lived in many different places and continents, he in America, I in Africa. At times we must have seemed almost out of touch, but the bond never really loosened: we went on sharing a sense of intellectual and spiritual affinity, and knew that we could count absolutely one upon the other. When in 1985 he retired from the rectorship of the Ecumenical Institute of Tantur, and I returned from Zimbabwe to become professor of theology at Leeds, Yorkshire's oldest university, we could once more meet almost regularly. It was a special joy to be able to arrange for him to preach and lecture in the university and, in particular, to feel the spell of some intensely powerful lectures on religion in Russia which he gave us in November 1992. I commented on them in my diary when the last, on Dostoevsky, had been delivered: 'His lectures have been an amazing spiritual experience and felt as such by staff and students alike. He is now intensely thin and appears almost wholly spiritualised and able in an extraordinary way to speak from within the Russian spiritual and intellectual tradition.' When Donald's illness made it impossible for him to prepare for publication this collection of his writings that he, I and many other people have been wanting for years, it seemed entirely natural that its arrangement should fall to me – some small repayment for all I have learnt from him over the years, and indeed have continued to learn as I put this book together.

Donald was born in Halifax in July 1923 in a very poor home – a 'Pennine village lad', as he sometimes described himself. His parents were loyal Anglicans and the moral soundness of that working-class Yorkshire Anglicanism, neither high nor low but certainly Labour-supporting, remained the ground beneath his feet all his life long. He was a Northerner and proud of it, never quite at ease in southern England. Tall (almost six foot six), athletic, so intellectually gifted that his teachers fought between themselves as to what subject he should specialise in, he seemed endowed with everything nature could offer. The history master won, and Donald sat for and achieved the highest prize the history field could offer a schoolboy – a Bracken-bury scholarship to Balliol College. He went up to Oxford for a single year before entering the army as a private.

The war took him to Asia, to India and then to Ceylon and Hong Kong. These Asian years were enormously formative – more so than he can quite have realised at the time. They set his consciousness firmly within a world context and, while strengthening his Christian identity, turned him into a Catholic. In India it became obvious to him that nothing less made full sense if one was to be a Christian at all, and he already identified himself as a Catholic while there, although he was only received into the Church, at Blackfriars, on returning to Oxford in 1946.

Oxford proved a decisive influence. On the one side was Balliol, with two of the greatest historians as his tutors – Christopher Hill in modern history, Richard Southern in medieval. Immensely seriously as Donald took modern history, his principal expertise lay for the time in the Middle Ages, and Dick Southern became a dear friend and the model for him of all that a historian should be. On the other side was the influence of Blackfriars Priory at a time when its community was at its most lively and stimulating. Richard Kehoe instructed him in his own inimitable way, and Donald always remained grateful and fond of that brilliant, self-effacing scholar who so soon disappeared to keep sheep on a Northumbrian farm. But many others, especially Conrad Pepler, Victor White and Illtyd Evans, became a permanent part of Donald's world, just as the cold library at Blackfriars, with its windows overlooking St Giles, remained one of the places where his mind was formed.

In the summer of 1947 he married Dorothy Tordoff, just a 'Pennine village lass' whom he had known since school-days. She had found her own way to Catholicism. Without Dorothy's sensibly practical support and unfailing love, together with that of their children, Donald could have lacked the homely security which always balanced in his life a certain care-not-for-the-morrow adventurousness.

The following years were ones of an internal struggle over vocation – between medieval historian and interpreter of the intellectual quandaries of the twentieth century. Initially, while paid to be the first, his heart lay in the second as he immersed himself in Europe's postwar spiritual struggle. He visited Germany and France, wrote *Recent Thought in Focus* (1952) – a guide to all the -isms of the mid-twentieth century ('your book about everything', Victor White called it a little mockingly) – and made a number of translations from German, such as Bochenski's *Contemporary European Philosophy* and the *Life of Edith Stein*, who was ever after one of his special saints. In those years Donald became truly a citizen of contemporary Europe. The two volumes of *Selection I* and *Selection II*, which he edited with Cecily Hastings in 1953 and 1954, still provide a wonderful collection of the most stimulating theological and religious writing of that period, in many ways foreshadowing the best of Vatican II – something hardly to be found elsewhere in anything published at the time in Britain.

Donald had been appointed lecturer in British history at Edinburgh University in 1948. Here his friendship with the Dominicans continued, especially in the person of Father Anthony Ross, with whom he helped to establish the historical journal, *The Innes Review*. But in 1953, Donald's professional medieval interests returned to the centre of his life. He moved to the University of Keele in that year, and for the rest of his life Keele and the nearby village of Betley provided an anchorage – a place where he came to feel he belonged. Lord Lindsay,

Keele's first vice-chancellor, had been Donald's Master of Balliol, and the special ethos Lindsay established at Keele, with its stress on an interdisciplinary 'foundation year', was one which appealed to Donald's naturally interdisciplinary temperament. In 1954 he published a new translation of Dante's *De Monarchia* as a help to students unfamiliar with Latin, and he then researched his one major academic work, a life of Archbishop Thurstan of York, published in 1964. Here was Dick Southern's pupil most clearly at work creating a composite picture of a twelfth-century religious culture, appropriately a Yorkshire one.

About the time that *Thurstan* was published, however, Donald decided that he could not spend the rest of his life becoming an ever-more distinguished medievalist. Almost overnight he switched his academic interests to the twentieth century, and to Russia in particular. Just as he had learnt medieval Welsh and Irish in order to feel competent to teach early British history, so now he set himself to learn Russian. His central concern with the history of the spirit remained unchanged and he became, above all, an interpreter of the deep complexities within Russian Orthodox Christianity, something he had always cherished since first encountering Julia de Beausobre's *Flame in the Snow*, an account of St Seraphim of Sarov, in the 1940s. This huge academic shift came as part of Donald's response to the mood of the 1960s. Later in life he would at times describe himself as 'a Sixties person', and it was indeed somewhat characteristic of the 1960s to abandon a well-trod path and launch into a less predictable field of academic expertise. This linked appropriately with his visits to the Santa Cruz campus of the University of California and a growing preoccupation with all the world religions, especially those of Asia. Nowhere was the Sixties spirit more powerful than in California.

After some to-ing and fro-ing between Keele and Santa Cruz, Donald abandoned the former for the latter, to hold through most of the 1970s a chair in history and religious studies and to be, for three years, chairperson of the Santa Cruz religious studies department. He and Dorothy enjoyed in California a second honeymoon period, and these years were some of the most fruitful in his life – the time when his personal understanding of religion and the spirit acquired its mature shape. But here, as almost always, Donald was still more the teacher than the scholar. With the exception of *Thurstan*, all his published writings have been born out of an attempt to help the less scholarly to understand reality. It is for the wider human community that he lived, wrote and taught, rather than for academe – which helps explain the more than 100 articles he published in the *Tablet*. Among his other community services, he became a prison visitor. But at no point was his wider concern more evident than in his delighted participation in the 'Penny University', which met regularly in the Café Pergolesi in Santa Cruz, and was open to anyone who chose to attend. The reading and interpretation of *The Brothers Karamazov* in the Café Pergolesi was without doubt a high point in his life. He describes the experience in Chapter 5. It was at that time too that John Todd asked him to write a book on *Holiness*, published in 1981. By far the best known of his works, it has recently appeared in a new edition.

Donald could well have stayed in California, but his five children (four daughters and one son) had all decided that they preferred to be English. Donald and Dorothy did not wish the Atlantic permanently to separate them from their family. Soon after their return to Britain, however, Donald was offered the rectorship of the Ecumenical Institute of Tantur, Jerusalem, and this became the final stopping-point on his institutional pilgrimage. For four years (1981–5) he was absorbed not only in presiding over an often awkward community and coping with its mixed bag of international scholars but, at a more creative level, in relating to both Arabs and Jews, his neighbours in the Holy Land. He has described some of the Tantur experience in a little-known but moving book, *The Testing of Hearts* (1989).

At Tantur, to his surprise, Donald was asked to 'preach' retreats, and after retiring in 1985 he found himself invited to do so quite often, especially by Anglicans. In a way, this represented the culmination of his personal intellectual trajectory – a teacher of the spirit, able to call upon an extraordinarily rich knowledge of Christianity, both Western and Eastern, as well as of all the other main religions. He wrestled internally with their relationship, always anxious to avoid any sort of paternalism or triumphalism in relation to traditions other than his own, but none the less committed to Jesus and to the Catholic Church which he never regretted entering, much as he disagreed with some of its more autocratic aspects. But his wider teaching was not only given in retreats, as any *Tablet* reader is aware. He commented – often pretty sharply, even unpredictably – upon many issues of society and politics, but he was never a party man, either in secular or ecclesiastical affairs. His commentary upon the predicament of contemporary humanity has been simply that of someone who sees more deeply into things than, at times, seems bearable. The devout, the left-winger and the conservative, could all, on occasion, be angered by his refusal to travel even one step along the road of allowing moral respectability to those who misuse power or affluence in any context.

Donald certainly practised what he preached. There was an unworldliness in all that he did, a complete inability to set about feathering his own nest or promoting himself. Even so, a world-wide network of people have been influenced by him. Of his former writings, only *Holiness* is widely known. Fortunately, Darton, Longman and Todd has just published *Triumphs of the Spirit in Russia*, a book upon which he had been working for years – the culminating achievement of his concern as a historian to make the inwardness of Russia better understood in the West. That, with *The Beatitude of Truth*, *Holiness* and *The Testing of Hearts* constitute, in Donald's own judgement, a satisfactory 'quartet' of his spiritual legacy.

The Beatitude of Truth has been put together as a selection of articles to represent the very best of his thought, while witnessing to his own life's pilgrimage. A few were already written in the 1950s, but most date from the latter years of his life. The book has been divided into three sections, following a sermon preached in the University of Leeds which seems a suitable prelude for all that follows: particularly appropriate both because of its wide sweep and as a message offered to fellow academics in his own homeland of the West Riding. The sermon's title has become the book's title too. It represents precisely what Donald has sought throughout his academic and teaching life: to adhere tenaciously to truth in all its depth and complexity, to share it unceasingly with others and to experience that from the truth, and only from the truth, comes genuine happiness.

Part I consists of a number of longer pieces, mostly lectures, but including a study of Bede to remind us of Donald's earlier years as a medieval historian. Part II is made up of briefer, more wholly personal and even autobiographical, articles. Part III focuses upon a central preoccupation of Donald's later years – an understanding of the relationship of the great religions as positive vehicles for interpreting God and the action of grace. Donald did not believe in a secularly-framed science of comparative religion, nor did he regard all religions as 'the same thing really'. He was a Christian whose life was profoundly committed to the following of Christ within the Catholic Communion. But he saw other religions, and indeed every serious human commitment to truth and goodness, as possible ways to enter into a mystery which can certainly not be confined within the limitations of a traditional Catholic theology, and he greatly welcomed the opening of doors, however cautious, achieved by the second Vatican council. In meeting with believers of other traditions, he was sure that he had much to learn and much to share – and that the last word in any dialogue can never be with us or with them, but always with the truth, love and grace which is in all and above all.

Donald was certainly saddened by any suggestion that inter-faith concerns had weakened his own discipleship of Jesus. He wrote to me in September 1996:

I hope you will make it clear that my belief is that Jesus is, indeed, the Way, the Truth and the Life, everything that is said in John's Gospel but which is so misused by fundamentalists – whether Protestant or Catholic. I believe that the human family will tear itself to pieces unless the whole family learns to love unconditionally, and that the way to do that was opened up by the life, teaching, death and resurrection of Jesus, by the one, final sacrifice for the whole creation. Creatures that we are, we are incapable of such unconditional love. Only God is so capable and so it is only through God's grace mediated by Jesus that we can be saved. But it is part of such grace that Jesus has opened up for us the treasures of other religions and, indeed, the treasures of all Creatures who are longing for unconditional love – to receive it and to give it (Matthew 25 above all).

He spent the months of his illness studying the New Testament with the Greek text before him, and focusing his gaze on a gallery of portraits opposite his bed – Conrad Pepler, Anthony Ross, St Seraphim, Edith Stein, Sri Ramana Maharshi and others – faces of those who had for him come best to represent the ongoing incarnation of the spirit of Jesus within the history of humanity.

Donald died at home in the little upstairs study he called his 'dugout' on 3 May 1997, nine months after being diagnosed as suffering from inoperable cancer. While his strength slowly ebbed away his spirit shone out with an ever purer flame as he focused mind and heart upon the great essentials. The words 'love' and 'friendship' came back on his lips again and again. On the final Sunday of his life he was immensely pleased to see a first copy of *Triumphs of the Spirit in Russia*. Desperately weak as he was, he could still read through the Foreword by Bishop Kallistos and then point out one or two very special pages. One was page 212 with the lovely story of the Russian peasant soldiers in 1914 who explained why they had not shot at the advancing Prussian cavalry: they did not mind firing at a thousand yards because they knew they would hurt no one, but at two hundred yards 'it would have been a great sin'. Another was page 190 and the phrase of Pavel Florensky *proshloe ne proshlo* – the past has not passed away. Only 'the dross' passes, Donald commented. What is of value is eternally preserved.

Finally Donald asked me to bring him from the bookcase on the stairs his *Recent Thought in Focus* published 45 years before and then pointed at the wonderful quotation from Aelred of Rievaulx on friendship in heaven. It was a last testimony for all his friends.

This is the great and wonderful happiness that awaits us in heaven. God has created between himself and his creatures, between the manifold orders and degrees of angelic spirits, between the innumerable types of Saints, an all-embracing friendship, so that each one loves the other as himself. The result is that as each individual rejoices in his own happiness so he finds joy in the happiness of his neighbours; and the beatitude of each individual is the beatitude of all, and the *sum total* of the beatitude of all is enjoyed by *each* individual.

ADRIAN HASTINGS

1

The beatitude of truth

(1987)*

I should like to begin this evening's sermon by sincerely thanking all of you of the Leeds University Christian community for inviting me to preach here, and I wish to thank you also for the hospitality you have shown towards us. You have faithfully fulfilled the injunction of St Paul, 'Remember always to welcome strangers'. And after I leave you this evening I hope you in turn may have reason to recall the words with which the apostle concluded that injunction: 'for by doing this some people have entertained angels without knowing it'.

As your appointed ἄγγελος, your angel or messenger, for this evening, I hope to bring you a message which is especially appropriate for the start of the university year, since I take it that the vocation of a university, even in this barbaric age, is to search for truth; and that members of a university, therefore, are people who have already responded to the call of truth. Yet what we university members are called to is not the same as that which is the primary concern, of, say, technical experts. They are concerned to make a series of true observations which will be useful to mankind in changing the world for man's benefit. But our vocation is towards the very source of all true observations, the truth itself, which we long for not primarily for its use to us but, above all, because we believe it is in the truth that we live, move and have our being. This means that here, at the very beginning of our search, we are confronted with a paradox: since our being depends upon the truth, since we will cease to *be* as human beings if we depart from the truth, it follows that in order to preserve our human being we may have to lose our lives rather than depart from the truth. Being, in truth, is more than life.

That, surely, was the import of Jesus' words to Peter as recorded

*For further information on the source of each chapter, see References on pp. 226–36.

1

by John the Evangelist at the end of his gospel, in an episode which affords us the classic meaning of call, or vocation. Jesus said to Peter:

'I tell you most solemnly,
when you were young
you put on your own belt
and walked where you liked;
but when you grow old
you will stretch out your hands,
and somebody else will put a belt around you
and take you where you would rather not go.'[1]

In these words he indicated the kind of death by which Peter would give glory to God. After this he said, 'Follow me'.

Like Peter, each one of us was called into being by the truth before the foundation of the world. And the end to which we are called is also the truth, because truth is both alpha and omega, the beginning and the end.

Moreover, like Peter, none of us in our beginning, when we first respond to the call, can envisage where we are going to be led – if we *could* see those places to which we shall be led, but where we would rather not go, perhaps our hearts would fail us and we would faint.

Speaking for myself, at least, I have to acknowledge that when in my youth I envisaged the life of the scholar, of the intellectual, which seemed to stretch before me, what I foresaw was very different from the reality that subsequently emerged. In 1940, for instance, the image of the intellectual impressed upon my mind was derived from such well-known figures as a Lytton Strachey or an H. G. Wells. The kind of life they represented was filled with the latest books on every variety of subject and in many different languages, and was conducted almost entirely by way of reading, writing and discussion with like-minded people, often at irregular hours and in rather disordered surroundings. Those physical surroundings and, indeed, one's own bodily condition (so the conceit ran) could be ignored by a genuine intellectual, because such factors have no essential bearing on the workings of one's mind.

By the grace of God, however, in that year 1940, I came across a book entitled *La vie intellectuelle* written by A. D. Sertillanges. It proved to be one of those books that change one's life. Put simply, Sertillanges stated that the vocation of an intellectual embraces every aspect of one's daily life. Nothing one does, at any moment whatsoever of the day or the night, is without consequence in one's search for truth. So as not to betray one's calling, therefore, one's every breath, one's every thought, word and action has to be ordered towards the truth. The consequences of this thesis are not to be realised, of course, by any series of syllogisms, but only by trying to put them into practice over the whole of one's allotted span. It is not the person who speculates but the one who *does* the truth, as the Evangelist says, who comes to the light.

You may imagine how odd these statements appeared to a budding thinker of that period, for whom Strachey and Wells were models. But even more disconcerting was Sertillanges' following statement. He said that an intellectual should spend as much time as possible in the open air. Why on earth did he say that? The answer he gave may also seem odd at first sight: it is that thinking is not simply the function of an isolated human faculty named reason or intellect, but is the work of the whole person, all of whose faculties need to be engaged if the truth is to be known. And that happy state of affairs is best achieved when one spends time in the open air breathing oxygen sufficient to ensure the purity of one's blood. Because the condition of one's blood conditions the quality of one's thinking, or, to quote Wordsworth, the sensations are:

> felt in the blood and felt along the heart
> and passing into the purer mind
> with tranquil restoration.

The significance of what Wordsworth and Sertillanges say is that they make us realise that we are responsible for even the chemistry of our blood. If, for instance, we take into our bodies what is bad for them by eating and drinking foolishly, then our body chemistry deteriorates and our blood becomes jaundiced and bitter, as a consequence of which our thoughts also are likely to become bitter. That sense of joy which gives birth to true thought is impossible if we ourselves are bitter and if we fail to honour these temples of the Holy Spirit which are our bodies. Or, as Jesus tells us,

'The eye is the lamp of the body. It follows that if your eye is sound your whole body will be filled with light. But if your eye is diseased your whole body will be all darkness. If then the light inside you is darkness, what darkness that will be!'

And just as we have to be careful as to what we take into our bodies, likewise we must exercise discrimination over what we allow into our thoughts and our feelings. What we choose to read, for example, or what we consume through the television tube, is never an indifferent or neutral matter; either we shall be edified and recreated by it or else we shall be disedified and trivialised by it. Also, throughout the ages, discerning human beings have always known how deeply we are affected, for example, by the music to which we subject ourselves. Some of you may be familiar with those fateful words of Lenin about Beethoven's music:

I know nothing more beautiful than the *Appassionata*. I could hear it every day. It is marvellous, unearthly music . . . But I cannot listen to music often; it affects my nerves. I want to say amiable stupidities and stroke the head of the people who can create such beauty in a filthy hell. But today is not the time to stroke people's heads; today hands descend to split skulls open, split them open ruthlessly, although opposition to all violence is our ultimate ideal.

And if these words of Lenin provoke in us the wish that he had indeed chosen to listen more to Beethoven and had consequently stroked people's heads instead of splitting their skulls, then let us not be too pharisaical about it. Rather let us bethink ourselves of all the various kinds of noise that we ourselves both emit and receive daily in our noise-filled world, which in their turn also lead, though by less obvious paths, to the splitting of skulls – to say nothing of the hardening of our own hearts.

If I am to attempt to summarise Sertillanges' teaching, then, I would say it is that the moral virtues are of fundamental importance in the search for the truth – more important by far than the possession of a quick brain; for it is only the pure in heart, as Jesus says, who will see the truth. Hence our whole being has to become what our Hindu friends call *ekâgratâ*, or one-pointed, meaning that every available cell of our being has to be directed towards the truth – so much so that we ourselves become transformed, as it were, into signposts pointing beyond ourselves towards what is utterly beyond the power of human vision. The way in which we discipline ourselves to becoming so one-pointed was delightfully illustrated on one occasion by Archbishop Ramsey. When asked how long he spent each day in private prayer he replied, 'One minute. But it takes me half an hour in silence to get to that one minute.'

A precondition for this one-pointedness, this readiness to worship the source of all truth, is a habit of reverence for all creation that is far removed from the mind-set of those who are fashionably thought of as intellectuals.

In this regard I am reminded of an amusing yet revealing incident recounted to me by the late Sir Edmund Whitaker, one of the most distinguished mathematical physicists of an earlier generation and a contemporary of Bertrand Russell. Sir Edmund told me, 'One day, when we were both young fellows of Trinity College, Cambridge, Russell burst into my room in a state of great excitement – I remember he was clutching a tin of corned beef in his hand. He said to me, "Whitaker! I have just discovered a principle which invalidates all previous human reasoning".' After a pause Sir Edmund commented, 'This discovery seemed rather to please than to distress him'.

Such an attitude of irreverence and disrespect as that adopted by Russell towards those who in the past had struggled for truth eventually proves to be self-defeating, because it makes light of one profound and inescapable feature in the human desire to know. I am referring to the vein of sadness and tragedy which runs through all our efforts to know, whether those efforts be directed towards knowing one another, or knowing one's self or knowing God.

I puzzled in vain over this feature of our longing for the truth for many years, until one day when illumination came to me. It came, surprisingly enough, from St Thomas Aquinas' commentary on the beatitude, 'Blessed are those who mourn'. There St Thomas says that this is the special beatitude for those whose calling it is to extend the boundaries of knowledge – for intellectuals, in other words. St Thomas' assertion is, to say the least of it, intriguing, and naturally provokes one to ask why intellectuals are to be classed as those who mourn. The answer Thomas gives is that, whenever our minds yearn towards some new truth, then we become afflicted with pain, because our whole being wishes to protect the balance of inertia and comfort which we have established for ourselves; and the pain is a symptom of our distress at its disturbance. Moreover, we experience a sort of bereavement when those formulations, images and symbols through which we had in the past appropriated truth have now to be abandoned. For those formulations, images and symbols have, over the years, become part of ourselves. To lose them feels like losing part of ourselves. And we mourn that loss as we would mourn the loss of a limb.

Of course not everyone wearing the label of intellectual is capable of such authentic mourning. I am thinking, for example, of a star of the English academic world whom I heard proudly declare, 'I am incapable of sticking to any opinion for more than 20 minutes. After that I just get bored with it.'

But to those for whom thinking is a serious matter and not an excuse for titillation, Thomas Aquinas' commentary serves as a complement to the thesis of Sertillanges. For just as Sertillanges insists that the intellectual vocation demands not simply the exercise of one human faculty but the ordering of one's whole life, so, according to St Thomas, the intellectual life itself, far from being a life of self-indulgence, of wallowing in endless discussion, will necessarily be one of asceticism, of readiness for truth's sake to abandon what one has long held dear and become attached to.

Such readiness is by no means so easy, or so widespread, as the liberal society party-line would have us believe. To acknowledge that you were wrong about some important issue dear to your heart is extremely demanding and, therefore, extremely rare – not so easy or so frequent, strangely enough, as the readiness to confess to sin. Some years ago, for example, I pointed out to a friend of mine that a beautiful section in one of his books hinged upon an assertion of fact which was not correct. He was mortified when he realised that what I said was true, and he promised to alter it in later editions. There have been many subsequent editions of his book – but no alteration. It is not easy to abandon a beautiful piece of one's own writing.

By contrast, think of what nobility of mind was displayed by the late Cardinal Bea, one of the giants of the second Vatican council. For most of his adult life, Bea had been a professor of biblical studies – a very thorough, sound, rather conventional expositor of Scripture.

Then one day he appeared as usual in his regular class and, to the astonishment of his students, began his lecture by saying that he had now come to realise that the principles upon which he had based his scriptural exegesis for nigh on 50 years were misguided, and he would therefore have to begin all over again.

That, it hardly needs saying, took a great deal of doing. But even Bea's action was almost as nothing compared with a further affliction that seems to descend on all of us at some time when we try to answer the call of truth. After all, Bea had only to acknowledge an error which could be put right. But what do you do when you have striven over your whole lifetime to seek the truth, invested all your energies in the search, and then one day you are overwhelmed by the feeling that the very longing to know which has inspired you was an impossible one, and that all your striving has been in vain?

This terrifying experience is common, so it seems, to truth-seekers in all the world religions. Zen Buddhists, for example, name it 'the Great Doubt', that stage which, significantly enough, immediately precedes the breakthrough into *satori*, or enlightenment – though it has to be noted that the connotation of our word 'doubt' gives too negative an impression of the Buddhist meaning, since the state of mind indicated is in no way passive but fiercely positive in its determination to hang on.

Here, in the Western tradition, the very word we use to indicate the crisis we have come to is itself significant. We speak of a *crux* of knowledge – a cross, a crucial moment. And the word is appropriate because crucifixion is the intrinsic form of human knowledge. The trajectory of our search always brings us to a point where – limited, conditioned beings that we are – we are brought face to face with the unconditional. And whereas we can be content to have values such as justice and mercy and gentleness to some degree and on certain conditions, with truth it is not so. The demand of truth is unconditional, absolute. If we dare to face the truth, it strips us of attachment to anything less than itself.

'He was bewildered unto death', is how St Mark describes the Great Doubt that the Son of God experienced in the Garden of Gethsemane when he was brought face to face with the unconditional will of the Father, stripped of every support except truth. And throughout the Christian centuries one hears in thousands of hearts the echo of that agonising cry in the Garden, none more haunting than that terrible sonnet of the poet Gerard Manley Hopkins:

No worst, there is none, Pitched past pitch of grief,
More pangs will, schooled at forepangs, wilder wring.
Comforter, where, where is your comforting?
Mary, mother of us, where is your relief?
My cries heave, herds-long; huddle in a main, a chief
Woe, world-sorrow; on an age-old anvil wince and sing –
Then lull, then leave off. Fury had shrieked 'No ling-
ering! Let me be fell: force I must be brief!'
O the mind, mind has mountains; cliffs of fall
Frightful, sheer, no-man-fathomed. Hold them cheap
May who ne'er hung there. Nor does long our small
Durance deal with that steep or deep. Here! creep,
Wretch, under a comfort serves in a whirlwind: all
Life death does end and each day dies with sleep.

When there is no worst, when rational considerations no longer offer any foothold, the only choice for a human being is either to abandon oneself to despair or else to exercise the virtue of courage, and to hang on.

Courage is not usually high on the list of virtues regarded as indispensable for intellectuals, but surely courage *is* quite indispensable at this crucial point of the Great Doubt. For here we find ourselves on the edge of an abyss by no-man-fathomed, as Hopkins puts it. Here we no longer have anything visible or tangible to sustain us, so our only hope has to be in what no eye has seen nor ear heard nor human mind conceived. And the door to that hope is opened by the exercise of courage, which is itself a form of faithfulness.

Yet if *we* do not abandon truth, we shall discover the truth has not abandoned *us*. On the contrary, it is at precisely this moment that we make the most wonderful discovery of all. We discover that what we had thought of as the story of our search for truth was, in a deeper sense, the story of the truth seeking us out. We see that our longing for truth was not something generated by us but must have been implanted in us from the beginning. The seed of hope had already been secreted in us before ever we answered the call to spend our lives searching for the truth. It was our response that caused the seed to germinate; and that seed comes to fruition in the form of the special beatitude for those who mourn; because now after the Great Doubt, as the gospel says, those who mourn will be comforted.

What sort of conclusion or comfort, then, may an intellectual expect? May he or she, for example legitimately look to be elected a member of the British Academy? Or to be awarded a Nobel Prize? Or to be hired for a salary of £100,000 a year? The answer is that if any of us should look, even out of the corner of our eye, for any such rewards, it is a sign that, in Jesus' words, our eye is not single – and we are not filled with the light. It means, rather, that we are not by nature truth-seekers but merchants, businessmen, members of what the Hindus call the *vaishya* caste. We mistook our *dharma*, which was to have spent our lives as honest traders in the bazaar or market-place.

However, for the truth-seeker whose eye is single, there can only be one legitimate consolation for the mourning that has afflicted him: that is, the gift of truth – ever more truth, ever deeper truth – nothing else. According to the Christian tradition, that gift is not an abstraction but a person, the Holy Spirit, of whom Jesus said, 'I will not leave you comfortless but I will ask the Father to send you Another, who will be with you for ever, the Spirit of truth . . . who dwells with you and is in you . . . and who will guide you into all truth' (Jn 14:16–17, 18, 26).

Consequently the whole aim and the consolation of the Christian life is to acquire the Holy Spirit, the Spirit of truth. This fact about the Christian life is frequently not recognised because whereas, within the economy of the three-personed God, the Son images the Father and the Spirit images the Son, the Holy Spirit remains unimaged by any other person of the Trinity. The Holy Spirit, therefore, as person, remains unmanifested, hidden; for just as the air itself remains invisible to us but acts as the medium through which we see and hear other things, so the Spirit does not reveal to us his own face but shows us always the face of Christ. The Holy Spirit is transparent, pointing not to himself but always to the risen Christ.

The Holy Spirit will not be manifested as person until the restoration of all things, until the final redemption. In that moment his image will be revealed as the whole company of saints taken together, all those who have been deified by the action of the Spirit. But even now, as St Paul tells us in that magnificent eighth chapter of his letter to the Romans, we are aware that all who are moved by the Spirit of God are already the sons and daughters of God, and that through our inarticulate groans and the groans of the whole creation the Spirit himself is pleading for us; and God who searches our inmost being knows what the Spirit means.

It is that same reality to which St Paul is pointing in his letter to the Corinthians when he writes, 'Eye hath not seen, nor ear heard, neither have entered into the heart of man the things which God hath prepared for them that love him. But God hath revealed them unto us by his Spirit, for the Spirit searcheth all things, even the deep things of God' (1 Cor. 2:9–10) – or the depths of God, as we might well translate that marvellously poetic Greek phrase, 'καὶ τὰ βαθη τοῦ θεοῦ' – the very depths of God.

The Spirit, then, fulfils Jesus' promise to lead us into all truth, that great and wonderful promise, as the second letter of Peter describes it: 'ἵνα γευλσθε θείας κοινωνοι φύσεως' – so that you may become partakers of the divine nature (2 Peter 1:4) – sharing in the very life of God, plunging ever deeper into the unfathomable being of God.

And if our immediate reaction to these promises that we may become sharers in the divine nature is a faint-hearted suspicion that such a transformation is impossible, then let us learn otherwise by studying the lives of those who *have* had the courage to believe the promises, the people known as saints. I am thinking, for instance, of the man who, of all known to me from the last 1000 years, I find the most remarkable – the Russian saint Seraphim of Sarov. We have a very detailed, and entirely creditable eye-witness account of how, in November 1831, Seraphim was transfigured by the Holy Spirit in just the same way as Jesus was transfigured on the mountain in the presence of Peter, James and John. And yet even that radiant episode is not what I find most remarkable about St Seraphim.

For the most riveting evidence, from Seraphim's life, of how a human being may actually share in the divine nature comes from the time when he had himself gone through his Great Doubt, that time of trial immediately preceding the breakthrough into the risen life. After that breakthrough it became Seraphim's habit to greet all whom he met with the words, '*Radost moya! Christos voskres!*' 'My joy! Christ is risen!' During this last period of his life, his own breath like a breath of the Holy Spirit, Seraphim's every word, every silence, every gesture, proved to be a source of healing to those who came near to him, whether they were sick in their bodies or distressed in their minds. And when someone asked him why such healings were now so much less frequent than they had been in earlier days he replied, 'It is because we have wandered far from the spacious vision of the early Christians' – and have become insensitive to the touch of the Holy Spirit.

Yet witness to the fact that the Holy Spirit still continues to work even in our own day, as in the days of Jesus and Seraphim, was given to my wife and me only three weeks ago. A Danish man with whom we have recently become friends was describing to us his experience in 1945 as a teenager in the Danish underground. He was captured by the Gestapo, and they tortured him in an effort to extract from him the names and plans of his underground comrades. Unlike almost everyone else in that situation, he did not pretend that he did not know of their names and future plans. 'Yes,' he said. 'I do know them. But you yourself must realise that I cannot tell you.' And so after further threats and torture, he was placed in the death-cell to await execution. Alone in the cell, so he told us, he had no fear, but was filled with such peace that is beyond human understanding – and his cell itself was completely filled with light – the light of the Holy Spirit. For us that was a sign that our friend had indeed received the Holy Spirit, the Consoler, who is promised to those who mourn for the truth's sake.

Let us pray for one another that we, being truth-seekers, may likewise receive that consolation, the gift of the Holy Spirit.

Part I

Part 1

2

St Bede

(1959)

Many saints, from the moment of their conception, are the occasions of pious prophecy and miraculous visions; for the rest of their lives they are the subjects of spectacular graces and astonishing intuitions. Their writings and sayings are organised into systematic guidebooks to the heights of spirituality, and their treasured relics become the means of wonderful cures, dramatic conversions and terrible punishments. None of these things happened to St Bede. No fuss seems to have been made of his birth; even his parents' names are unrecorded. We are not told of his being favoured by visions; nor did he work miracles – though it is, perhaps, typical of him that he should be the beneficiary of one, which he mentions casually, almost shyly.[1] After his death no cult of him swept the country; not until 1899, in fact, some 1200 years afterwards, did the Church officially recognise him and grant him the title of doctor. On the face of it, Bede is not the most promising subject for study in a series on the mystical tradition.

Yet one wonders how many of the older saints are as likely as Bede to make spiritual life intelligible to men of our day, for his is the spirituality of the technician; the man who serves his apprenticeship quietly, steadily and conscientiously mastering the necessary skills and only revealing his consummate achievement in the last decade of his life. Our contemporaries who are rightly sceptical of short-cuts to wisdom and look doubtfully on youthful lyricism might well be reassured as they glance at the titles of Bede's early works: *De arte metrica*, *De orthographia*, *De schematibus et tropis*, etc. Like a craftsman bending over his last, Bede applies himself assiduously to the dry details of learning, to getting his quantities right and mastering his references. With each fresh treatise he perfects the chief tool of his trade, his Latin prose-style, which becomes ever more exact. As he frees his Latin prose from all those superfluities and adornments upon which his contemporaries prided themselves, so when incorporating the work of other men into his own he cuts out all irrelevant material and goes straight to the nerve of the subject. As a result, the story of his spiritual growth does not tell of how a youthful vision had to be clung to despite the dark clouds which came with the realities of experience; on the contrary, the darkness and incomprehension are dispelled with the years, so that the note of youthful joy grows stronger, his mind moves with increasing ease and flexibility, until at the last he can say:

> It is time for me, if it be His will, to return to my Maker, who formed me, when as yet I was not, out of nothing. I have lived long, and my merciful Judge has well disposed my life. The time of my departure is at hand, for my soul desires to see Christ my King in His beauty.[2]

There is an economy in these dying words of Bede that befits the manner of his living. Only a boy of seven when he was entrusted to the monastery of Wearmouth, he spent the next 55 years until the day of his death (24 May 735) either there or in the house at Jarrow. Fifty-five years of monastic duty – the office, manual work and teaching – a routine scarcely ever broken. There was the journey to York. Otherwise he worked away unceasingly at his scientific treatises, his hagiographies, biblical commentaries and the *Historia Ecclesiastica*. It is upon the last of these, quite rightly, that Bede's fame is based, for it is in the proper sense of the term an epoch-making study of history. But one feels that Bede would be pleased if at least one or two of the thousands who read his history would turn sometimes to the 'mystical' aspect of his teaching – to what he himself regarded as of highest importance.

However there is a sense in which it is misguided, and even in a measure an offence to the memory of Bede, to speak of *his* mystical teaching at all. For though he was a teacher he was at every instant conscious of being a Catholic teacher, whose duty it is to come ever closer to the mind of the Catholic Church: whoever wishes to be united to God must first become united with the Church, learn its faith and be imbued with its sacraments.[3] Then when a person, in fear and trembling, assumes the office of teacher and begins to announce

16

Catholic truth to the unlearned, he must above all things avoid giving to that teaching some special interpretation of his own – that would be to ape the pagan oracles.[4] It is, in fact, this habit of sullying the purity of Scripture with human fictions that made heretics so detestable to Bede:[5] for him, heretics are the little foxes referred to in the Song of Songs who destroy the vines, that is, who lacerate the simple minds of faithful Catholics; it is the duty of Catholic teachers to seize them before they can do much damage.[6] His burning zeal for the purity of the Catholic faith accounts for the one outburst of real anger from this usually serene man, on the occasion of his own orthodoxy being called into question by the 'babbler' David.[7] And for the same reason it is most inaccurate to cite him, as frequently happens, as a representative of 'Benedictine spirituality', for there is not the remotest suggestion in his writings that he recognised any schools of spirituality – the very notion would smack to him of conventicles rather than of the Church.[8]

Of course, all Catholic teachers bring out fresh treasures from the inexhaustible stock of Catholic wisdom, according to their own times and their own temperament – but if one is not to confuse the proportions completely and be unfaithful to Bede, one must stress that the main body of his writings consists of a conscientious repetition of basic biblical texts and the standard comments of the Fathers. Rarely does he venture an opinion of his own; his was not a brilliant, original, speculative mind – the theology of the incarnation, for example, or of the Trinity, receives no exciting development at his hands – and his own attitude is frequently only to be inferred from the way he treats his authorities. When one finds, for instance, that he omits from his rendering of Adamnan's *De locis sanctis* the disgusting story of the Jew who threw an icon of Our Lady into the privy, one can infer something about Bede's temperament. His omission of the story is the silence of a fastidious spirit. But such aspects of his temperament are usually to be inferred rather than demonstrated.

Fortunately we do not depend upon inference to realise that it was Bede's close attachment to tradition that led him to the Scriptures as the beginning and end of a Catholic's spiritual life, for he says as much quite plainly. How, he asks, can anyone boast of being a Christian who does not, to the limit of his capacity, devote himself to study of the Scriptures in search of Christ?[9] The very first thing a Christian must do, if he wishes to arrive at contemplation of the divine majesty, is to seek strength from those two breasts of the Church, the Old and the New Testaments.[10] Everything he receives there will be a source to him of peace and charity,[11] for the will of God is our peace and only in sacred Scripture can we be sure at all times of discovering God's will.[12] At the same time let no one imagine that he can arrive at an understanding of the Scriptures if he reads them hastily and negligently – Bede has severe things to say of gifted men who harbour this illusion – the Scriptures must be studied constantly and diligently.[13]

So faithful was Bede to his own advice, so close was he to the Scriptures, that it would be inadequate to speak of him interpreting the world in the light of them; it would even be inadequate to describe the Scriptures as the spectacles through which he saw the world, and nearer to the truth to say that the Scriptures were the eyes with which he beheld it. And if one wishes to glance to see that world for oneself, one can scarcely do better than to look long at the illuminated pages of the Lindisfarne Gospels, the gospels produced by the community at Lindisfarne which Bede himself visited, for which he wrote his life of St Cuthbert and which, in return, inscribed his name in its Book of Life. The words '*In principio erat verbum*', for instance, are *seen* when they appear in the Lindisfarne Gospels to contain depths of meaning which they are not seen to contain when they appear in the clipped, efficient form of modern type, devoid of any penumbra of suggestion. Within the initials one finds trumpet-patterns, whorls, triangles and lozenges, and birds and animals inter-laced, as though foreshadowing the whole wealth of forms and life that was to issue from the Word; and this whole microcosm is highlighted by the interplay of colours used for the illumination . . . green, mauve, yellow, red and pink. In a similar fashion the world revealed by Scripture was for Bede full of many layers of meaning – literal, allegorical and tropological. And just as the purpose of the illumination was to ensure the greatest impact of the words upon the eye and mind of the reader, so the purpose of biblical study, for Bede, was to allow the interior, or mystical, meaning of Scripture to make its full impact upon the heart of the devout reader.

The images used by Bede to characterise the relationship between the literal and the spiritual meanings of Scripture are remarkable:[14] the literal is a veil which has to be drawn aside to reveal the spiritual sense;[15] it is the bark one must strip off to come to the pith;[16] it is the shadow of the allegorical truth.[17] When one translates the literal sense into the spiritual it is like the change of water into wine,[18] like rolling the stone away from our uncomprehending hearts.[19] Or again:

> A honeycomb is wax containing honey; but the honey in the wax is the spiritual sense of the divine words in the letter, which is properly described as a dripping honeycomb. The honeycomb is dripping indeed since it has more honey than its waxen cells can contain; for such is the fecundity of the sacred Scriptures that a verse which is usually written down in one short line would fill many pages if one examined it more closely and tried to bring out how much sweetness of spiritual understanding it contains within.
>
> Let us give an example: the psalmist says, Praise the Lord, Jerusalem. In the literal sense, the psalmist is urging the citizens of that city, in which stands the temple of God, to sing the Lord's praises. In the allegorical sense, Jerusalem, the Church of Christ, is spread throughout the whole world. Tropologically, that is, according to the moral sense, each holy soul is rightly named Jerusalem. Anagogically, that is as signifying the highest things, Jerusalem is the habitation of the heavenly kingdom, which consists of holy angels and men.[20]

From these examples, the danger of Bede's approach is obvious: that just as the wealth of colours and patterns in the illuminated initials of the Lindisfarne Gospels may distract the eye from the words themselves, so Bede's zeal for the spiritual sense may deflect our attention from the literal meaning. Indeed, his references to the literal meaning are almost slighting,[21] and as a result he sometimes denatures an event of scriptural history. The story of Christ raising Jairus' daughter, for instance, he takes as an allegory of the fate of the synagogue, represented by Jairus, the leader of the synagogue; and not once throughout his commentary on this incident does he betray any sense of the time and place of the incident, of the anguish in Jairus' heart, the sickening delay in getting to his home and, finally, the tender solicitude of Christ over the girl, telling her parents to give her food.[22] The personalities of the drama, and the drama itself, melt into the moulds of allegorical types.

This by no means isolated example of Bede's manipulation of the literal sense[23] is the kind of scriptural exegesis which makes modern scholars dismiss his allegorising as a quaint aberration which he shared with his age. But to shrug off such a large proportion of Bede's work in this way is to fail to grasp that, for Bede, the Scriptures are primarily the means of spiritual edification rather than a field for historical expertise. The latter should not be neglected, certainly – but it remains secondary. Convinced that all the Scriptures, even the names and locations of places that occur there, abound with spiritual significance,[24] Bede impressed the names and places, numbers, colours and shapes of Scripture so deeply upon his heart that his heart itself became Holy Land, filled with the spiritual significance of the places and events that occurred there. It has been pointed out that the word 'sacrament' is a favourite word with Bede in this connection, and that for him it means, not 'the outward and visible sign of an inward and spiritual grace', but rather the inner and spiritual meaning of an external fact, or narrative, or name.[25] Consequently Bede traces out upon the hearts of his readers a kind of spiritual geography derived from the geography of the Holy Land: Ephra, Beth-horon and Seboim, for instance – the three vulnerable points of the Israelite position attacked by the three companies of the Philistines – are the concupiscent, wrathful and rational areas of man respectively;[26] again, the building of the temple of Solomon[27] is the external event corresponding to the transformation of the soul into the temple of God, and the four-square stones of the temple, the measurements of it, the kind of wood used for the beams, the decoration with gold and silver, the vestments of gold and violet and purple and scarlet twice-dyed,[28] all this wealth of form, number and colour has its corresponding inner and spiritual meaning. Or, as he puts it in another passage:

If our conscience, once it is purified of its vices, rejoices in having God dwelling there, then it is truly to be called Jerusalem. What are the gates of this Jerusalem except the senses of our body, that is, sight, hearing, taste, smell and touch? . . . These on the sabbath day we are ordered to shut so that we may take our leisure with God, occupying ourselves in psalms and prayers.[29]

But nowhere does the 'wondrous sacramental concord'[30] of nature and history achieved by Bede's allegorical method strike such an immediately authentic note as in that chapter of his *Reckoning of Time* which he devotes to the typical or mystical significance of Easter-time.[31] Coming at the end of a long scientific work of great technical complexity, this chapter fuses the external and internal into one so that we see at a glance what Bede on another occasion described as 'the fair harmony of things'.[32] For the events of Easter-time in the heavens and upon earth bespeak the Easter mysteries enacted once in the Holy Land and re-enacted each year by the Church in her Easter rites. We have the token for entering upon the Easter ritual when the spring equinox assures us that God's Son has opened up for us the paths of light and destroyed the powers of darkness, as the sun itself gains the victory over the shadows of night. This is the first month of the year's cycle, the same month in which the world was created,[33] and in which man was set in paradise; the same month in which man who has strayed from paradise is made anew – for now the Lord makes all things new. Thus the great sacrament of Easter is celebrated at every level of creation – in the mounting power of the sun, reflected by the waxing of the moon, in the renewal of vegetation on the face of the earth, and in the renewal of life within the soul of the faithful, that is, in the Church. This is already a participation in the great Eighth Day of the world, when the souls of the just will enter into that eternal rest won for them by Christ their King, whom they now behold in his beauty.

There we have the climax of humanity's spiritual life envisaged by Bede. Inevitably the question arises, are these heights of mystical perception within the reach of everyone, or only of a few? Certainly Bede held that only a few are capable in this life of penetrating into the secrets of heavenly contemplation, and he issues a warning to those who have not achieved consummate virtue at the human level: they should not presume to meddle in divine things lest they come to harm, falling into heresy, for instance, or into despair.[34] But the context of the warning makes it quite clear that it was to those who wish to know God's particular secrets that his warning applies, and not to those who seek the normal means of perfection. In fact there is not the slightest trace in Bede of spiritual snobbism, of any sugges-tion that there is a special way of spirituality for a few specially gifted people; the categories of fragmented individualism underlying such an assumption are totally foreign to him. So intimately shot together are all members of the Church that it is virtually impossible to say when the virtue of one begins and the virtue of another ends. Each of us is in the same position as a stone in the building of the temple, resting on some and supporting others.[35] Even those who are least polished (are, indeed, rather insensitive and mule-like)[36] have their part in furthering the work of edification and redemption when they humbly and patiently offer their shoulders to bear the burden of fraternal charity.

It is true, of course, that Bede holds to traditional teaching on status, and that the orders of the married, the continent and the virgins are to be placed in an ascending order of dignity.[37] It is also true that there is a select group of people who achieve such perfection in the active life, and the virtues it demands, and that they are granted the grace of divine vision.[38] But of this latter grace, as of what are usually termed 'mystical experiences', Bede has little or nothing to say.[39] And considering the monastic audience he was usually addressing, it is notable how rarely he alludes to the special privileges of the monastic status, whereas he is constantly reminding them of the part which the simple faithful, the laity, have to play in the Church. They are all aware, he remarks, how many people of lay status are leading lives of outstanding virtue while many dedicated from childhood to the religious life are seen to have fallen into sloth. Again, he says, all the faithful are truly priests,[40] and in a heart-warming sermon preached on the Nativity of Our Lord he speaks of how the title of pastor is not confined to bishops, priests and deacons or rulers of monasteries, but is rightly applied to all the faithful who keep watch over their tiny homes.[41] Such a delicate sense of the sanctity of everyday duties was rare among Bede's contemporaries, and rarer still was the ability to express it as he did:

> We must aim, then, by good living to hasten to behold the face of our Creator in such a way that we never in any wise desert our neighbour who is running along with us, but let us take care to appear before the face of the Lord all together with him.[42]

No one, therefore, whatever his status or however limited his talents, need fear that Bede's spiritual teaching is too rarefied for him. Indeed the diffident especially might find in him the ideal teacher. To begin with, he is always ready with a word of encouragement: he assures us, for instance, that we need not despair if, through ignorance and weakness, we fail to achieve the good we aim at, so long as our actions are rooted in goodwill.[43] Similarly with the involuntary thoughts which distract our minds: they are to be treated as a nuisance, like flies that keep on buzzing around one – but we can take comfort from the fact that, though they take the edge off our vision, they do not blind us.[44] We must bear in mind, moreover, as Bede is never tired of reminding us, that growth in the spiritual life is not sudden: it is a slow growth, like that of a young tree;[45] also like a young tree, it is a tender thing, with most of its strength underground in the darkness, hence we must hesitate before revealing our spiritual aspirations lest the tender shoots become corrupted and wither.[46] At the same time we must be sensitive to every touch of grace, and ready to respond at the crucial moments of growth.[47] And it is absolutely essential to root all our spiritual aspirations in *hope*[48] – the unshakeable hope that we shall achieve our desires with the help of God. There is nothing more execrable than lack of hope, for without it our courage in the fight of faith is completely sapped.[49]

The importance that Bede attaches to hope needs to be insisted upon because it explains a feature of his writings that has puzzled, and even shocked, some scholars: the severity with which he condemns Pelagianism. But this is not surprising, even in so tranquil a soul as Bede, when we recognise that Pelagianism, with its teaching that man of his own goodness can do good, drives people to despair. When they find out that unaided they do evil, instead of throwing themselves upon divine grace, they tend to give up hope. Scholars are agreed that the Pelagian controversy was a live one in the England of Bede, but have tended to speak of it as though it affected only the people of learning; Bede's vehemence against Pelagius, and his joy over those of the faithful who were brought back from 'heresy and despair', suggest that it may even have been an immediate pastoral issue. The hope of ordinary people hung upon it.

We have now shown that even the humblest have their role in the common work of building the temple and have seen how dependent each one is upon the other even for doing his own work. It remains to describe the means that the individual must adopt, according to Bede, if he is to be made perfect. It goes without saying that he constantly recalls us to the central Catholic teaching that to be perfect means to love God and one's neighbour – love of one's neighbour coming first in the order of time, and love of God being prior in dignity. It also goes without saying that the traditional teaching on asceticism is repeated over and over again: praying, fasting, vigils, are indispensable aids to spiritual growth. All this is common to the tradition that Bede absorbed so thoroughly, and has to be taken as read. But a striking feature of his teaching which gives it a peculiar nuance – and a very English one at that – is the emphasis he lays upon practical moral behaviour as a means of purification.[50] And among these injunctions of practical morality there are three which recur so persistently in Bede's writings that they give his spiritual teaching a character of its own: these are, the need to control one's tongue, the need for mutual correction among the faithful, and the need to give alms.

Presumably as a result of living for so many years in a monastic community, Bede had come to realise vividly that the tongue is the greatest source of discord in the human community.[51] From the use of the tongue for purposes of detraction almost the whole human race lies in danger;[52] so we should bear detraction patiently and try not to provoke those who malign us[53] because the tongue is a fire, and the abuse of it can burn down the carefully planted woods of virtue – its corrosive effects are to be felt in almost all aspects of human behaviour.[54] We should not, for instance, quickly start talking after a time of prayer, since that is to dissipate the fruits of our devotion,[55] and such promiscuity is destructive of chastity – a virtue of the tongue no less than it is of the body.[56] How strongly Bede felt that the control of the tongue is a *sine qua non* of purity may be sensed not only from the number of occasions when he cites 'idle words' as illustrating aspects of sinful behaviour – and the number is enormous – but also from the fact he even speaks approvingly of a pagan philosophical discipline in this regard. This was the Pythagoreans' practice of making the master's disciples keep silence for five years.

But there is a time to keep silent and a time to speak out, as Bede notes; and the time to speak out is when we see one of our brethren committing sin. For a person who holds his tongue when he sees one of his brethren sinning is no less a sinner than the man who refuses forgiveness to a penitent sinner. In fact, failing to correct and refusing to forgive are but two sides of the same coin, since a person

24

cannot be forgiven until he has been corrected and is penitent. Similarly, forgiveness should not be discriminately accorded, but only when the sinner is ready to do penance.[57] Bede himself, as we have seen, demanded public restitution of his own good Catholic name from his detractor David, nor did he hesitate to demand that his own diocesan bishop, Wilfrid, should join in the restitution since he had tacitly shared in the detraction.[58] Bede's action is totally misunderstood, moreover, unless it is seen as arising from his charity towards the two transgressors, because the duty of correction is not one that he allowed to be undertaken lightly. Above all, we must make sure that we do not undertake it out of hatred – which is so much more deadly than, for instance, anger: anger may be a motive for genuinely wanting to correct a person, but hatred never can be. Again, before pointing out some fault in one of our brethren, we should examine ourselves to discover if we ourselves have never been guilty of the same fault: if we never have, then let us reflect that we also are human, and might have been guilty in that way.[59]

What a magnificent corrector Bede must have been, with his quiet penetration into human self-deceit. Equally penetrating and bold are his observations on the third of the practical issues which we have claimed as characteristic of his teaching, that is, the need for almsgiving. And the boldest of these observations are to be found in his commentary on Nehemias, where the extortion wreaked upon the poor by their governors gives Bede the opportunity to tell the secular and ecclesiastical leaders of his own day some uncomfortable home-truths.[60] Here he is even prepared to abandon his beloved allegorising entirely, and insist that Nehemias' threats against the rich for oppressing the poor are to be taken quite literally: anyone who makes exactions of the poor in their time of distress will be shaken out of the lap of God; even our just claims at such a time must be waived if we ourselves wish our Father to forgive us our debts.[61] Once more he is prepared to insist upon the literal meaning, a little later in the same commentary, when he tells his monastic readers that they must make sure on feast days to put aside some portion of their food to be given to the poor and to pilgrims.[62] For nothing is more apt than generous alms-giving to cure a person of spiritual aridity and sterility.[63] And unless a man stretches out his hand to give to the needy, it is in vain for him to stretch out his hands to God in search of forgiveness of his sins.[64]

This image of the hands stretched forth, giving and forgiving, may well stand in our minds as typical of Bede's spiritual teaching, bringing home to us how all events in this world – even the humble movement of the hands – are charged with intimations of that divine order wherein 'All things are double one against another'.[65] Bede did not have the quick fluency of some other saints in speculating about the secrets of that order, but he did know what contribution to it was demanded of his particular talents. It was, for the most part, a craftsman's contribution of regular attendance upon the everyday moral demands of the work. He knew that his own hands were but a shadow of the divine craftsman's hands – for God is the ultimate craftsman.[66]

3

The Catholic Church and the Nazis

(1975)

I

For an historian it can be one of the strangest experiences to read books by colleagues about some period one has personally lived through, or about some people whom one has known personally. As one reads one's colleague's description of those periods and of those people, one often undergoes the same eerie experience as when gazing into a mirror that is reflecting a scene through a series of distorting and reversing mirrors. One is aware of who or what the mirror is meant to reflect but at the same time realises that no one who sees only this mirror could come anywhere near knowing the original that is being reflected.

For example, after the second world war I met and worked with a number of French Catholics who made their mark on the intellectual and political life of France during those post-war years, and I came to know them reasonably well. So I was interested, one day, in the university library at Santa Cruz, to come across a book about them written by a young scholar. As I began to turn over the pages I grew more and more astonished and angry, because it became ever clearer to me that the young man did not know what he was talking about. It was not that he made mistakes of dating or quotation – on the whole he made few mistakes – it was that he did not even begin to understand the world he was talking about; he had got the whole of it wrong from the very beginning. How it can happen that a person may make no factual errors in writing about the past, while at the same time getting it all wrong, is something of a puzzle and points to some extremely complex and subtle aspects of truth in historical studies.

But there is no doubt that it does happen, as anyone can testify, for instance, who reads descriptions of a world one has known from the pen of someone who never knew that world personally. How many of us, for example, who were members of the working-class world of Northern England during the 1930s recognise the accounts of our everyday life that have been written subsequently by outsiders? Very often there is missing from such accounts an element which used to permeate the *whole* of our existence, so that anyone who ignores that element must inevitably get the *whole* story wrong. The element of humour, for instance. Obviously humour was not the dominant element in that world, which many outsiders can only see as one of unrelieved grimness; but the people actually living in it could not afford to find it unrelievedly grim. After all, that was the only world they had got – and so they had to see the funny side of things. However, for an outsider to point to the funny side of such an existence would seem almost indecent or patronising, yet the picture becomes distorted unless one does so; because although the element of humour was not the dominant one, it was a constant undercurrent which affected the whole. This is what one means by saying of such a picture that it may not contain any errors in details, but at the same time it is all wrong – it is wrong from the beginning.

Yet there is no need to labour the obvious difficulty of convincing someone that a certain description of a world one has known is all wrong, even though one cannot put one's finger on anything incorrect. Because it is plain fact that one cannot put one's finger on a permeating element or an atmosphere. This is perhaps the reason why an historian has to have a 'good nose': it is above all the smell of a particular world which one has to learn to detect, and if one fails to do that then, no matter how correct one's particular observations may be, the whole description is wrong. And more and more of the books on the Churches under Hitler that are appearing nowadays lack precisely this permeating element – for example, Gordon Zahn's books *In Solitary Witness* and *The German Catholics and Hitler's Wars*, or even J. S. Conway's *The Nazi Persecution of the Churches*. The reader who lived through the period may well admire the erudition of these authors, but is bound to reflect that neither of them seems to have known the smell of fear which can transform a superficially comprehensible situation into a nightmare.

Sometimes, of course, a reader has the opposite experience, the recognition beyond a doubt that the author *knows* what he is talking about. I myself had this experience, for instance, when reading Delzell's book about Mussolini's enemies: I had scarcely read more than a few pages before I realised that Delzell knew what he was talking about. So I was not surprised, on turning to the Introduction, to discover that he had fought all the way up Italy with the American forces during the war: the smell of his experience and the world out of which it arose had seeped into the pages of his book.

This fundamental point is worth insisting upon, because there is now a danger that historians, in their obsession with objectivity, will produce a sterilised portrait of, say, Hitler which will slot him conveniently into a series of would-be conquerors, and gradually smooth away the pain and sense of outrage – the brimstone smell – which mention of Hitler produces in those whose lives brought them into contact with the brimstone. Significantly enough, Hitler himself foresaw that if he were victorious then the cruelties of his regime would be smoothed over and treated objectively as by-products of the historical process that are inevitable in the wake of a world-conqueror. He pointed to the way in which historians, while duly deploring Genghis Khan's slaughtering women and children, never-theless spend most of their time admiring the genius of a man who could so bestride the world. With his usual cunning, Hitler had seen the truth of the popular saying, 'The other man's toothache is easily cured', and that historians in particular show professional equanimity in bearing other people's troubles.

But even those historians who usually cultivate a Voltairean sang-froid when dealing with the past are sometimes driven by the force of events to adopt a very different, much more passionate, tone when evoking events in which they were themselves involved. Listen, for instance, to the words that Trevor-Roper uses to describe the death of Himmler:

It was an appropriate death, as appropriate as the barbaric funeral of Hitler and the silent, secondary death of Goebbels; appropriate to his character – for it was squalid and delayed – and appropriate to the functions which he could no longer exercise. The terrible high-priest of Hitler, who had once served the altar, expounded the mysteries and presided over the human sacrifices with such undeviating devotion, having once yielded to doubt, had become a mere wandering shadow, a ghostly sacristan, fitfully haunting the shrine he could no longer tend. Now the god himself had perished; the temple had been utterly destroyed; the faithful had been scattered, or converted, and the suicide of the exiled priest is the natural end of a chapter in history, the history, it seems, of a savage tribe and a primitive superstition.[1]

Though he himself had not been in the thick of the fight, nevertheless, as this passage testifies, Trevor-Roper had been near enough to the brimstone to know the smell.

II

Nor is his imagery inappropriate or exaggerated in the attempt to record the reality of the Hitlerite epoch. At the time, any less apocalyptic idiom seemed totally inadequate as a representation of what had emerged from the depths of history – the 'Beast from the Abyss', as one contemporary entitled his account.[2] Indeed, almost every account written during, or immediately after, the war, seems to contain a reference to the demonic forces at work in Nazi Germany – whether it was Gerhardt Ritter with his *Dämonie des Machtes* or Eduard Hengstenberg with his *Michael gegen Luzifer*. Furthermore, under the impact of their recent experiences, people were beginning to perceive the demonic at work in many spheres of modern life and in past ages. Among biblical scholars, for instance, Heinrich Schlier stressed the part that was played by the forces of darkness in resisting Christ's redeeming work, while in England Rosalind Murray was drawing attention to the way in which St Paul and the early Christians had to wrestle not so much against principalities and powers but with the powers of darkness, with wickedness in high places and with evil spirits. It was, in fact, a phrase from St Paul's letter to the Corinthians which I heard quoted time and again in Germany during my visits there in the years immediately after the second world war – a phrase that has haunted me for 30 years as I have tried to grasp its significance. That phrase was 'the discernment of spirits'.

Time and again I asked Germans the question which, in those days, was on everyone's mind: 'How could such terrible things happen in one of the world's most cultured countries?' And time and again the answer would come back '*Was uns gefehlt hat war die Gabe der Unterscheidung der Geister*' – 'What we lacked was the gift of the discernment of spirits'. Naturally I understood what, in the literal sense, they meant by this phrase: they meant that they had under-estimated the power of evil that had been awakened in Germany by the rise of the National Socialists. But for more than a quarter of a century the phrase has haunted me, and as I turned it over in my mind, I always suspected that there was more to it than the literal sense. Yet the profounder meaning of it only began to emerge for me a quarter of a century later, with an incident in the locker-room of the Sports Center of the Santa Cruz campus. There one day I heard an instructor talking to a student about *Justine* (which I later discovered was a novel by the Marquis de Sade). He was saying that from the novel one could learn that, ' . . . once you can eat shit, then you can do anything'. The instructor, I might say, was commending this process as one of liberation, as if to say, once you have broken through the barrier that divides shit from food then there are no limits to what you can do.

But for me the remark took on a darker meaning and it instantly, if obscurely, associated itself in my mind with a lack of the spirit of discretion, or *discretio spiritum*, as the Vulgate translates that phrase of St Paul in the letter to the Corinthians.[3] Searching for the roots of that obscure association, I turned towards the roots of the word *discretio* and discovered, to my astonishment, that it is derived from the Greek word *skhor* which means 'shit'; so the person who lacks discretion in the deepest sense of the word, is one who does not recognise shit for what it is; who, in the words of the regimental song of the Royal Army Ordnance Corps, 'Can't tell sugar from shit'; who is so devoid of discretion that he will eat shit as if it were sugar.

This was all of a piece with the readiness of the Nazis to use precisely this imagery. So Hitler, for instance, spoke of himself as a magnet whose task it was to draw to himself the steel elements from the shit-heap of the German nation. And I also remembered how frequently the guards in the concentration camps would greet incoming prisoners with the remark that they must stop thinking of themselves as Doctor This or Professor That or Minister So and So because here, ' . . . everyone is just shit. And the sooner you realise that, the better.'[4] Moreover, the guards took special delight in forcing Jews to clear up shit, instinctively realising that Jews, with their tradition of fastidiousness, were particularly vulnerable to this form of humiliation: for a people who live by distinctiveness, by drawing proper lines of demarcation between the clean and the unclean, the failure to distinguish between sugar and shit threatens to plunge them into a world of chaos (*tohu wa bohu*) where each person will lose his identity.

In our day a very similar process of subjugation and humiliation has been put into operation by certain Marxist students in the German universities. They have discovered that, if only they can once get relatively unpolitical students to shout an obscenity at their professor, even as one of a crowd, these same students can then be easily manipulated into revolutionary activity because, as the Marxists explain, they have broken through the *Shambarriere*, the barrier of shame, and are now capable of anything. To the Marxist students, of course, as to the instructor in the Santa Cruz locker-room, the fact that someone is now capable of doing anything is a matter of congratulation; to the Jew who was in the camp, or indeed to anyone with experience of what iniquity people are capable of, it is likely to be a cause of fear and trembling.

III

As I reflected on these parallels, I at last began to see the deeper significance behind the statement of my German informants after the war – that what they had lacked on the eve of Hitler's coming to power was 'the gift for the discernment of spirits', *discretio spiritum*. This became easier to understand one day when a group of my German informants began to speak of how one aspect or other of the Nazi upsurge had momentarily, at least, attracted them: for one it was the stress upon healthy moral values as opposed to rootless cosmopolitanism; for another it was the hope of establishing a community not riddled by class exclusiveness, etc. But one of their number, they said, Carl Josef, had never been taken in by the Nazi promises even for a moment. They remembered how, one day, they had all been discussing what elements in the Nazi upsurge one could take up and incorporate when he, who was normally silent, said, 'You cannot have any truck with such people. You only need to hear their cry, "Germany awake! Perish the Jews". You don't need to know anything more.'

'You don't need to know anything more.' This is the crucial injunction which so many intellectuals ignored, because it is part of the intellectual's professional deformation that he is driven to know more than he needs to know. Years ago the poet Gerard Manley Hopkins expressed the force of the injunction so clearly when he said that we must ' . . . cleave to that which is good and not even give evil a hearing within ourselves'. Such a statement is, of course, a sort of heresy for most intellectuals, who take it as a sign of tolerance to give everything a hearing, no matter how evil it may be, foolishly imagining that no harm can come from just entertaining evil ideas, not realising how ambivalent such entertainment can prove – since it is rarely clear who is Salome and who is Herod. Also their tolerance is based on the illusion that they can separate ideas from action.

In the Middle Ages people had a much better grasp of the evil power of ideas and of their fatal fascination. This they used to show by the way in which they would present the fascination of evil, of the Devil. If you look at the portals of many of their churches you will find sculptured on them, greeting you, as it were, the figure of a beautiful young man. But when you look at the same sculptured figure from the other side you will discover that it is ugly and menacing. It is evil – the beautiful young man turns out to be the Devil. Those medieval artists knew full well the fascination of evil and the urgent need of the capacity to discern spirits – as, indeed, did the mystics who were their contemporaries. The Devil, according to *The Cloud of Unknowing*, has only one nostril, lacking that division which in a human's nose separates one nostril from the other and which symbolises the spiritual insight by which one knows how to distinguish ' . . . the good from the evil, the evil from the worse and the good from the better before he passes judgement on anything that he has heard or seen done around him'.

This passage from *The Cloud* links up, of course, with what we discovered at the beginning – that one of the prime requisites for an historian is to have a good nose. While evil and its menace are still at a distance one is able to smell from afar what is cooking in the cauldron of world history. Otherwise one's fate will be that of one of Hitler's closest advisers, Albert Speer, who later tried to explain how it was that he fell for Hitler; he tells us, 'Hitler had taken hold of me before I had grasped what was happening'.[5] Because he had not been content to cleave to that which is good but had given evil a hearing within himself, Speer woke up too late; by that time, evil had already got its hooks into him. It is to prevent such a thing from happening to us that we need the gift of the discernment of spirits, so that when evil is approaching us we can smell it at a distance and know it for what it is. Or, as Elizabeth Wiskemann expressed it, being taken in by Hitler had ' . . . really nothing to do with belonging to a school of thought, it was a matter of being able to grasp that Hitler's wickedness was possible'.[6]

To take the most obvious and horrifying example: suppose that those Germans whose dislike of Jews was a factor in their voting for Hitler in 1933 could have seen the end-term of their attitude, would they have acted as they did? If in 1933 they could have foreseen that the road they were being tempted to take would inevitably lead, within 12 years, to the destruction of six million of their fellow human beings, would they not have refused to take that first step? Because it has to be remembered that the first step then, as now, was usually of no seeming consequence – just one of those 'small acts of cowardice' with which, according to Dr Hautval, 'all of the terrible things of the world begin'.[7] How noiselessly that first step might be taken is movingly illustrated in Karl Stein's book *The Pillar of Fire* where he describes his homecoming in 1934 from his medical studies in Munich.[8] Alighting at the station of the little Bavarian town which had been his Jewish family home for generations, Stern describes his walk home in the company of his father and how their fellow citizens whom they encountered divided themselves into those who still greeted the Jewish couple with the traditional '*Grüss Gott*', those who no longer did so, and those who, out of a sense of a new-found solidarity with the Jews, had now begun to 'greet'. It is with such small acts of cowardice or courage, greeting or not greeting, that the first step is taken, a step whose consequences can only be foreseen with the spirit of discernment.

IV

It is sometimes forgotten how easy it was in the early days of the Nazi regime to imagine that such acts were of no great significance, since it was thought that the regime would soon pass. For instance, the military attaché of the Soviet embassy in Berlin was maintaining, as late as 30 January 1933, 'that a Hitler regime is out of the question for the foreseeable future'.[9] This judgement was shared by many others because it took a long time for the National Socialists to secure a totalitarian hold upon the country. Churchmen, for example, could be excused for thinking that they had revealed the cracks in the totalitarian façade of Germany when, in October 1934, their opposition secured the dismissal of August Jäger who had been appointed by the Nazis as administrator of the Reich Evangelical Church. The conflict had arisen because of Jäger's attempts to get rid of the Protestant Bishop of Württemberg, Theo Wurm, and his colleague in Bavaria, Bishop Hans Meiser – attempts which led to a storm of protest throughout Bavaria and Württemberg on the part of Protestant congregations and to Jäger's dismissal. It seemed at the time as though a firm stand was sufficient to make the Nazis hesitate.[10]

Again, as late as August 1937, the Protestant Bishop Dibelius was found not guilty by a panel of judges of the charge of having broken the Conspiracy Law – and this although the charge had all the power and prestige of the Gestapo behind it. More remarkable still when the Nazi Minister for Church Affairs, Hans Kerrl, tried to get Dibelius sent to a concentration camp, the Minister of Justice prevented him from doing so.[11] Later, in March 1938, that thorn in Hitler's flesh, Martin Niemöller, was virtually acquitted of the major accusations against him which had led to his arrest at Hitler's personal order.[12] It is true that Niemöller was immediately arrested as he came out of the courthouse – nevertheless these incidents show that the National Socialists did not have anything like such a firm grip upon Germany as, say, Stalin had upon Russia at the same period. And they help us to understand how easy it was for those who did not wish to face up to the essentially evil nature of the regime to take refuge in the illusion that it would soon pass. Even many Jews – those who had most reason to gaze at the movement with the utmost clarity – did not take its proper measure. The great Jewish exodus from Germany did not get under way until late in 1938; and even later than that there were some who still imagined that they would soon be returning.[13]

But our intention here is not to blame those people from every section of the community in the German nation who were blind to the nature of National Socialism. People of every nation and class were similarly afflicted.[14]

Rather the rest of this lecture will be devoted to asking how far one particular community in Germany responded to the challenge to discern the spirits that were abroad in the land during the 1920s and 1930s. We have chosen to take a closer look at the Roman Catholic community in Germany because at first sight, certainly, it would seem that the Catholic community responded to this challenge extraordinarily well. Not only were there scarcely any prominent Catholics in the Nazi movement,[15] but it has been said of the Catholic bishops, for instance, that no other group of men of similar weight in German public life maintained such a resolute stand as early as they did.[16]

V

The fundamental opposition between Catholicism and National Socialism had, of course, been recognised from the very beginning by many Catholic thinkers,[17] and this opposition had received somewhat flamboyant expression in 1923 when Hitler's collaborator in the Munich *putsch*, General Ludendorff, had used the occasion of his trial to launch unrestrained attacks upon the Catholic Church. Nevertheless it was not until 1930, once the Nazis had become a power in the land, that the opposition began to take shape at the grass-roots level. In the autumn of that year a priest in Kirschhausen, in the diocese of Mainz, preached a sermon against the whole philosophy of National Socialism, and made it clear that anyone who subscribed to such a philosophy thereby placed himself in a condition where he was deprived of the Church's sacraments. The priest was denounced to the Gauleiter of Hesse by a Nazi sympathiser, and the Gauleiter saw that here was an opportunity to cash in on the ever-popular rabble-rousing theme of clerical interference in politics. He protested to the priest's superior, the Bishop of Mainz, Dr Mayer, but received in reply more than he bargained for – a lucid and unambiguous statement of the gulf that divides National Socialism from the Catholic faith.[18]

The theme of the bishop's reply was soon taken up and developed in more formal fashion by one after another of the German bishops in their pastoral letters. The first to do so was Cardinal Bertram, Bishop of Breslau, in the pastoral which he issued on 1 January 1931; and he was followed in February by Faulhaber of Munich and then, during the rest of the year, by the bishops of Cologne, Paderborn, Freiburg, etc.[19] Each member of the hierarchy treated the theme in his own way, but the net result was to make it clear to even the simplest German that membership of the Nazi party excluded a person from the sacraments of the Catholic Church.

This resolute opposition to National Socialism on the part of the Catholic bishops was accompanied in their pastorals by a steady encouragement of their flocks to vote for the Centre Party, the only party besides the Social Democratic Party which never wavered in its loyalty towards the democratic institutions of the Weimar Republic. For the next two years these spokesmen for the Catholic community in Germany continued to warn their people against the paganism of the National Socialists and the atheism of the Communists, right up to and including the pastorals issued in preparation for the Reichstag elections of 5 March 1933.[20] But then, on 28 March of that year, there was published an instruction from all the bishops of the Fulda Conference in which they recognised that the new regime to emerge from the 5 March elections, headed by Hitler, was the legitimate superior of the German people (*rechtmässige Obrigkeit*), and thereby entitled to obedience from the people, including Catholics; consequently the ban on Catholics being members of the Nazi party was removed.

VI

What had happened in the three weeks preceding this declaration to account for a reversal in policy that can only be described as drastic and fateful?

The clue to answering this question is to be found in a letter

written by Cardinal Bertram, in virtue of his position as president of
the Fulda Conference (the conference of bishops from the northern
half of Germany), and dated 25 March. This letter, sent to all bishops,
included the instruction on the changed policy towards the Nazi
party which was issued three days later to the public at large. It ended
with the words: 'The urgency of the situation compels us to take
rapid action. Hence I am sending the draft of the instruction in
duplicate. If any changes need to be made please send the amended
version back by return of post. If not, the answer "Accepted" or
"Rejected" can be sent by telegraph.'[21]

It hardly needs to be underlined what a remarkable letter this is:
here was a major change being proposed in the policy of the German
Church towards the National Socialists, and the bishops were being
asked to endorse this change by return of post! The letter alone is
sufficient witness to the feverish state in which Bishop Bertram found
himself – to say nothing of the bishops who accepted Bertram's
proposals. For although the bishops did fall in line with Bertram,
many of them did so with heavy hearts and against their better
judgements.[22] This was specially true of the Bishop of Eichstätt, Graf
von Preysing, who protested in the sharpest manner against the way
the whole operation was being carried out. And almost immediately
he began to compose a masterly memorandum in preparation for the
Whitsun Conference of the Fulda bishops to be held on 31 May.[23]
This memorandum laid out, one by one, the points at which National
Socialism was diametrically opposed to the teachings of the Catholic
Church, and insisted that a detailed list of these points should be
drawn up and issued as a pastoral from all the bishops so that the
Catholic faithful should be provided with a crystal-clear exposition
of the limits of their adherence to the new regime. Above all he
warned against being taken in by words whose traditional association
drew up people's loyalty towards them, words such as 'God', 'Christianity', 'morality', 'justice', etc. – words which were now being used
by the Nazis in a perverse sense precisely in order to deceive believers.

Von Preysing was not, in fact, able to persuade his fellow bishops
to adopt his proposals, but from these months date the disagreements
between him and Cardinal Bertram. They were to be at loggerheads
for the next 12 years,[24] especially after 1935 when von Preysing
moved from the quiet Bavarian town of Eichstätt to become the

Bishop of Berlin. Indeed, the tension between these two was to increase so constantly during these years that on several occasions von Preysing seriously considered resigning his see in protest against Bertram's weak-kneed approach to the Nazis, but was each time persuaded to stay on by his old friend in Rome, Pacelli, who was soon to become Pope Pius XII. The first occasion which drove him to the verge of resignation was when he was baulked by Bertram in the late 1930s in his desire to draw up a bill of accusation against the Nazi regime, listing their offences, and his wish to issue it as a pastoral in the name of all the German bishops. The second occasion was when Bertram sent a personal greeting to the Führer for his birthday in the name of all the bishops without consulting any of them.[25]

The dramatic conflict between these two prelates is heightened by the contrast in their personalities and their background. Von Preysing came of aristocratic stock, being related to the great bishop of Munster, Graf von Galen. He was not educated at a church school but, on the contrary, in his youth sat under a very anti-Catholic teacher. While still young he was taken into the diplomatic service of the Bavarian princes, and not until he was 32 did he decide to become a priest, being ordained very soon afterwards with the minimum of ecclesiastical training. He quickly became secretary to the archbishop of Munich. This rapid progress on his part was made all the easier through his aristocratic connections which also prompted him to see so sharply through the pretentions of Nazi demagogy. Well-informed by the traditionalists around the journal *Der gerade Weg* concerning the activities of the Nazis, he was already saying, in 1933, 'We have fallen into the hands of gangsters and fools'.[26]

In contrast to this was Bertram's personality, as can be seen immediately simply by glancing at photographs of the two men – von Preysing's face is firm, with steady eyes and strong jaw, whereas Bertram's face is narrow, his nose thin, the eyes hesitant, mouth small and chin weak. Bertram himself came from a lower-class, clergy background; he spent almost the whole of his youth in ecclesiastical institutions, where he acquired the scholarly training that enabled him to compile his learned history of the bishopric of Hildesheim, the first volume of which appeared in 1899 and the last in 1925. He was essentially a man of the desk, and used to claim in his later years that he had never taken a day's holiday since becoming a bishop.

But the key to Bertram's behaviour throughout his after life – and by 1933 he was already 74 years old – is to be found in the story of his early days. He illustrates particularly well the truth of the maxim that historians should always examine with special care the first 25 years of the lives of the people they are studying.

VII

Bertram was born in Hildesheim in 1859,[27] and from the very time that he began to take notice his life was dominated by the *Kulturkampf* which Bismarck was waging against the Catholic Church. He saw the Jesuits expelled from Prussia; he saw about 1,000 parishes in Prussia deprived of their regular pastors, and of the twelve bishops only four still remained in their dioceses by 1878. Drastic restrictions were placed on what preachers were allowed to say from the pulpit; theological students were obliged to attend the university, and seminaries were placed under state control, or, in many cases, forced to close. This affected young Bertram very personally because it meant that he was unable to pursue his priestly studies in his native diocese of Hildesheim and had to go to complete them as a sort of ecclesiastic refugee in the Church centres of Würzburg, Innsbruck and Rome.

As a result, Bertram was haunted for the rest of his life by this memory of the *Kulturkampf*, and he often said that he would never do anything which might lead to his Catholic flock having to endure a similar period of persecution; above all, as he said to one Jesuit, he would never allow things to come to such a pass that once again the faithful should have to die without the ministrations of a priest.[28] His vivid memory of the *Kulturkampf* led Bertram into some extraordinary behaviour during the Nazi period, when we find him time and again replying to colleagues who were pressing him to take a firmer public stand against the National Socialists, that on the contrary, it was essential to play it cool otherwise they would bring another *Kulturkampf* down upon their heads. For example in 1940 it was brought to his notice that the Security Forces reported a marked lack of enthusiasm for the war among the Catholic priests of his diocese, as compared with the attitudes of the Protestant pastors, and so he warned his clergy to be more circumspect in case, by their words or their deeds, they should provoke another *Kulturkampf* and all that would imply. And he was saying this at a time when the most terrible things imaginable were happening throughout the land, including his own diocese, where priests and laymen were being thrown into concentration camps, deeds in comparison with which Bismarck's measures were mildness itself. But Bertram was so obsessed with his memories that he could not see what was happening before his very eyes. Yet he continued to assure his critics that, 'The craziest people are precisely the ones who need the most delicate handling'. It is no wonder that von Preysing said of him: 'The virtue of prudence counts for much more with the Bishop of Breslau than the virtue of truth'.[29]

VIII

This sketch of Cardinal Bertram's personality may indicate how fateful it turned out that someone of his character should have occupied the crucial position he did, as President of the Fulda Conference of bishops, in 1933. Just how crucial that position was is highlighted when we think of how differently the divided bishops would have behaved if von Preysing, and not Bertram, had been the one to sway them in virtue of his office. However, there were other factors at work that we must also touch upon if we are to understand even their behaviour. Because just as there was no proper, regular consultation among the bishops, so there was no consultation or mutual trust among the other three groups involved in the German Catholic dilemma, that is: their Centre Party in the Reichstag; the Vatican; and the faithful, as the general body of Catholics were called.

Why, then, was there so little consultation and trust among these various groups within what was generally thought to be an extremely united organisation?

Once again we have to trace the causes back to the *Kulturkampf* and the surprising fact that it was actually a Catholic – the Bavarian Minister of Cults, Johannes Lutz – who drew up the *Kanzel-Paragraphen* for Bismarck.[30] The *Kanzel-Paragraphen* were those clauses in the new laws which made it so easy for the government to punish legally almost any comment from the pulpit which touched critically upon government policy.

The authorities in the Vatican never forgot this collaboration between a Catholic politician and Bismarck in a strategy directed against Rome, and the Vatican ever afterwards distrusted that breed of German politician. So in 1878, when Pope Leo XIII decided to put an end to the Church's estrangement from modern society, and to come to terms with both French republicanism and Prussianism, he did not use the Centre Party, or even the German bishops, as his channel of communication with Bismarck. Instead he resorted to what is nowadays called personal diplomacy in order to reach some sort of agreement with Bismarck, keeping the German bishops and politicians in the dark. Not unnaturally, when the Centre Party leader Windorst discovered what had been going on behind his back, he became enraged and henceforward the Vatican's distrust for Centre Party politicians was well and truly matched by their distrust of the Vatican.

As one illustration of the baneful effects of this mistrust we may refer to the reception of Leo XIII's Bull issued in 1894, *Plaeclara Gratulationis*. This Bull is a fascinating document – though almost no one seems to have heard of it – on account of its clear delineation of the evils inherent in the practice of conscription, which had by now been introduced into most European countries, and the madness of imperialism which had seized most governments in Europe. The far-sighted German Prince Löwenstein was so impressed by the deep sanity of the Bull's assertions that he tried to have it publicised as one of the main themes for the annual assembly of German Catholics, the *Katholikentag*, due to be held in 1895. But he was sharply rebuffed by the head of the Centre Party, Professor Graf von Hertling, professor of philosophy at Munich University, who was later to become the prime minister of Bavaria. Hertling judged rightly that such a discussion in 1895 would be seen in Berlin as an attack upon German imperialism; and, in any case, he considered that it was not the business of the pope to tell German Catholics how they should behave within Germany; that was a matter for decision by the Centre Party.[31]

It would take a long time to detail all the misunderstandings that characterised the relations between the Vatican and the Centre Party over the next 40 years. But it is worth noticing that the Vatican became further alienated during the first world war when the Centre

Party, in an attempt to prove its patriotism, tried to manipulate the Vatican as a German weapon against the Allies. The height of their impertinence was reached when the Centre Party's publicist, Erzberger, coolly suggested that it would be a good idea to remove the patriotic Cardinal Mercier from his position as Primate of Belgium and put in his place Monseigneur van Heylen, the Bishop of Namur, who would have been subservient to the German occupying forces.[32]

The net result of this history of distrust was that by 1933 there was hardly any consultation taking place between the Vatican and the Centre Party. This left a gap between the two into which the archschemer von Papen managed to insert himself, and to present himself as spokesman for German Catholicism – although he had in fact deserted the Centre Party earlier, and although his snobbish brand of Catholicism was not shared by one Catholic in a hundred. But it was he who, on 7 April 1933, went to Rome with proposals for a Reich Concordat with the papacy of such a nature that the Cardinal Secretary of State, Pacelli, said they were like a pistol pointed at his head. Of course Pacelli did not say this in public, and Centre Party politicians were not in the least aware of Pacelli's feelings about the Concordat. All they knew was that Rome was once more negotiating behind their backs, this time with a deserter from their ranks in the shape of von Papen; and most of them felt then, as the few survivors do to this day, that they were being sold down the river by Rome. By 4 July, the day that the Centre Party dissolved itself, they were a demoralised group of men, in no mood to rejoice over the Concordat that was signed on 20 July.

IX

But if the Centre Party politicians were a demoralised group by this time the same does not seem to have been true of the fourth element in the situation, whom we have left until last, and who received scarcely any mention in most histories of this period – that is, the Catholic faithful, the lower ranks who still practised their faith. In a word, they appear to have been the most trustworthy people, yet none of their leaders were prepared to trust them to behave faithfully.

And here we turn once more to Cardinal Bertram, because the

reasons he gave in 1933 for the need to relax the ban on Catholics being members of the Nazi party were all variations upon the theme that to retain the ban would have meant asking more of the faithful than they could be expected to bear. He pointed out, for instance, that it was the custom for uniformed members of the Nazi party who were Protestants to march to their churches in a body and attend services in formation, whereas Catholics were forbidden to do so and consequently many Catholics had taken to attending Protestant services and were likely, therefore, to be lost to the Church. Again, he said, the Nazi party supplied footwear, clothes and food to party members and their families; and if the ban on party membership were rigidly enforced, such people would be put in the impossible position of having to choose between their loyalty to the Church and the practical advantages of being members of the Party. Furthermore, he asked his colleagues to consider the fact that there were 400 Catholic newspapers in Germany which employed all told some 100,000 people; if the Nazis were given an excuse for closing these newspapers down, the livelihood of some 300,000 people would be placed in jeopardy, taking into consideration the workers' families. And which of them was prepared to take responsibility for such a disaster?[33]

The crucial question here is whether or not Bertram's judgement of what the faithful could stand was correct. At this point it should be remembered that throughout all the elections of the Weimar Republic, and despite all the temptations from extremist parties, the percentage of Catholic voters supporting the Centre Party never fell below 40 per cent. This means that throughout all those years some four to five million Catholics stood solidly behind the Centre Party in its loyalty to the Weimar Republic. Equally, of course, this means that over half the nominal Catholics were regularly voting contrary to the advice of their pastors. But 40 per cent is a good basis on which to build some sort of opposition, especially in view of the fact that the predominantly Catholic districts 'resisted the lure of National Socialism far better than the Protestant ones';[34] and certain fervently Catholic areas, such as that around Cologne-Aschen, proved real bulwarks of the faith against which Hitlerism proved impotent.

But there are further indications that the body of the faithful was more ready for spiritual resistance than the bishops gave them credit

44

for. To take one instance, those Catholic papers and journals which most boldly skirmished against the Nazi party enjoyed an enormously increased circulation during the years immediately following the Nazi seizure of power.[35] The weekly *Die Junge Front*, for example, was founded in 1932 and in the early days gained a circulation of some 30,000. It had acquired as many as 100,000 subscribers by 1934, when it was closed down because of a cartoon which it published under the caption, 'Goliath despises the people of Israel', where Goliath was depicted as an unmistakable Nazi.[36] And as if to prove that they were undaunted, almost the same group of editors from *Die Junge Front* began virtually the same paper the following year under the name *Michael*. Within six months it had achieved a circulation of 330,000 before it also was suspended, this time for 'lack of National Socialist content'.[37] Nor was this support for Catholic resistance an isolated phenomenon, because during the same period the journal of the Catholic intellectuals, *Hochland*, doubled its circulation, as did the radical Catholic *Rhein-Mainische Volkszeitung*.[38]

No less active were the Catholic trade unionists associated with their newspaper *Kettelerwacht*. It was they who, on 13 July 1934, chose to stage a demonstration at Bishop Ketteler's grave in Mainz at the very hour when Hitler was making an address by radio to the whole German nation; as many as 20,000 Catholic workers made the pilgrimage to Ketteler's grave. Moreover, by the time their newspaper *Kettelerwacht* was suspended in 1938, its circulation had risen to 100,000.[39]

In the year 1935 representatives of all these groups – youth organisations, Trade Unionists, academic associations, etc. – met in Mainz. The *Verbände*, as these groups were called, had for years been the pride of German Catholicism, ever since they were formed in the age of Bismarck as a bulwark against his policies. This year they were presided over by a famous physicist, Friedrich Dessauer, a man of tremendous personal courage scarred by numerous operations for the skin cancer that he had contracted through his work on X-rays. He was also one of the editors of the *Rhein-Mainische Volkszeitung* which had come out so strongly, on 4 April 1933, in defence of the Jews. It was under his inspiration that the *Verbände* in Mainz issued a *cri de coeur* to the German hierarchy then gathering for their annual meeting at Fulda. This moving cry from the heart of the German laity in

1935 listed the sufferings of the German people under the new regime and asked that their pastors, the bishops, should draw up a clear directive of how the faithful were to behave in face of each of the threats now facing them. The message from the *Verbände* ended with the haunting phrase that, unless this were done, then the faithful would have to endure 'martyrdom without mandate'.[40]

In reply, on 15 August, the bishops sent a message full of solicitude and warm feelings but totally inadequate to the near despair that had prompted the request; and it can be said not unfairly that the faithful were indeed left to endure 'martyrdom without mandate'. And from that moment onwards the Catholics were in retreat, a well-conducted retreat, but a retreat none the less.

X

In conclusion, therefore, what are we to say in answer to our question about how the Roman Catholic community in Germany responded to the challenge of discerning the spirits that were abroad in the land during the 1920s and 1930s? Contrary to what has now become fashionable opinion they did remarkably well: the bishops, the clergy, the Centre Party, the Catholic workers' movement, the intellectuals, those sorts of people nowadays described as 'activists', did, to a large extent, see the evil in Nazism well before it got a grip upon the country. It is not at all difficult now to compile a whole corpus of statements by Bertram, Sproll, Walter Dirks, Waldemar Gurian, Nikolaus Gross – even, upon occasion, von Papen[41] – in support of such a judgement.

Why, then, did the German Catholics prove to be so impotent to change the course of events?

One reason, surely, is that it is not sufficient simply to see the evil that is approaching you and your family; you must also see that which is threatening to get its hooks into other people as well. And here one notices how very rarely any Catholic voice was raised to ward off the blows that were threatening those people who were not members of the Catholic Church. When, for instance, Nazi thugs murdered a Communist miner at Potempa in August 1932, the Catholic voice was not heard in protest. When at Hitler's orders his rivals within the Party, and many others not within the Party, were butchered during the 'night of the long knives', there was silence once more. Even the continued persecution of the Jews did not call forth any sustained chorus of disapproval. Certainly Cardinal Faul-haber had preached his famous Advent sermons on Judaism in Munich Cathedral, and Wilhelm Neuss' devastating refutation of Rosenberg's racial theories had sold more than 200,000 copies;[42] but both Faulhaber and Neuss, sickened though they were personally by the attacks on Jews, concentrated in their public expositions on the doctrinal errors embodied in Nazi racialism rather than upon the cruelty to flesh-and-blood Jews that was being carried out. It was not really until 1942 that official spokesmen of the Church stated clearly that it is the Church's calling to raise its voice in protest not only when Catholics themselves are being persecuted but when human beings, simply as human beings, are being deprived of their God-given rights. This was the theme of Faulhaber, Frings and the other bishops during 1942 and 1943,[43] and it marks a tremendous step forward in their recognition that discernment of spirits cannot stop at the threats to one's own integrity.

In fairness, of course, we have to remember that until the war brought enemies of Nazism into some sort of comradeship, the different religious and political groupings in Germany were so deeply divided that it would have been almost unthinkable – even imperti-nent – for a representative of one group to have spoken up on behalf of another group. To begin with, these groups virtually never met one another socially: Catholics went to Catholic schools and Protestants to Protestant schools; Socialists had their comics for Socialist children and Communists had theirs for their children; Jews went to Jewish doctors and Catholics to Catholic doctors; all along the line they tended to meet only people of their own religious or political colour, whether they were worshipping or playing or being ill; and so they harboured the strangest notions about those outside their own com-munity. Moreover they often had good reason to be suspicious of those outside. The Catholics whom we have been discussing, for instance, had long been conscious of their minority status – in the Second Empire, as one Jewish observer has said, 'the difficulty of reaching a leading position in the councils of the nation was much greater for a Roman Catholic of strong convictions than for a German

47

of Jewish descent who had professed Protestantism'.[44] Again, during
the period of the Weimar Republic, the Catholics had been harassed
and ridiculed over the issue of Church schools, the Concordat, their
doctrinal teaching, loyalty to Rome, and many other issues, at the
hands of Free-thinkers at one time, of Socialists and Communists and
Protestants at other times. To anyone conversant with the concrete
realities of Weimar (as opposed to the abstractions of moral hindsight),
the notion that a German Roman Catholic bishop might have taken
it upon himself to act as a spokesman in defence of, say, a Socialist
or a Protestant is fantastic. It would have overtaxed all imaginations;
indeed, were it to have happened in the 1920s, any bishop who
might have taken it upon himself to be such a spokesman would
probably have been considered impertinent and his motives treated
with suspicion. In Weimar Germany it was up to the Communists
to speak on behalf of Communists, and Jews to speak on behalf of
Jews, and Catholics on behalf of Catholics. The lines of loyalty were
firmly drawn and it was not until the different groups began to
experience persecution in common that they began to draw
together.[45] The first lesson was eventually and painfully learnt by the
German bishops during the Nazi period – but a second lesson may
never have been learnt, to judge from the Germans who after the war
ascribed their failure to prevent Nazism to their lack of discernment of
spirits. Because, as we have seen, large numbers of them did recognise
the evil abroad in the form of Nazism, but they nevertheless failed
to resist Nazism in any very effective manner. Once more this is the
sort of judgement that is easily made in retrospect; and one needs to
point out that the very concept of resistance (which people nowadays
tend to treat as though it was available, fully worked out, from the
beginning of time) had not been elaborated by the 1930s. It was still
fused with guilty thoughts of rebellion and disobedience, and was
only slowly hammered out on the anvil of Nazism; symptomatic of
the difficulty of fashioning such a concept is that in Russia, where
there was the same need for it, it seems never to have been fashioned
at all.

XI

Perhaps the failure to achieve any effective resistance is best illustrated by the case of Bishop von Preysing. Because here was a man who, as we have seen, was never deceived about Nazism and had a very clear picture of what needed to be done. But even he was ineffective; and it is a sign of the ineffectiveness that, if it had not been for the researches of subsequent historians, we should still be ignorant of his desire for an open confrontation with the Nazis or of his letter to the pope, now well-known, in which he asked the pope to say a word on behalf of the Jews.[46] For the fact is that he did not resign his post when Bertram congratulated the Führer, nor did he commit himself in a public fashion to the defence of the Jews. In his case, as in many others, it was not discernment that he lacked, nor, quite clearly, did he lack courage. What was missing was the ability to translate his perceptions into effect at political level. If the dying nurse Cavell made it clear that patriotism is not enough, then the story of the German Catholics makes it equally clear that discernment of spirits likewise is not enough.

Nor do we need to search long to determine at least one factor in German Catholicism which lay at the root of the inability of Catholics to set their perceptions into motion. That factor was memorably brought out for me soon after the war when I spent a whole night talking to someone in Cologne, who had never compromised himself under Hitler, about the dilemma that had faced Christians during the period of the dictatorship. Eventually, just as the light before the dawn was picking out the shape of the great cathedral facing his house, I asked him what one could *do* in such a situation? '*Nichts*,' he replied, '*Man kann nur leiden*' – 'Nothing. One can only suffer.' Looking back on that reply I have come to see it as a symbol of a strand in the tradition of the German Catholics that paralysed them when it came to doing something effective. Suffering in silence was thought of, in the circumstances, as an adequate response to their dilemma. Not, of course, that this paralysing factor was confined to Catholics: it was also influential in the case of those Jews who went to their deaths with hardly a murmur, or those Protestants who recognised Hitler as evil but felt they had to endure him rather than get rid of him. But the power of this tradition of silent suffering among German Catholics is underlined very clearly by the case of von Preysing, because he realised the need to break out from it and take public action, but was still hamstrung by the tradition.

Another side of the same coin of suffering is that the German bishops were so fearful of what might happen if their flocks were asked to suffer. As we have seen, they even rescinded the ban on membership of the Nazi party for fear of the dilemma in which the laity might otherwise be placed. Once more, it was not through personal fear. They put themselves at risk, for example, to protect the printers and distributors of the papal encyclical attacking the Nazis, *Mit brennender Sorge*. And it was their policy at all times, when issuing any message or pastoral that they knew would anger the regime, to read it out first in their own cathedral church before it was to be read out in the parishes by the lower clergy. They hoped in this way, so to speak, to draw the fire upon themselves and to protect their charges who, if accused by the regime, could always plead that they had simply followed the orders of their bishops in reading out the offending message.[47]

XII

So no one can reasonably question the courage of the German bishops. But this attitude does raise another question which takes us into the depths of theology. This is the question of whether it may not be wrong for those in authority to adopt such a protective attitude towards their charges who are being threatened with suffering. While no responsible person would directly will suffering upon another, are there not circumstances in which one would allow one's charges to suffer and die rather than protect them if that involves sin? This is a hard possibility to have to face: what father would allow his son to suffer and die if he could prevent it? Here a Christian inevitably reflects that, according to Christian teaching, this is precisely what God did: there was no other way of saving humanity from sin than that his Son should suffer and die.

Perhaps in the end *this* was the ultimate lack of discernment on the part of the German bishops, that they were not prepared to trust their people to withstand the evil spirits abroad in Germany. We have already quoted some of the evidence about the behaviour of the Catholic laity which suggests that more of them were ready to be martyrs, i.e. witnesses to the faith, than their superiors gave them credit for. One might add that in the weekly *Der gerade Weg* (19 June 1932) Father Ingbert Naab proved to be one of the first to coin the concept of *Widerstand*; in his opinion there was sufficient firm opposition to the Nazis on the part of Catholics to have ensured that one German in every six would have supported a movement of resistance. And some support is given to Father Ingbert's estimate when we learn that between 1933 and 1945 only 600,000 men and women in Germany left the Catholic Church, in spite of all the tremendous pressures they were under to do so – a much smaller percentage than the numbers of Protestants who left their Churches.[48] All of which suggests that the Catholic bishops had a greater number among the faithful who were prepared to stand by them than they had calculated, if only they had been ready to trust them.

But discernment of spirits is not in the end a matter of calculation; if it were, it would be rendered unnecessary by the statisticians and their computers. Nor is it, as my post-war informants seemed to assume, simply a matter of being aware of the evil spirits abroad in the land. The German Catholics in general, and their bishops in particular, *were* aware of them in 1933. What the bishops seem to have been less aware of is the Holy Spirit at work among the people to sustain them in their cleaving to the truth. For the discernment of spirits does not only mean the gift for seeing evil approaching when it is still at a distance; it also means having confidence in the power of the Spirit of goodness and truth to overcome that evil.

4

Is there a *locus classicus* for theology?

(1982)

I need to begin by explaining that I am not a professional theologian
and have never taken a single course in theology, much less completed
a *Doktorarbeit* in the subject. At the same time I realise that even those
of us who are amateur theologians stand under the threat voiced by
the Dominican Père Brückberger when he said: '*On n'a jamais entendu
dire que le bon Dieu ait foudroyé un tout petit théologien – et c'est grand
dommage*'.

I don't know how far all of you would agree with Brückberger
that it is a great pity for no theologian to have been thunderstruck
on account of his errors. I can only agree with him in the sense that
it would have been better for many of them to have been thunderstruck by God who is merciful than to have been struck, as so
often, by their fellow theologians, in whom the quality of mercy has
frequently been strained.

In any case, although I would not need to explain to a group of
theologians what I had in mind if I were to use the term *locus
theologicus*, perhaps I do need to offer some explanation of what I
have in mind when speaking of a *locus classicus* for theology.

The term *locus theologicus* gained currency amongst Western theologians through the systematic work of Melchior Cano, when he was
identifying what he called *sedes argumentorum*. By this he meant to
say that if, for example, you were treating the question of original
sin, then a *locus theologicus* for you would obviously be the treatment
of the matter by St Augustine. Similarly, if you were talking about
limbo, St Augustine's works would again be a *locus theologicus*. In the
same way, for a discussion of the doctrine of analogy you would go
to St Thomas – and so on.

Then, by an extended use of the term, I expect you would say that within Muslim theology the *locus theologicus* for the Muslim teaching on paradise is in the work of Tabari. Similarly, in Jewish theology it is the work of Maimonides – his Thirteen Articles – which would serve as the *locus theologicus* for Jewish teaching on faith.

But what I want us to ask is a very different question. The *locus theologicus*, traditionally, is that place in the writings of some theologian within a particular tradition which serves as an authority, a point of inception whenever a certain issue is to be discussed. My question, however, is a wider one. It is whether there is a *locus* for theology itself, and not simply for certain issues within a particular tradition. This wider, more embracing *locus* I have chosen to characterise as classical in the broad sense of the term, as when one speaks of some work of art or thought as classical – in the same way that one describes Machiavelli's *Prince* as the classical treatise on tyranny.

However, when one speaks of a *locus classicus* in regard to some classical achievement in art or thought, one is using the word *locus*, or place, in a metaphorical sense, which is several steps removed from the literal sense. In the literal sense the word means the physical place in which one lives, moves and has one's being; where one eats, sleeps, works, and eventually dies. By a short metaphorical step from the literal sense the word further means the place of position that one occupies in the social order. It was awareness of being conditioned in this second sense that recently led Père Congar to write a most interesting short article called 'On being a theologian' (which I recommend you to read). One of the reasons why I think that article is especially interesting is because Congar is now old; and I notice that it is true of theologians as it is of retired generals or retired diplomats or retired politicians, that when they retire they begin to say things which somehow or other they never quite said when they were younger, when they were perhaps in the midst of their professionalism. And age seems to be a great help in ridding people of their *déformation professionnelle*.

What Congar wrote was this:

My questions, my documentation have remained too clerical. At the Brussels Congress Jean Pierre Jossua said that we have the theology of our way of life. How true this is! I am dedicated to paper, to books, to the regular life. Above all I'm too tied to the middle class from which I spring . . . I'm not really in touch with the workers or the poor.[1]

It was through an awareness of this second sense, denoting social position, that I first began to ask myself in what way, and how completely, does social position determine the intellectual positions that we take up? I was amazed, for instance, to discover how unquestioningly two of my great heroes among twelfth century ecclesiastics took up what we should call jurisdictional positions – though they experienced them as theological positions – simply by virtue of their occupying the *cathedras* of York and Canterbury respectively. These I had to study very intensely and in great detail in the course of producing my biography of Thurstan, Archbishop of York. And what amazed me about both Thurstan and St Anselm was that in spite of being such highly gifted scholars, and holy into the bargain, neither of them seems to have harboured any hesitation about swearing to defend the rights of the churches of York and Canterbury against all comers in regard to the primacy, and to precedence at coronations and other occasions, even though neither of them appears to have studied the issues objectively beforehand. And I could scarcely avoid noticing the irony that the churches of York and Canterbury held opposite and conflicting positions on almost every issue that these saintly archbishops had to swear to when they were installed.

Since first noticing how close a connection there invariably is between taking up a social position and taking up an ideological position, I have observed the connection in many different spheres – in universities, diplomatic circles, political parties, and so forth. And it was through such observations that I came to ask myself whether the same might not apply even beyond the metaphorical place, which is social, and hold equally of the literal place, that is, the actual physical position which we occupy. And the answer came, vividly enough, the very first instant that I saw the buildings of Tantur. As soon as I saw it set upon this hill I spontaneously characterised it in my mind as a Crusader castle, and I asked myself whether the Institute, in consequence of its position and the corresponding architecture, may not have inherited also the mentality of the Crusader; that is, a distinct remoteness and an inclination to look down from the height of Tantur upon the concerns of the local people.

Interestingly enough it is precisely this which is denied by David
Maria Jaeger in his Introduction to the excellent Tantur volume,
Christianity in the Holy Land. He writes that his Introduction does
not represent some kind of 'official', or indeed 'unofficial', position
of the Ecumenical Institute at Tantur – for he says the Institute 'of
course, has no positions'.[2] I believe the Orthodox Patriarch Diodorus
had a different opinion, at least to judge by his face, when I presented
the volume to him and he saw the large Crusader cross that domi-
nates the front cover of the book. And I also believe that, given the
time, I could tease out certain theological options characteristic of
Tantur theology. And certainly we cannot accept unquestioningly
David's 'of course' as the last word on the subject. After all we live
in a city, Jerusalem, where even within our religious orders there are
very different theologies which seem to be closely tied to their
physical situation; one constantly discovers that the branch of an order
established in East Jerusalem, for instance, has a noticeably different
theology from the branch of the same order in West Jerusalem. Nor
is this surprising, because the history of intellectual enterprise provides
so many instances of parallel influences at work. Think only, for
example, of the institution which, perhaps more than any other, has
shaped Western intellectual history – that is, Plato's academe; think
of that grove, far from the moiling streets of Athens, where Plato and
his aristocratic companions strolled up and down. And then consider
how unlikely it was that in that place they should have developed a
theology in which God is a liberator of the oppressed. Or indeed
how unlikely it has been for such a theology to have developed in the
academies or seminaries of Europe, which have been characteristically
remote, head divorced from hand, institutions whose teachers have,
in Congar's words, been 'too clerical, dedicated to paper, to books . . .
out of touch with the workers or the poor'.

But before we go on to ask if there is a classical place in which to
do Christian theology, perhaps it would be useful, an enlightening
comparison, to speculate about other faiths in order to see whether
the very content of those faiths demands of their theologians that
they should live in a special place. And, conversely, whether there
are places where it is virtually impossible for them to do their theology
properly, having regard, as I said, to the content of their particular
faiths.

I think that Tertullian had something like this in mind when he asked, 'What has Athens to do with Jerusalem?' And Tertullian's cry has been echoed in a brilliant book by the Russian theologian Shestov which has the title *Athens and Jerusalem*. Shestov's thesis is that Jerusalem represents the place of revelation and Athens the place of dialectic, and that there is a contradiction between these two places: that you can't have both Jerusalem and Athens. As an example of what he means by the difference between revelation and dialectic, he points out how differently a question is posed in Jerusalem as opposed to Athens. Take the question, 'What is man?' In Jerusalem, it is formulated as 'What is man, that thou art mindful of him and that thou carest for him?', where the immediate reference is to God. The instant direction of one's mind is on the vertical plane. In Athens, by contrast, the question is one of definition and dialectic, 'What is man?' From which we get the answer most common among the Greeks: 'Man is a rational animal, capable of laughter'. That answer is on the horizontal plane. In consequence it seems to me that there may well be something in the notion that Judaism has no place in the European university, an institution that has developed from the academe and which works in the manner of dialectic. And for this reason, the proper place for a Jewish theologian is in the Yeshiva because he does not really belong in the university. And if Judaism finds itself in the university, it is only by an accidental series of events.

I dare say that the same would be true of Islam for slightly different, though not wholly different, reasons. On account of the content of the Islamic faith, Islam has no place in the academe as it has developed in Western Europe. Consequently, the proper centre of Islamic learning is Al Azhar; and the manner in which teaching is done there shows that Al Azhar is the place in which Muslim theologians are properly situated by virtue simply of the content of their faith.

In Hinduism, the place would be different again, according to its content. Certainly, that is true if you take the Upanishads as the basis of Hinduism. Because the content of faith in Hinduism is essentially related to the guru, and the guru is one who has the enlightenment. He is not simply teaching propositions to his students, or exercising their minds in dialectic. His task is to form the students in every aspect of their lives, for in Hinduism there is no distinction between the doctrine and the way. And Hindu teaching is Sadhana, instruction about how you go along this way. So the appropriate place in which to study Hinduism is the ashram, where the teacher, the guru, is responsible for the whole life of the disciple.

So I think if we bear those comparisons in mind, it enables us to pose more precisely the question about the proper place, the *locus classicus*, for Christian theologians. But before we go on to ask that same question, in more detail, of Christianity, perhaps it is worthwhile for us to run over quickly in our minds the actual places in which Christian theology has been carried out over the centuries, at the same time pondering how far the actual places have corresponded to a *locus classicus* such as may be demanded by the content of the Christian faith.

If we do this it seems to me that the first great Christian theologian, St Paul, proved able to do theology in any place whatsoever. He was such a great wanderer. Sometimes he did it in the synagogues, sometimes he did it in the prisons, sometimes he did it on ships. He simply did it everywhere. But Georg Kretschmar, one of our Advisory Council, has just edited a book entitled *Klassiker der Theologie*, dealing with the centuries up to the time of the Reformation, and if you go through the list of people who are considered classical theologians by Kretschmar, you will see that theology after Paul comes to be very concentrated in certain limited places.

First of all, with people such as Origen and Irenaeus, it becomes concentrated in the bishop's *cathedra*; the physical place in which they find themselves doing theology is around the bishop's *cathedra*. And then you find it moves to the monastery. I do not mean to say that they abandoned the other places entirely, but it is in monasteries especially that theology is pursued. And then with Aquinas and Scotus and Ockham, theology moves into the university. Afterwards, for the Catholic world, it moves for the most part to the seminary, and in the Anglican world, for example, it moves into the colleges of Oxford and Cambridge. That is where Anglican theology has traditionally taken place.

However, before going on to pose the main question, it needs to be said that I am not doubting that theology can be done in any place whatsoever by theologians of sufficient virtue. I do not absolutely deny that one could produce a great theological work even in the Hilton Hotel, but I think that's an unlikely place for theology;

and as far as I can establish no considerable theological work has been produced there. At the other end of the scale, in a place very different from the Hilton Hotel, a great deal of the most convincing theology of the twentieth century has been produced in the concentration camps of Germany and Russia. Now I am not suggesting that, because this has happened, therefore the camp is the *locus classicus* for doing theology. I am just saying that in fact the concentration camp is where a lot of the most convincing theology of our century has taken place.

I'm not recommending it, because obviously those are places where it is very, very difficult to reflect. In such places you receive plenty of experience but you do not get much chance to reflect upon it, and I'm reminded of the question which was put in an Oxford philosophical paper. Some of you may remember it. The question was: 'Is it possible for a man to be happy on the rack, the torturer's rack?' And one undergraduate answered very simply, 'Yes, if he is a very good man and it is a very bad rack'. In other words, such extremes cannot be invoked as the norm.

So I want to ask you, 'Is there a *locus classicus* for theology which is determined by the content of the Christian faith?' When we ask ourselves this question, we have to begin by asking ourselves what is absolutely fundamental for Christian faith? And the fundamental affirmation of the Christian faith seems to me the affirmation that ultimate reality is Trinitarian. That is to say: ultimate reality is revealed to be *koinonia* of three Persons.

If we are going to do Christian theology, therefore, it seems clear that we must at the same time be experiencing some analogous *koinonia* which, in its turn, entails that the Christian theologian must always have his or her place in community. You must do Christian theology in the Church. A Christian theologian must stand within a community and within a tradition. To be a loner is not consonant with the content of Christian faith; and I think it is instructive to observe what has happened to a number of Christians who have tried, so to speak, to combine their own tradition with the tradition of the Sannyasi in Hinduism or the Zen master in Zen Buddhism. Always, as you watch the trajectory of their lives, you see that they move further and further away from this sense of *koinonia*, because essentially the tradition of the Sannyasi in Hinduism and Zen Master in Zen Buddhism is one of individualism. A Christian theologian, therefore, needs to be in constant physical touch with communities, and this demands sharing, sharing in all aspects of the communal life – not simply the liturgy, for example, but also in all the common work. And probably there is something to be said for always joining in the most common, menial, physical work, such as doing the washing-up, the cleaning of rooms and similar tasks. I always thought that one of the dangerous aspects of the life of certain religious communities which I have known, mainly communities of intellectuals, was that some of the professors there were, as they used to say, 'excused the liturgy'. In fact, those professors were the very last people who should have been excused the liturgy, because the more they were excused the liturgy, the sharing in everyday menial work, and so on, the more inevitably they were pulled away from that *koinonia*, the constant experience of which was absolutely essential for enriching their theological reflection on that *koinonia* which is the fundamental revelation of the Christian faith.

The second question I would ask you is this. Traditionally, as you know, revelation has taught us that God is Father. But it seems to me that at the present moment a tremendous change is taking place in our perception of the world. We are coming to realise more and more that to affirm that God is our Father is not to say that God is exclusively masculine. We are coming increasingly to realise that God, as revealed to us in Scripture and tradition, is not exclusively either male or female. I say 'coming to realise' because apart from one or two remarkable exceptions such as Lady Julian of Norwich, the feminine in God has been almost eclipsed in the Christian tradition. The truth of this was vividly brought home to a very sensitive, gifted missionary, Vincent Donovan, as described in a marvellous book entitled *Christianity Rediscovered, An Epistle from the Masai*. Donovan was a missionary among the Masai for 18 years and his book is called *An Epistle from the Masai* because it was the so-called pagan Masai who taught Donovan many fundamental things about his Christian faith which he had never realised previously. In fact, he says time and again that he himself had never realised these absolutely fundamental things, it was the Masai who taught him.

For the Masai there is only one God, *Engai*, but he goes by many names. Sometimes they call him *male*, sometimes *female*. When he is kind and propitious they call him the black God. When he is angry the red God. Sometimes they call him rain since this is a particularly pleasing manifestation of God. But he is always the one, true God. They asked if we did the same. I had to admit that for us, also, God goes by many names, and that in the long history of the Bible the same is true. Indeed, I was to find from research as a result of this question of theirs, that the Jews called God on occasions fire, breeze and God of the mountain. They were a bit incredulous to learn that, for all practical purposes, we leave the female out of God, and we consider him only as male, which is, of course, as patently wrong as considering God only female. God is neither male nor female, which is an animal classification, but certainly embodies the qualities which we like to believe exist in both. If the Masai wanted to refer to God as she as well as he, I could certainly find nothing theologically incorrect about the notion. Their idea seems much more embracing and universal than ours – and not a whit less biblical:

'Does a woman forget her baby at the breast, or fail to cherish the son of her womb? Yet even if she forget, I will never forget you' (Is. 49:15).[3]

This eclipse of the feminine is hardly surprising when you think of the low position in which woman has been placed by Christian theology, as a result perhaps of theology having been almost exclusively located in bishops' schools, in monasteries, seminaries and celibate colleges. There has been a very good study made by Elizabeth Borissen on the position of woman in St Augustine and St Thomas, which shows very clearly the way in which the low position of woman in their theologies is often based on a very crude and inadequate biology. Is this sad story of the eclipse of the feminine – and it is a sad story – not a warning to us to pay heed to the words of Rabbi Simeon in the Zohar when he says, 'The *shekhinah* (the presence, or glory, of God) cannot take up its dwelling where male and female do not dwell together'?

It follows that the *locus classicus* for doing theology is a place where men and women live together. And I would ask whether the lopsidedness of Christian theology in all sorts of ways, many of them hidden from our conscious minds, cannot be traced back to the fact that through the centuries almost all Christian theologians have lived their daily lives separated from half of the human family?

Have those theologians not also been generally located in a place cut off from regular contact with a further presence, which is fundamental for understanding Christian revelation? I am referring, of course, to the presence of children. Speaking of them the gospel says:

> And they brought young children to him, that he should touch them; and his disciples rebuked those that brought them. But when Jesus saw it, he was much displeased, and said unto them: 'Suffer the little children to come unto me, and forbid them not, for of such is the kingdom of God. Verily I say unto you, whosoever shall not receive the kingdom of God as a little child, he shall not enter therein.' (Mark 10:13–15)

What a revelation to humankind Our Lord's attitude towards children proved to be has been beautifully expressed by a writer of our day, the Russian André Sinyavsky, who writes:

> Why were infants so important for the new era? Children had never been so much in evidence. Now for the first time, an infant became a symbolic figure – quite apart from the main symbol of the crucifixion – and His mother with Him: Mother and Child . . . There we have a child who seems to be not in the past but still ahead of us in future prospect. The germ not of history but of eternity, and through the birth of his Mother a constant reminder that in God the Child is never extinct.[4]

When he produced that paragraph Sinyavsky was obviously reflecting not only on the infancy narratives, but also upon what we are told in the gospels of St Mark and St Matthew, of how, if we are going to enter the Kingdom of Heaven, we have to become as little children – and that we musn't turn children away, because it's from them that we have to learn what it is to live. Can we ignore the fact that the words of the Lord are quite categorical on this subject?

There has been a very good book written on this subject by Simon Légasse called *Jésus et l'enfant*; Légasse sums up the message of his book in these words: '*Les enfants sont les meilleurs témoins de ce qu'on peut considérer comme le message essential de Jésus*'.[5]

Jesus would not have had to say those things to us so categorically, were it not of course that he knew (since he knows what is in our hearts) that we would resist them; and we resist them now as the disciples resisted them then. Nor can I forget in this context that among the first pieces of advice I received when I was coming to Tantur was a long screed from a former scholar here. Much of the burden of his advice to me was that I should exclude children from the place, on the grounds that they interfered with the work of the theologians. And indeed, I was told by another scholar when she was here about two or three weeks ago, that when she was here some years past, the children became such a nuisance in the coffee and tea room that a group of the scholars demanded that they should have a different tea room where they could go and meet on their own – and in a curious kind of way I don't think she realised the implication of what she was saying when she asserted, 'We called that "the celibates room"'!

But how you can live in accordance with the teaching about being children if you are for ever hiding yourself away from children? So I think that there is a third element here. It follows, therefore, that the place for a Christian theologian is in a community, a genuine community where the members share one another's lives. It must also be one where men and women are together, and it must be one where children are not hidden away.

Now you can probably think of many other contents of Christian faith which point us towards some such *locus classicus*, some physical location – maybe towards some social position also, as being the most favourable one for doing Christian theology. I mean for example, if we read Matthew 25 we see that the Lord again is quite categorical when he tells us that, at the end of the day, what will be asked with regard to our time on earth is whether we fed the hungry, whether we gave drink to the thirsty, whether we took in the strangers, whether we clothed the naked, whether we visited the sick, whether we visited the prisoners. And if you take up a position, a physical or social position, which deliberately places you out of touch with these, can you still be in a position to do Christian theology? Or does it mean to say that, in the end, as a result of having put yourself in such a remote position, you don't know what you are talking about? Because not knowing what you are talking about is the fundamental *déformation professionnelle* of all of us who make our living by the use of words. How true this is was brought home to me when I was talking with Father Nicolas, who is the head of the association of Mother Teresa's Mission of Charity, a group working with people who are suffering particularly terrible physical illnesses. I told Father Nicolas that I would like his help in reflecting on the matter of suffering. His response was such an arresting one. He said to me, 'Well, Donald, I did work for two years among the dying in Calcutta with Mother Teresa but you know it is now seven years since I did so, and I'm beginning to forget what it was really like'. He said, 'If you put yourself out of touch with that kind of suffering, you begin to forget what it is really like'. So maybe this *locus classicus* to which the content of our faith points us, will also in some way require that the community of which we are members is helping to feed the hungry and to look after the sick and to visit prisoners and to do all those kinds of things which are spoken of in Matthew 25.

What does all this say to the theologian? Well, the most obvious thing it says is that the theologian has to ask himself, 'Am I in the right place?' And it may well be that a change of place is the only thing that will enable us to cease being blind to certain basic things about our faith. Just over a year ago, when I was in California, I was on a panel with Professor McAfee Brown who explained to us that he had recently been in Latin America, as a result of which he said, 'For the first time in my life, after spending some months among the marginalised of Latin America, for the first time in my life, I began to understand the Bible'. I said to him, 'What do you think it was in the previous 50 years of your reading the Bible that prevented you from reading it properly?' But I didn't really get an answer to that.

The second thing is, if I think I am not in the *locus classicus* for doing theology, does that mean that I must keep quiet until I'm in the classical place? And this question also came out on the afternoon I mentioned when I was on that panel with McAfee Brown. Because a pastor said, 'Look, in my parish there are lots of people who work in armaments. But I have come more and more round to the position where I'm against all nuclear arms. But if I preach against nuclear arms they will probably throw me out of the parish, or I will lose my parishioners, and that won't do any good. Should I modify my preaching in order to make it acceptable to them?' And McAfee

Brown replied, 'I cannot answer that question, because I am not in your position'. Now that answer seems to me to be a way out which is not legitimately open to us. In other words, no matter what position we are in, we have to try and witness to proclaim truths of our Christian faith. Because it may well be that daring to speak out from the wrong position is the one way which will force us to recognise that, if we are going to continue preaching the Gospel, then we cannot do so from the position in which we find ourselves. The place we are in is the wrong one, and so we have to change it.

Finally, perhaps I should say this. It may be that the search for a *locus classicus* for theology is no more final than was Melchior Cano's search for an ultimate system of *loci theologici*, and that the example of the first Christian theologian, St Paul, is the one to which we should pay most respect. That is to say, there is no exclusive *locus*, but that the classical position (if that's the right word) is the one that St Paul adopted whereby he was prepared at any and every moment to change if the Gospel demanded it. His *locus* was one where he was instantly ready for dislocation. So if what I say is true, then all of us should stand in perpetual readiness to be dislocated, because it is only by being dislocated that one is enabled to see and to witness to the truths of our faith.

5

The Karamazov brothers as teachers of religion
(1979)

The Karamazov brothers are the best teachers of religion in the late twentieth century; better, I am certain, than contemporary theologians. *The Brothers Karamazov* is at its best in *sobornost*, in the community of *seekers*. It has been my privilege during this last year to receive instructions from *The Brothers Karamazov* in such a community, and I came to realise that the novel is the most wonderful way of raising religious issues in the minds and hearts of our contemporaries. More important, I am convinced that *The Brothers Karamazov* cannot be appreciated if it is read in isolation. It must be read in community, each sharing insights into the meaning of this profound statement with other members of the community. After all, there is something dissonant about reading a book in isolation whose theme is 'each is responsible to all'. When Dostoevsky published his novel, it appeared in instalments in a monthly journal, and the segments were often read out aloud in the families of subscribers to the journal. Moreover, Dostoevsky himself read portions to his second wife before she transcribed the words for publication. He frequently offered public readings of chapters to large audiences. Like everything else that is worthwhile, *The Brothers Karamazov* is meant to be shared in community.

The two communities with which I have read Dostoevsky's novel during the past year were a class of university students in the University of California, and the people at the Penny University. The Penny University is held in the Café Pergolesi at the end of Pacific Avenue in Santa Cruz. It is named for similar gatherings in eighteenth-century coffee houses where, for a penny, customers could join in the discussion. At Santa Cruz's Penny University, sessions are held at five o'clock every evening, when a professor talks for half an hour.

After the talk, anyone can take part in the discussion, which goes on amidst the hissing of espresso machines and moving customers.

Needless to say, these groups brought different interests and backgrounds. The students at the University of California were all between the ages of 18 and 23, almost entirely drawn from prosperous families, and committed to studying *The Brothers Karamazov* for credit to finish degrees. Those in the Pergolesi were of all ages and kinds, some very young, some grandmothers and grandfathers, some veterans of the Vietnam war and others of the second world war. One day a couple of professors of psychology dropped in; the local flower-seller was almost always in attendance, and at a later date two Steinerite priests appeared. But all of them were there purely out of interest, and if they saw no point in what was being said, they simply walked out; there were no external sanctions.

Yet the problems of studying *The Brothers Karamazov* were very similar for the two communities. As one sceptic said when he saw more than 50 students signing up for the degree class, 'How on earth can you have a discussion involving 50 people?'; and in regard to the Pergolesi gathering, 'How on earth can you hold a discussion with no guaranteed clientele and no assurance that the people will have read the text?' The solution adopted for both groups was similar, and one that I imagine can be more generally applied: you put into a hat a number of slips on each of which the name of one of the characters is written; then you ask each member of the class to draw out a slip and be responsible for making sure that the rest of the group does not misrepresent or misunderstand that character. It is also helpful to have a number of miscellaneous slips for, say, a geographer of the novel and a chronologist of the novel, and so on. The effect of this device of having slips is much the same as the effect of the prospect of imminent death: it marvellously concentrates the mind. The member responsible for the character reads the novel with unprecedented intensity, and comes to feel a genuine sense of responsibility for seeing that justice is done to his or her character. And when you have a whole group sharing so intense a reading, they notice details on such a scale that all become aware of the superficial manner in which they have habitually read on previous occasions.

Indeed, after listening to contributions from the geographer and the chronologist, I am forced to wonder if many of the novel's critics could pass a simple examination in the geography of Skotoprigonevsk, or on the time-sequence of the story. Nor can such details be dismissed as insignificant pedantry. For one thing that our geographer brought home to us quite memorably, as a result of reconstructing the geography of Skotoprigonevsk, was how much Alyosha is the mediator in a deep sense of the word, constantly moving between the monastery and the Karamazov home, or between the Suishkin cottage and Katerina's drawing-room, always reconciling. In the same way, when the chronologist pointed out to us that the Devil appears to Ivan at the very moment when Smerdyakov dies, there was a sudden burst of awareness among all of us as to what 'synchronicity' might mean. That gave rise to a prolonged and lively discussion of how the notion of synchronicity is related to the sense of what *kairos* means in the holy Scriptures – the day of the Lord. And we came to the conclusion that, if only we open our eyes in the manner in which Dostoevsky intended, then we come to realise that each moment is the day of the Lord, because the kingdom is among us.

Which brings me to a truth about *The Brothers Karamazov* which I have seen no one mention, and that is the novel's consummative power within Dostoevsky's own life, itself the supreme reason why the novel is such a perfect medium for discussing religion. Throughout his life Dostoevsky was striving to make a breakthrough out of one prison after another, and at the end of 40 years he made the final breakthrough by *The Brothers Karamazov*. Dostoevsky knew various prisons: literally in the case of Peter and Paul Fortress and the camp to which he was condemned at Omsk. Metaphorically he was imprisoned in his gambling, in nineteenth-century scientific positivism, in his passion for Suslova (with whom he had an abortive affair in the 1860s), in his sense of guilt towards his natural father, his 'little father', the tsar, and his heavenly Father. His outrage at such imprisonment, and his protest against it, is nowhere more eloquently expressed than in *Notes from Underground*, where he says of the Job's comforters who came to the Underground Man:

> They'll call out to you, why protest? Two and two do make four. Nature doesn't always ask your advice. She isn't interested in your preferences, or whether or not you approve of her laws. You must

accept nature as she is, with all the consequences that that implies, so a wall is a wall, etc., etc.

But good Lord, what do I care about the laws of nature and arithmetic if I have my reasons for disliking them, including the one about two and two making four? Of course, I won't be able to breach this wall with my head if I'm not strong enough. But I don't have to accept a stone wall just because it's there and I don't have the strength to breach it.

Significantly enough, at the time at which he was gathering himself to write *The Brothers Karamazov*, Dostoevsky was absorbed in reading the book of Job, which itself tells the story about how a man protests against the imprisoning walls of traditional religion and eventually breaks through into a new and deeper awareness of God. He breaks out of 'God' into the freedom of God. It is equally significant that Dostoevsky was intrigued at this time by the work of the mathematician Lobachevsky, who showed that one need not condemn oneself to the two-plus-two-equals-four prison of Euclidean geometry, because there are alternative geometrics if only people have the courage and imagination to protest against the constricting walls of Euclidean geometry and break through them.

In fact, Dostoevsky's life is the story of how he wrote himself out of one prison into the next and then out of that into another, each breakthrough being punctuated by the publication of some memorable work: *Poor Folk*, *Crime and Punishment*, *The Possessed*, *The Gambler*, etc. And yet each breakthrough led him nearer to the ultimate prison walls: those constituted by his own supreme gift, his psychological insight. Theodore Reik said that Dostoevsky 'knew more about human psychology than the whole of the International Psychological Association put together'. This is true. But it is no less true of him, as of us all, that the greatest gift or blessing is also the greatest curse unless we can get beyond it. This is evident in Dostoevsky's case through the incredibly skilful way in which he shows how almost all of us, most of our lives, are caught in psychological mechanisms. We imagine, for instance, that we are freely and selflessly loving someone, and then some event happens as a result of which we find ourselves hating that same person for no apparent reason – as though a control button inside us had simply been switched. What was love becomes hate; what was humility becomes pride; what was compassion becomes cruelty; and what was revenge becomes compassion. The psychological laws controlling the mechanics are depicted by Dostoevsky with unparalleled and unerring skill so that it seems in the end as if his characters only break through one set of prison walls to face a yet more inexorable set, until reaching the ultimate set, the one that proves to you by Euclidean reasoning that your very desire to break through is itself the wall. It is a wall even more immovably subject to mechanical laws than any of the previous ones.

This would have been the last word of Dostoevsky had it not been for the miracle of *The Brothers Karamazov*. For there *is* something miraculous about the fact of Dostoevsky's being able to integrate and bring to consummation all that terrible experience of his – his mother's death, his father's brutal murder at the hands of his serfs, himself being taken up and then cruelly dropped by the literary establishment, his enduring mock execution, his years in the prison camps, and the deaths of his children. When we also add his gambling fever, his torture at the hands of Suslova, his fortnightly epileptic fits and his emphysema, and then remember that in the midst of all this he was having to pay off his brother's debts and support one improvident relative and hanger-on after another, then one must acknowledge that any psychologist or sociologist who knew the laws of his science would have to conclude that there was no earthly hope for any individual in the middle of that mess.

Yet we all know that it is not the psychologist or the sociologist, or even the theologian, who had the last word, but Dostoevsky himself – or, more exactly, God speaking through him. Only in this way can we account for the miraculous achievement and also explain why, when once *The Brothers Karamazov* was completed, Dostoevsky had nothing more to say and do on this earth, and so he died. For this reason alone, I do not believe there could have been a sequel to the novel. It may well have been that Dostoevsky's plans included the further adventures of Alyosha, but after the funeral feast for Ilyusha there was nothing more for him to say. At this point Dostoevsky's situation was like that of a believer in the Orthodox Church at the height of the liturgy, who has come to church with plans for going on pilgrimage as soon as the service is over. But then at the climax of the liturgy he realises, 'This is it'. *Tat rvan asi*. Why should he now go anywhere? Since here and now it *is*, '*This is reality*'. In like manner, it was right and fitting for Dostoevsky to die once he had completed his work; for as one critic has observed, it is well that he never went on to write the projected second volume, ' . . . because otherwise not only Russian literature but also Russia and mankind would have exploded and evaporated'. As in many other respects, so also in this respect, *The Brothers Karamazov* matches that other great work of psychological integration and spiritual consummation, Dante's *Divina Commedia*. Dante, too, faced every painful experience of his life, and by the very process of writing them into the *Commedia*, managed to achieve personal integrity. The achievement of the wholeness and holiness of the great artist is simply the inner aspect of the process by which a great artistic work is achieved, which manifests wholeness and holiness to humankind. It will be remembered that Dante was also finishing the final cantos of the *Commedia* in his very last days, and that according to his sons the manuscript of those final cantos was only found after his death by a miraculous intervention.

The reader of the *Divina Commedia* accompanies Dante on his long journey through hell and purgatory, and finally emerges into the clear light of paradise, breathing deeply, taken further and further into the empyrean, finding then that breath of God which moves the sun and the stars and the human heart. So, too, the reader of *The Brothers Karamazov* is led through Dostoevsky's own hell and purgatory into the clear air.

In Dostoevsky's earlier writing, we are in the world of the underground man who cannot break out from the fetid, tuberculosis-ridden, dark, gloomy prison of the modern industrial city in which there is scarcely a blade of grass to be seen; but in *The Brothers Karamazov*, along with Alyosha, we are delivered from that world:

His soul, overflowing with rapture, was craving for freedom and unlimited space. The vault of heaven, studded with softly shining stars, stretched wide and vast over him. From the zenith to the horizon the Milky Way stretched its two arms dimly across the sky. The fresh, motionless still night enfolded the earth. The white towers and golden domes of the cathedral gleamed against the sapphire sky. The gorgeous autumn flowers in the beds near the house went to sleep till morning. The silence of the earth seemed to merge into the silence of the heavens. The mystery of the earth came into contact with the mystery of the stars. Alyosha stood, gazed and suddenly he threw himself down upon the earth. He did not know why he was embracing it. He could not have explained to himself why he longed so irresistibly to kiss it, to kiss it all, but he kissed it weeping, sobbing, and drenching it with his tears and vowed frenziedly to love it, to love it forever and ever. 'Water the earth with the tears of your gladness and love those tears', it rang in his soul. What was the weeping over? Oh, he was weeping in his rapture even more over those stars which were shining for him from the abyss of space and he was not ashamed of that ecstasy. It was as though the threads from all those innumerable worlds of God met all at once in his soul, and it was trembling all over as it came in contact with other worlds.

The parallel between this passage and Dante's last words, '*L'amor che mueve el sol e l'altre stelle*' ('The Love that moves the sun and the other stars'), is so striking as to leave us in no serious doubt that the Italian poet and the Russian novelist had each experienced the same touch of final integration.

In the novel, of course, Alyosha's rapture is a realisation of the truth in Father Zosima's homily:

Many things on earth are hidden from us, but in return for that we have been given a mysterious inward sense of our living bond with the other world, with the higher, heavenly world, and the roots of our thoughts and feelings are not here but in other worlds. That is why philosophers say that it is impossible to comprehend the essential nature of things on earth. God took seeds from other worlds and sowed them on this earth and made his garden grow, and everything that could come up came up, but whatever grows is alive and lives only through the feeling of its contact with other mysterious worlds; if that feeling grows weak or is destroyed in you then what has grown up in you will also die. Then you will become indifferent to life and even grow to hate it.

Clearly the opening into this spiritual world, including this earth transfigured, is by way of the gate of forgiveness, as surely in *The*

Brothers Karamazov as in the *Divina Commedia*. As Father Zosima says in introducing the passage just quoted, 'My young brother asked forgiveness of the birds: it may seem absurd, but it is right none the less, for everything, like the ocean, flows and comes into contact with everything else. Touch it in one place and it reverberates at the other end of the world.' Nor is this revelation lost even upon Ivan, the character in the novel who seems most irredeemably lost in the city of Euclidean logic with its unyielding rectilinear pavements and its asphyxiating lack of free air. Speaking to Alyosha he says, 'I want to live and I go on living even if it is against logic. However much I may disbelieve in the order of things, I still love the sticky little leaves that open in the spring, I love the blue sky.' It is as though Ivan were the unhappy orphan that Dostoevsky had in mind when he wrote in his journal, 'Children must be born on the soil and not on the pavement . . . a nation should be born and *sprout* on earth, on the soil upon which corn and trees grow. There is something sacramental in the earth in the soil.' For Dostoevsky the heavens opened when he bowed down and kissed the earth.

I am convinced that the pilgrimage which brought a wholeness, an integration, to Dostoevsky's life came easier to the two communities with whom I read *The Brothers Karamazov* than to professional literary critics. The subject before us is the transfiguration of life's experiences by God's work – Dostoevsky's life and our own. The critics – the Soviet ones in the van, followed by the Western ones – usually concentrate on technical questions about the use of different voices, choice of imagery, plot and subplot, etc., as if deliberately to focus on the secondary matters so as to avoid the all-important question which my unspoilt companions asked straight away and never ceased to ask: 'What is it *all* about?' For once we ask that simple, fundamental question, we begin to realise that *The Brothers Karamazov* is about everything. In answer to the above question, for instance, one person said, 'It is all about humiliation'; another said, 'It is all about money'; another said, 'It is all about food'; yet another thought, 'It is about fools for Christ (*yurodivi*)'. To another, the killing of the father was central. For someone else, the refrain, 'Each is responsible for all' was the crucial theme, in answer to the nihilistic slogan of Ivan Smerdyakov that 'Everything is permitted', once you get rid of God. Another person maintained that the novel presents us with a theology of faces.

Of course, each of these persons was correct. There is a whole theology of faces embedded in *The Brothers Karamazov*. One has only to remember Father Zosima's account of the terrible fate he had seen in Dmitry's face and how he had sent Alyosha to Dmitry in the hope that Alyosha's 'brotherly face' might help to save him from that fate. And he did this partly because Alyosha's face had always reminded Zosima of his own brother's face, which in his memory had served as a guide upon the precious path of his monastic calling.

But perhaps the most memorable of all passages for a theology of faces occurs in Zosima's exhortation to the monks:

> Every day and every hour, every minute, examine yourself and watch over yourself to make sure that your appearance is seemly. You pass by a little child, you pass by spitefully with foul language and a wrathful heart; you may not have noticed the child, but he has seen you, and your face ugly and profane will perhaps remain in his defenceless heart. You may not know it, but you have perhaps sown an evil in him and it may grow.

Here the reference to the seed stirs our memory of the verse from St John's gospel which stands at the head of the whole novel, 'Verily, verily I say unto you, "Except a grain of wheat fall into the ground and die, it abideth alone; but if it die, it bringeth forth much fruit".' The same verse of the gospel had been quoted by Zosima in an earlier section of the discourse, and although that is the only instance in the whole novel when these actual words of Scripture are quoted again, nevertheless the theme of them keeps returning throughout, as though the verse itself is a seed which has fallen into the ground and is present underground the whole time, bursting forth with the fullness of truth on certain occasions. One such occasion is at the very end of the novel, at Ilyusha's funeral, when we are made to realise that the previous seed is Alyosha himself and that he has already begun to bring forth much fruit in the form of the transfigured children. And I use the word 'transfigured' advisedly, because in his reference to the face Dostoevsky sometimes uses the word *obraz*, which is also the Russian word for icon and is the basic constituent of *preobrazhenie*, the Russian word for transfiguration.

There are many more instances throughout the novel where the face is a means of salvation, as when Grushenka says to Alyosha, 'But I have looked at you a hundred times before today. I began asking everyone about you. I couldn't forget your face: I carried it in my heart.' Similarly, later in the novel, it is the appearance of Alyosha which drives away the Devil from Ivan – ' "You did drive him away" ', says Ivan to his younger brother. ' "He vanished as soon as you appeared. I love your face, Alyosha. Did you know that I loved your face?" ' And how vital it is, for redemption, to remember the face is illustrated by Alyosha's own failure to do so. It is during the episode when Rakitin is trying to drag him down the path of perdition, apparently with success:

> ... and suddenly his brother Dmitry's face flashed through his mind, but only for a fraction of a second, and though it did remind him of something, of some urgent business which must not be put off for a moment, some duty, some terrible obligation, this reminder made no impression on him, did not reach his heart, and immediately slipped his memory and was forgotten. But Alyosha remembered this long afterwards.

Because he failed to hold the face in his heart, he slipped further down that path of perdition. Here, once again, we notice that for Dostoevsky there is an essential connection between the face and the heart and remembrance; hence one can scarcely avoid seeing here a connection with traditional Orthodox teaching on the prayer of the heart. It is essential that the Jesus Prayer move from the lips to the mind and then descend from the mind into the heart. The same is true of the remembered face.

There is quite a stunning moment in the court, at Dmitry's trial, when the public prosecutor says to Alyosha:

> 'And why are you so absolutely convinced of your brother's innocence?'
>
> 'I couldn't but believe my brother. I knew he wouldn't lie to me. I could tell from his face that he wasn't lying to me.'
>
> 'Only from his face, is that all the proof you have?'
>
> 'I have no other proof.'

'And you have no proof whatever of Smerdyakov's guilt except your brother's words and the expression on his face?'

'No, I have no other proof.'

This passage has a finality about it that reverberates with the finality of Jesus' appearance before the Grand Inquisitor, or, indeed, his appearance before Pilate. For whereas members of the establishment, whether priests or governors or lawyers or doctors or policemen, are reduced to grubbing around for proofs of truth and for evasion of truth, Alyosha is able to go straight to the truth, unerring, through his brother's face.

Alongside those in the group who stressed the significance of a theology of the face, a still larger group maintained that the novel is 'all about' humiliation, and how the way of humility is ultimately the only way to recover from some deep humiliation. 'Bowing,' said one of our Buddhist companions, who practices bowing as a spiritual exercise. 'This novel is about how to become humble through bowing'. And certainly the deep meaning of humility is revealed through Father Zosima's prostrating himself at Dmitry's feet, 'with full conscious deliberation, even touching the ground with his forehead'. But false humility and its terrible consequences in further humiliation is displayed in Katya's bowing deeply before Dmitry, going down on her knees at his feet – 'with her head touching the floor'. And between the extremes of these two bows are many others in the story – some half-bows and some failed-bows, each of them filled with hidden meaning, and all of them answering Dmitry's question – 'Dmitry stood for a few seconds as though thunderstruck: the elder had bowed down to him – what was it all about?'

It became clear, in an unspoken fashion, to each of us reading the book, that humiliation is an experience we had all undergone. How right Dostoevsky was to put his finger on humiliation as an endless source of bitterness that never dries up throughout the length of one's life – unless the bitterness can be transformed into sweetness through humility and forgiveness. Otherwise, as we see in the case of every single character in the novel, from the elder Karamazov through Zosima to Smerdyakov and Alyosha, there is set in motion an inexorable cycle of humiliation and revenge, followed by claims to honour disguising shame which then seeks justification in claims to dignity bolstered by contempt for others; and this in turn keeps the cycle in motion by inflicting further humiliation.

There are at least 50 sections in *The Brothers Karamazov* where it is the infliction or the memory of humiliation which keeps the wheel of fate bearing the characters in the novel upon this cycle of bitterness. Indeed, there is a sense in which this theme runs throughout the whole of Dostoevsky's writings, as it does throughout his life, from the publication of *The Double* in 1846, through *The Insulted and Injured* in 1861, to *The Adolescent* in 1875, on the eve of his beginning to write *The Brothers Karamazov*. And still in 1875, in spite of all the prison walls he had broken through during the previous 30 years, Dostoevsky had not yet managed to make the final breakthrough out of the psychological dimension, where all events are mechanistically determined, into the world of the spirit where all relations grow in organic freedom.

That breakthrough was made through his writing *The Brothers Karamazov*. This is not to say, of course, that his previous writings had been in vain (though each of them is incomplete in the way that all preparatory work is incomplete), but rather that through his previous writings he had been gathering the weight of his experience into one point, a centre of integration through which the whole impetus and meaning of his past life might flow. What other writer, for instance, at the first attempt, could in such an unerring fashion have depicted the Devil in the manner in which he appears in Ivan's nightmare, as Ivan's perfect double? Consider the irony: Ivan, all intellect and good taste, and proud of it, complains that the Devil sent him is so stupid and vulgar. As Ivan's double, the Devil says, ' "You are hurt first of all in your aesthetic feelings and, secondly, in your pride. How could such a vulgar devil come to visit such a great man?" ' Again, what terrible energy is released as the double comes closer and closer to Ivan, ever more threatening the nearer he comes! At the same time, the closer Ivan comes to accepting the Devil as his double, so the closer the double comes to vanishing forever in a whiff of smoke.

' "I forbid you to speak of the Grand Inquisitor!" cried Ivan, colouring all over with shame.

"Well then, what about the Geological Upheavals, remember? That was a lovely poem."

"Shut up or I'll kill you." '

Dostoevsky had begun to work on this scene 30 years earlier when he composed *The Double*; even then he held in his hand the thread which would lead him out of the maze of psychology if only he would hang on to it. That thread is given in the words of Petrushka, ' "Good folks live honestly. Good folks live without falsity, and they never have doubles. God doesn't afflict honest folk." ' Put another way, when the double vanishes one becomes honest and integrated. Then, as Alyosha says over the exhausted Ivan, ' "God will conquer" '. Only God can overcome the shadow, the double, in the light of his simplicity.

This gift of discrimination by which a person can distinguish between the reality and the shadow, between the true and the false, is a gift which finally enabled Dostoevsky to present one true image which he had been struggling all his days to represent – that is, the presence of a 'fool for Christ', a *yurodivi*. The first intimation is to be found in Makar Ivanovich. His most ambitious attempt at depicting a character as a fool for Christ is Prince Myshkin in *The Idiot*. That attempt was a failure. Dostoevsky realised that it was a failure, significant because it helps to explain the next stage of his effort to integrate foolishness for Christ's sake into his own being and into his writing. In *The Brothers Karamazov* all the characters who make any claim to be fools for Christ – old Karamazov, Mikhail, and Father Ferapont – are all portrayed in such a way as to make a mockery of the claim.[1] It is as though Dostoevsky sought to illustrate the truth of St Seraphim's warning that only those who are exceptionally firm in intellect and character should undertake foolishness for Christ.

One might maintain that, by the time he came to write *The Brothers Karamazov*, Dostoevsky had ceased to admire *yurodstvo* – but to readers with even faint perceptiveness this is clearly not the case. *The Brothers Karamazov* is permeated with foolishness for Christ in the same way that a room is permeated with the smell of a perfume when the alabaster jar containing it is shattered; instead of being confined to one place, the perfume is now on all sides; it has become normal. Hence we understand why Dostoevsky underlines the health and 'normalcy' of Alyosha as compared with the sickness and angularity of Myshkin – he even intends to have Alyosha undertake marriage, an undertaking of which Prince Myshkin was incapable.

The process of integration is one of becoming whole and holy so that in the end there are no bits of experience left sticking out at an angle, unassimilated. Once this is recognised then it is possible to see that *The Brothers Karamazov* is indeed 'all about' foolishness for Christ – beginning with the time when Alyosha returned to Skotoprigonevsk not knowing why, and continuing with Zosima's refusal to duel, and Dmitry's not bothering to explain to the court why he did not return to Gregory, and, finally, with Alyosha's childlike behaviour with the children. The perfect fool for Christ is someone who is not regarded as just a fool (not for Christ, which is an ennobling role) but just a normal person being a fool.

In this respect, of course, Father Zosima is just a fool. Father Ferapont is a fool for Christ: the people 'had no doubt that he was a fool for Christ; it was the very fact of his being a fool for Christ that fascinated them'. To underline this, Dostoevsky makes us aware of Ferpont's rude speech, abrupt manner, his perception of evil spirits, and so on; but perhaps his most important and cunning characterisation is given when he has Ferapont say, ' "I am thinking of giving up their bread, for I don't need it at all, and going away into the woods and living on mushrooms or wild berries. They can't give up their bread here, and so they are still in bondage to the Devil." '

What a contrast here with Father Zosima! When Father Zosima began to stink in his coffin, one of the monks said, ' "He was not strict in fasting. He allowed himself sweet things. He took cherry jam in his tea. He loved it. Ladies used to send it to him." ' Dostoevsky is here drawing our attention to the fact that sectaries and false exemplars throughout the ages have always regarded food with suspicion, whereas the true faith tells us to find comfort in food. It is astonishing to discover on how many occasions throughout the novel one person or another takes food and immediately begins to feel better. Alyosha, on the way to Lake Street, 'took a roll he had brought from his father's and ate it on the way. This restored his strength.' Similarly, when Dmitry is returning from his exhausting expedition to Ilyinskoe,

> . . . he suddenly realised that he was terribly hungry. While the horses were being harnessed he ordered an omelette. He ate it all at once, ate a huge chunk of bread, ate a sausage which happened

to be available, and drank three glasses of vodka. Having thus fortified himself, he felt much more cheerful and his heart grew light again.

But the culminating illustration of how food is meant to be sacred comes appropriately enough in the final scenes. There the theme of bread is taken up once more, with Ilyusha's request that a crust of bread should be crumbled on his grave so that the sparrows might fly down upon it. But the point of the illustration comes with Kolya saying: ' "It is all so strange, Karamazov. Such sorrow, and all of a sudden – pancakes! The ways of our religion are unnatural." ' Alyosha, as is his way, does not reply immediately, but in almost the last words of the book he says to Kolya, ' "Don't get upset that we are going to be eating pancakes. It is an ancient custom, age-old and it is absolutely right." '

There is something to be said, therefore, in support of those people who affirm that *The Brothers Karamazov* is all about food – as well as in support of those who are inclined to see it as a theology of faces or a therapy for humiliation, and so on. But probably the most comprehensive vision is that which sees the novel as an invocation to remembrance. This is only to be expected when we know how deeply Dostoevsky was being influenced, during the time he was writing the novel, by that strange and wonderful man, Nikolai Fyodorov, of whom the novelist said, 'I have so thoroughly absorbed his thoughts that they seem to be my own'. Fyodorov believed that the root of man's misery and alienation was *forgetting*, and above all *forgetting the dead*. The task of humankind is to remember one another so intensely that the resurrection of the dead is a present reality. This reverberates like the guiding theme from the very beginning until the very end of *The Brothers Karamazov*. The early pages of the novel explain that Fyodor Pavlovich, the Karamazov father, abandoned his son Dmitry, 'because he simply forgot about his existence', and then soon afterwards 'forgot and abandoned' his other sons, Ivan and Alyosha. Here is the first forgetting, the monstrosity of a father forgetting his sons. In the same pages we have a liberal forgetting. Mitusov, a distant relative, makes the noble gesture of becoming Dmitry's guardian, but 'It so happened that having settled permanently in Paris he too forgot all about the child, especially when the

February Revolution broke out, which made such a strong impression upon his mind, and which he could never forget for the rest of his life'.

Nor is forgetting a flaw which affects only the wicked in the story. Alyosha, the hero, almost comes to grief through forgetting. On returning to the monastery where he finds Father Zosima so ill, for instance, Alyosha reproaches himself bitterly for having forgotten his elder through his preoccupation with the Karamazov imbroglio. But his subsequent forgetting entails yet more fateful consequences: he forgets about Dmitry after his conversation with Ivan, and for the rest of his life cannot imagine how he has done so, when he had known a few hours earlier how vital it was for him to find Dmitry and head him off from his fate. On two subsequent occasions he forgets Dmitry, because (as we showed in a previous quotation) he does not allow the memory of Dmitry to reach his heart. Again, he forgets the 200 roubles that Katya had given to him for Alyosha's father.

Meanwhile his brother Ivan also helps to seal Dmitry's fate. Ivan goes to Smerdyakov to find out what Smerdyakov had said to Katya that made her doubt Dmitry's guilt, and then he actually forgets to find out. ' "Good Lord!" Ivan cried suddenly, and his face darkened with anxiety. "Yes, I'd forgotten! Still, it makes no difference now" ' – but of course it makes all the difference, as the reader realises. Similarly the reader realises how crucial it was for Alyosha to have borne in mind Dmitry's puzzling gesture of pointing to the little bag hung around his neck, in which were the 1500 roubles which could substantiate his story. ' "How could I have forgotten it?" ' says Alyosha. ' "How could I have forgotten?" '

We, the readers, can answer Alyosha's question for him in words taken from the text. They are the words of the grieving peasant woman who has come to Father Zosima seeking consolation for the loss of her child, Alexey. ' "I have forgotten everything I have and I don't want to remember." ' People forget because they don't want to remember.

But if *The Brothers Karamazov* contains a severe warning to all against forgetting, it is even more a poem in praise of the beauty of remembrance. In those very first pages where Fyodor Pavlovich and Miusov are so monstrously forgetful, we learn by contrast that although Alyosha was only three years old when his mother died, nevertheless he remembered her all his life. And a few pages later, Dostoevsky evokes for us the moving image of Alyosha's mother, 'just as though she were standing alive' before us on a quiet summer's evening, by an open window and as the slanting rays of the setting sun turned towards the icon, praying to the Virgin to protect her child. This evocation reverberates throughout the novel, as when Father Zosima says,

> From the house of my parents, I have brought nothing but precious memories, for there are no memories more precious than those of one's early childhood in one's own home, and that is almost always so if there is any love and harmony in the family at all. Indeed, precious memories may be retained even from a bad home so long as your heart is capable of finding anything precious.

And then there is that terribly moving moment in court when old Dr Herzenstube (a man of *Herz*, or heart) is struggling to convey to the jury what it meant to him that Dmitry should have come back after 23 years to thank him for a pound of nuts given in the name of '*Gott der Vater, Gott der Sohn und Gott der heilige Geist*':

> 'And then I remembered the happy days of my youth and the poor boy without boots in the yard. And my heart turned over and I said, "You are a grateful young man, for you have remembered all your life the pound of nuts I gave you in your childhood". And I embraced him and blessed him and I wept. He laughed but he also cried, for a Russian often laughs when he should be crying. But he cried. I saw it, and now alas!'
>
> 'I'm crying now too, German. I'm crying now too, you dear old man!' Dmitry suddenly shouted out from his seat.

All of which leads us to the final scene of the book, Alyosha's speech to the boys at the stone, after Ilyusha's burial. Not only does this scene represent the consummation through remembrance of everything that has gone before in the story, but also it constitutes for Dostoevsky as a person the final point in his personal integration of all the experience accumulated by more than 50 years of the intensest living. Moreover, because it is a hymn, a hymn of praise, this chapter of the book cries out to be read aloud. And it is at this point that reading the novel aloud in *sobornost*, as opposed to reading it in isolation, makes all the difference in the world. We know the Hasidic warning about not writing stories down because then they can be taken away and read in isolation, in a cold and scoffing way, whereas it is only in warmth of heart that truth can flow from one human being to another. I have realised this ever since hearing two experts on Russian literature sneering at this last episode in *The Brothers Karamazov* as being senti-mental. One of those scholars spoke for both of them when he said scornfully, 'Karamazov and his boys! The redemption of the world through a boy-scout troop'.

None of us who had shared in reading the episode aloud at the Penny University could have spoken such crass words. There we all realised that the conclusion is a hymn to the sacred power of remem-brance, bringing together all those elements in the novel which had been transfigured in the course of the story: the earth, the humiliated, fools, birds, bread and children and the human face. The refrain of the hymn once heard can never be forgotten. It is repeated some 25 times within the space of two pages, the injunction *to remember* and not to forget, sounding antiphonally through Alyosha's speech and the boy's chorus in reply:

> 'Let us agree here at Ilyusha's stone never to forget, first Ilyusha, and, secondly, one another . . . I'm sure you will remember that there is nothing higher, stronger, more wholesome and more useful in life than some good memory, especially when it goes back to the days of your childhood, to the days of your life at home. You are told a lot about your education, but some beautiful, sacred memory preserved since childhood, is perhaps the best education of all. If a man carries many such memories into life with him, he is saved for the rest of his days. And even if only one good memory is left in our hearts, it may also be the instrument of our salvation one day.'

After joining in this hymn and hearing Alyosha's concluding invitation to go along hand-in-hand and eat pancakes in memory of the dead – ' "for it is an ancient custom, age-old, and it's absolutely right" ' – there was nothing left for those of us who had read *The Brothers Karamazov* together in the Café Pergolesi than to go and spend the evening eating pancakes together. Indeed it may well be that the test of whether a person has understood *The Brothers Karamazov* at all is whether she goes and eats pancakes with her friends when completing the reading.

Though in truth, one never finishes reading it. For as Père Congar once said, 'Every theologian should read at least the episode of the Grand Inquisitor once every year just to keep him on the way of truth'. I would take this further and suggest that if what I have been saying is valid, and *The Brothers Karamazov* really *is* the best book for raising religious issues of our age, then our theologians should be instructed to put away their own treatises for a year and spend the year's lectures in *lectio divina* with their students over *The Brothers Karamazov*. It might help some of them personally, following Dostoevsky's footsteps, to achieve integration. And those who now see no meaning in the Holy Trinity might learn from Dr Herzenstube that *Gott der Vater, Gott der Sohn und Gott der heilige Geist* can be found in the gift of a bag of nuts.

6

Spirit: a force for survival

(1994)

It sometimes happens that the person called upon to deliver a memorial lecture finds himself in an awkward situation, knowing that the person in whose name he has to speak was no more than remotely interested in the matters which the lecturer himself wishes to address. Fortunately for me, that is far from being the case, since at my first meeting with John Todd we both realised how close together were our respective visions of what it is to be a human being. And during the subsequent 40 years of friendship our visions grew ever more closely aligned.

Our starting-point was the realisation, more clearly grasped by John than by me, that humanity is in a perilous condition, threatened by forces of evil both from within and without. That peril will lead to destruction, so we thought, unless humanity is endowed with the spirit, the courage, to look without flinching at the forces of destruction, and yet to believe that some sort of redemption is possible. Our position was that to which Emmanuel Mounier gave the title *optimisme tragique*,[1] and what I have to say to you this evening is an elaboration on that title.

However, I recognise that there is very little agreement among the members of the human family themselves as to the nature of our condition. So I have decided to invoke extra-terrestrial help in an effort to find a point of view which does not suffer from the limitations imposed by our individual perspectives.

In order for us to achieve such a point of view, I would ask that we all envisage a company of extra-terrestrial beings who are gazing down upon the earth in this year of grace 1994. They have been thinking back over the last 200 years of the earth's history, intrigued by certain obvious and quite radical changes in the earth's appearance since 1794. They have been so puzzled by what they have observed that they have drawn up a report upon them.

The most striking change they report is that the earth has lost its dark side. For millenia upon millenia each part of the earth used to go into darkness and take its rest every 24 hours. But now, in 1994, the darkness is destroyed by great patches of light; and throughout the whole 24 hours there are myriads of tiny points of light moving around the dark side.

Also unmistakable is the transformation of the daylight surface of the earth. For vast areas that were once green have now become brown and grey, as if the earth itself were suffering from a severe skin disease. Moreover, just as there are myriads of dots of light endlessly moving throughout the night, so during the day there are myriads of small objects moving here, there and everywhere. These features represent an enormous change from what we discovered in 1794, says the ET report.

At that date we used to notice very little movement over the face of the earth; and whatever movement there was took place very slowly. But now it goes on without ceasing and at frantic speeds. The image it calls to mind is of an ant-heap that has been zapped by a petrol bomb, causing the ants to rush around in a frenzy, bewildered and out of control.

Alarmed at what we have seen, so the ET report goes on, and the likely consequences of the seeming madness if it were to spread beyond the earth, we decided to send some of our outstandingly intelligent members to the earth in order to find out, if possible, what has been going on there since 1794 that might explain the rapid, radical changes we had noted.

Our members, on returning from the earth, reported as follows. There can be no doubt that the source of the frenzy – the incessant movement and the craziness afflicting the earth – is to be found in the species of two-legged creatures who claim for themselves the title *Homo sapiens*.

Homo sapiens, for instance, is the creature responsible for having turned so much of the earth's green covering into those brown-coloured patches which we interpret as symptoms of the earth's skin cancer. They have, for example, cut down the forests at such a rate, and on such a scale – in Brazil, Canada, Russia, the Philippines,

Indonesia and countless other places – that they have destroyed innumerable other species of animals, plants and seeds which had taken billions of years to develop. In so doing they have severely damaged the atmosphere upon which their own lungs depend to keep themselves alive, and as a result they are rapidly asphyxiating themselves. By the same token they are destroying the thin layer of top-soil that covers the earth, and without which they themselves will starve to death.

Even more astonishing to us is their habit of killing one another, a habit that has become more ingrained since 1794. During the eighteenth century, for instance, on the continent of Europe, only a very small percentage of the population used to join in battles against others. And when they did so the casualties were numbered in a few thousands. But since 1794 more and more sections of the population have been conscripted into national armies – including on occasion virtually all the able-bodied males. Furthermore the killers do not only kill one another these days. Rather they kill those who have no weapons – children and old people especially. All told, in fact, the inhabitants of the most highly educated continent – that is, Europe – have killed one another to the tune of 100 million in what they call warfare.

But there is a yet more inexplicable and bizarre form taken by the human habit of killing. In some countries, as a matter of routine, they actually kill their own children in the womb.

Our reporters went on to say that they had questioned many of the two-legged creatures in an effort to discover if any of them were even slightly aware of how the behaviour of *Homo sapiens* might be judged by someone outside their own world. For the most part all they received in answer to their questioning was a blank stare, as though *Homo sapiens* finds it difficult to conceive that there is any world beside his own. Interestingly, however, our reporters did come across some persons whose family traditions required them to believe that outside their own little world there are other beings. Indeed, there is a Supreme Being, they maintain, who many centuries ago conveyed to them a series of commandments as to how they are meant to live. And as a seal upon his message the Supreme Being said: 'I have set before you life and death, blessing and cursing. Therefore, choose life, so that you and your children may live.'

Clearly the two-legged creatures have disobeyed the commandments and have continued to choose death rather than life. That is
why a special envoy was sent by the Supreme Being of whom the
following story is told.

This envoy was travelling through a district named Gadara when
he met a couple of two-legged ones who were possessed by demons.
Terrified by the presence of the envoy the demons fled out of the
possessed couple and entered into a nearby herd of swine which then
charged down the hill and plunged to destruction over a cliff into
the lake below. 'This story', so the final paragraph of our ET report
records, 'is known among the two-legged as the parable of the
Gadarene swine, and to us extra-terrestrials it seems to be a very
exact image of the mad dash towards the abyss which the two-leggeds
are now making.'

Since I am myself a member of the two-legged family which has
driven the extra-terrestrials to the brink of despair, I would like to
explain to them, as well as for my own satisfaction, how the process
they deplore has been experienced by those of us who have been on
the inside of the process, and have had to make decisions without
their privileged hindsight. I mean to show, at the same time, that the
last word does not belong to despair.

In a word, the image of the Gadarene swine presents only the dark
side of that unprecedented growth in knowledge and technology
which has taken place in the last two centuries, a growth which
has opened up hitherto undreamed-of possibilities in medicine and
education, in means of communication and in control of our
environment.

Take the case of medicine, for example. Because of progress in that
field only a small fraction of the women who used to die in childbirth
now do so, and the number of children who die in infancy has
likewise plummeted. In addition, diseases such as malaria, sleeping-
sickness, cholera and typhus, which used to decimate whole peoples,
have now been brought under control. However, the very success of
medical science has led to an exponential increase in the number
of human beings who have to share the earth's limited resources. But
we have failed miserably in the task of learning how to share those
resources, as a result of which the land, the sea and the air of the

earth are all becoming exhausted. So the advances in medicine which once promised health for all now threaten the health of all.

A similar story has to be told about the great increase in the variety, speed and efficiency of our means of communication, whether by trains or cars or aeroplanes, by telegram, telephone or Internet. The increase has meant that human beings now have infinitely more information at their disposal than any of their ancestors ever had.

By the same token, however, the power-centres of the world are enabled to use those new resources of communication to exercise control over their subject-populations to a degree unimaginable in previous times. Consider, for instance, how few of the authoritarian decrees issued by the French kings from Versailles in the eighteenth century were ever complied with in the French provinces, where many of the decrees were never even heard of. Or note how the people of my own West Riding simply ignored the Poor Law Act of 1832 for years, and how impossible it proved for London to enforce it. Yet news of similar dissent in our own day, whether in France or in England, would be communicated to the central authorities within seconds, and they could have their agents on the spot within the hour to enforce their decrees.

Through such an exponential increase in the means of communication, moreover, the power-centres no longer have to remain content with external obedience on the part of people who live at a distance. They have the means to quell dissent on the periphery in a much more radical, if subtle, manner. They can reach into the very souls of peripheral groups, and colonise them from within. Think, for example, of how English power established in London has in recent centuries uprooted Celtic cultures in Wales, Ireland and Scotland; and how England's apprentice, the USA, by means of its supremacy in information technology, is roaring across the earth like some giant, deranged combine-harvester uprooting every culture that stands in its way.

We are witnessing the culmination of that process, to which the Nazis applied a favourite term of theirs: *Gleichschaltung*. Taken literally it means shunting into line, and was initially passed off as an administrative measure to achieve efficiency – very much in the spirit of a British health trust chairman who lately made the sinister claim that the primary duty of doctors is not towards their patients but to the system they serve. On a world scale, according to the poet David Jones, it is in the name of *Gleichschaltung* that the current world-power considers itself:

> detailed to beat
> to discipline the world-floor
> to a common level
> till everything presuming difference
> and all the sweet demarcations
> wither
> to the touch of us
> and know the fact of empire.[2]

The climax of the process is imminent when the entire earth will be locked into the new Internet technology which will only work if there is available a common alphabet and a universal language. Who can doubt that the chosen language will be American, and even then in its poverty-stricken form? I wish to emphasise the world-wide poverty that will result therefrom; because it is easily forgotten that every age-old culture now being flattened has secreted within it some precious insights into the human condition. Those insights are embedded in its rituals and its language. Yet over the last few centuries, hundreds of those languages have perished, and with them have been lost seeds of wisdom – and lost for ever, moreover – in precisely the same way that so many plants, trees, seeds and species have also been lost for ever.

But what, then, is to become of the resultant monoculture? Ecologists have made us realise that biodiversity is essential to the richness of life – and, indeed, that a decline in biodiversity takes an ecological system closer and closer to a condition of stasis that is indistinguishable from death. Which leads to a paradox lying within the increase of power at the centre. It is that those centres themselves thereby become increasingly vulnerable. The most advanced societies on earth, for instance, would collapse completely if their supply of oil and electricity were to be interrupted. They would wither on the stalk within months.

Whether consciously or unconsciously, the masters of these advanced societies are aware of this threat to their very existence, which is why they are hag-ridden with anxiety. But since the prospect of their demise is too painful for them to face up to, they fall back upon a demagogic slogan in order to mask their own and others' anxieties. They describe those who call attention to humanity's perilous condition as 'scaremongers' and 'prophets of doom'. They comfort themselves by claiming that our ancestors before us used to voice similar forebodings, and yet those forebodings have not been fulfilled. A similar claim was made by the man who jumped from the top of a 30-storey skyscraper and who, as he fell past the seventh storey, exclaimed, 'Well, so far so good'.

However, such a nonchalant attitude must in the end lead to despair, because it represents a failure to search for the underlying factors which have precipitated our perilous situation. And so I will now venture to point to one or two of those factors.

As a preliminary to doing so I call your attention to one anthropologist's observation that the most profound change produced by a technologically advanced society upon people in a less technologically advanced society is a change in their manner of living in time, in the way they regard time, in the time they give to various activities of work and leisure and worship. An extreme example of such a change is that brought about by capitalist society through its fundamental axiom, 'Time is money'. In that one banal, blasphemous phrase, sacred time is abolished. And it is rapidly becoming clear that in capitalist society, even more than in Communist society, there is no time for sabbath – since with sabbath, time is a free gift, a space for celebration which cannot be fitted into a calendar where every second of every day, and every day of every year, has to be available for production and buying and selling. Celebration, like every creative engagement, requires its own time, which is not the time of accountants and the assembly-line but the time of musicians, artists and poets. The poet T. S. Eliot evoked that world of spontaneity and freedom when he wrote:

> Sudden in a shaft of sunlight
> Even while the dust moves
> There rises the hidden laughter
> Of children in the foliage
> Quick now, here, now, always.[3]

When time is defined as money it is abolished in much the same way as modern advanced societies also claim to have abolished distance. Those claims leave traditional societies feeling that they have been robbed of both time and distance, and therefore are denied room in which to breathe.

What all this suggests to me is that increasingly advances in technology call for human beings to change their life-patterns at a speed which is beyond the capacity of the majority of humanity as a whole.

At least, that is what the history of humanity seems to show. Consider, for a moment, the story which in one form or another is foundational for so many human societies. The form most familiar to Western society is the story of Adam and Eve. And out of all the innumerable commentaries upon that story there is one that rarely receives attention but is specially relevant to our theme. Briefly put, the interpretation of the story states that Adam and Eve were actually meant to eat of the tree of the knowledge of good and evil, but only in God's time, and not at a time of their own choosing. Their fault was to have snatched for the apple, impatient for what they desired, hoping they could speed up the process. In so doing they unleashed forces beyond their control that were to shape human destiny both for good and for ill.

Soon, so the story goes, man the gardener was displaced by man the hunter; then the hunter had to give way to the pastoralist, the pastoralist to the agriculturalist and the agriculturalist to the industrialist. And since the lead-time between one stage and the next grows shorter with each change, this inevitably means that the process of change speeds up exponentially right to the present-day, when we can observe industrial man being overtaken by the man of electronic signals.

Also noteworthy about each of these stages in human development is that the new man who emerges not only has an interest in discrediting his displaced predecessor – minimising the debt owed to him and the toll of his sufferings – but is also impelled to proclaim that his own arrival and his new technology herald the dawn of a new paradise.

This is particularly true when his triumph, as is almost always the case, is due to his superiority in the technology of weapons. That superiority gives rise to the illusion that the new weapons provide them with perpetual peace and security which, under their govern-ance, will then be dispensed to all who obey them.

The illusion may take the shape of the crossbow or the war-horse or, as in the case of Nobel of the Peace Prize, his explosives which he confidently maintained would put an end to warfare. But always there has been such illusion. And in no instance was that illusion more succinctly expressed than in a sermon preached in St Paul's, London, on Christmas Day, 1621, by the poet John Donne. Donne's sermon was in praise of reason, and one of his grounds for the praise was that:

> By benefit of this light of reason they have invented Artillery, by which means warres are brought to quicker ends than heretofore, and the great expense of blood is avoided; for the numbers of men slain now, since the invention of Artillery, are much lesse than before, when the sword was the executioner.[4]

Even as late as 1945, when the A-bombs were dropped upon Japan, there were some who maintained that the very awfulness of the latest weapon would inevitably drive humanity into the camp of peace. But that illusion also has now been shattered *pari passu* with our awakening to the reality that this latest instrument of destruction has placed humanity in a far more perilous situation than any it had encountered previously. For no matter how fearful previous tech-niques for killing may have been, none of them offered the possibility that humanity might thereby destroy itself. In earlier years a tribe might be destroyed, or even a nation, but there was never the fear that the whole of humanity itself might be destroyed. But which of us can be immune from such fear, now that instruments of germ-warfare have been invented that make atomic bombs seem almost like child's play? I had particular reason to think hard about the atom-bomb which was dropped just as Operation Zipper was about to land me and my comrades in Malaya, and which may well, therefore, have saved our lives. My ponderings during that period led me to realise that humanity was now in a position to commit suicide.

During the following months I formulated a question that was preoccupying me, and which I raised every now and again with my comrades: that is, 'Who, exactly, dropped the A-bomb?'

Not unnaturally my comrades mocked my philosophical musings,

saying, 'The fellow who pulled the lever, numbskull'. But then I
pointed out that he could not have managed it without the pilot
who guided the plane, and the pilot could not have guided the plane
unless someone had built the plane, etc. And so we traced responsibility for the A-bomb backwards in ever-widening circles, until
eventually my comrades gave in and acknowledged that the A-bomb
was the end-result of myriads of acts of injustice and cowardice by
millions of human beings which had gradually built up to a situation
where one could rightly say that the A-bomb had virtually dropped
itself, since it was simply the precipitate of myriads of small acts by a
whole host of human beings.

Though I did not recognise it at the time, I was already coming
to recognise that everything which manifests in the visible world is
the result of decisions made in the invisible world. That realisation
was later to be confirmed as regards that other most visible manifestation of death in the twentieth century, the Holocaust, by the words
of Mme Hautval. She was a French Protestant doctor, a survivor from
Auschwitz, who summed up her experience in the sentence, 'All the
terrible deeds in this world are the result of small acts of cowardice'.[5]

Whether cowardice is the only precipitator of death is open to
question – but it is certainly an element in it whenever we bow
down in the face of death and choose death rather than life. Strangely
enough, the most vociferous advocates of bowing down before death
in our own day are some whose profession it is to study life – that
is, biologists. A number of them have lately been assuring us
that human beings are no more than one species amid a myriad of
species destined to die out like every other species, so there is nothing
special about the species *Homo sapiens*. 'We know from the second
law of thermodynamics,' writes Professor Dawkins, 'that all complexity and all life, all laughter, and all sorrow, are hell-bent on
levelling themselves out into cold nothingness – we can never be
more than local and temporary buckings of the great universal slide
into the abyss of uniformity.' So, 'What is so special about human
life, given that we are close cousins of other apes and more distant
cousins of all animals and plants?'[6] That last question posed by Professor Dawkins did not, of course, anticipate an answer, being
rhetorical – but the answer is in fact embedded in his own vocabulary.
For when he speaks of 'cousins' he is using an idiom that characterises

humans, and he implicitly recognises thereby that there is something peculiar to human beings which is best expressed by thinking of us primarily as a family rather than as a species.

Is that not something which the classical biologists also recognised? For in Greek terminology there is attributed to the human being not only *bios*, life and *psyche*, soul, but also *pneuma*, spirit.

And here we come to the crux of the whole issue of resistance to the forces of death. We are brought face to face with the question: is everything totally subject to the laws of *bios*? or is there, indeed, *pneuma*, spirit, which is stronger than death?

In answer to that question I cannot refrain from quoting the words of a man from my own neck of the woods who also has his place in the story of this city of Bristol – James Nayler. In 1660, some two hours before his death, after he had been beaten up on his way home to Wakefield, Nayler said:

> There is a Spirit which I feel that delights to do no evil, but delights to endure all things, in hope to enjoy its own in the end. Its hope is to outlive all wrath and contention, and to weary out all exaltation and cruelty, or whatever is of a nature contrary to itself. It sees to the end of all temptations. As it has no evil in itself, so it conceives none in thoughts to any other. If it be betrayed, it bears it, for its ground and spring is the mercies and forgiveness of God. Its crown is meekness, its life is everlasting love unfeigned; and it takes its kingdom with entreaty and not with contention, and keeps it by lowliness of mind. In God alone it can rejoice, though none else regard it, or can own its life. It's conceived in sorrow, and brought forth without any to pity it, nor doth it murmur at grief and oppression. I found it alone, being forsaken. I have fellowship therein with them who live in dens and desolate places in the earth, who through death obtained this resurrection and eternal holy life.[7]

These words from Nayler, one of the early leaders of the Society of Friends, derive their power from the fact that he witnessed to the power of the spirit not only by words but also by his life and his death. The Greek word for such a witness is *martus*, martyr, a person who according to Albert Camus has answered the one absolutely fundamental question that every human being has to answer: Is life worth living? And Camus goes on to say that each human being, whether consciously or unconsciously, is making that choice by the way they live.[8]

In that sense it is now becoming clear that, not only does each human being face such a choice, but so does the human family as a whole. And it has to be acknowledged that a powerful case can be made, and has been made, for subscribing to the ancient Greek aphorism, 'Not to be born were best', especially now when not only is the incidence of suffering and cruelty upon the earth increasing, but through television and other means of communication its weight upon the heart of the human family is multiplied enormously. Surely it would be best, in accordance with the proposal of von Hartmann, the disciple of Schopenhauer, that humanity should co-ordinate all its energies in order eventually to annihilate this world which brings so much suffering and which, in principle, can never be redeemed.[9]

I do not see how such a proposal for collective euthanasia could be defeated by the power of any form of reasoning, or any philosophical or theological theory. Only a practical demonstration can nullify a theory, for in real life one showing is worth more than any number of theories. Happily such a showing is provided by the martyrs, those who witness to the truth, who manifest the truth, that there is a spirit which is stronger than suffering and death. And it is the glory of the twentieth century that just as it has provided in abundance the most powerful arguments ever for the human family to choose death, so it has brought forth such a cloud of martyrs, witnesses to the spirit, as has never been since time began. In Germany and the Soviet Union, and in other countries in Europe, as well as in Africa, Asia and Latin America, thousands of men, women and children have borne witness to the human capacity to resist the forces of death, to overcome the threat of death by choosing, like James Nayler before them, to live in the spirit.

But conversely, it is the misery of our century, and especially of our own generation, that we have failed to heed the witness of all those noble martyrs, their resistance against the forces of death. We have not heeded the words of the Czech writer Milan Kundera that, 'such resistance is the struggle of memory against forgetting'.[10] Indeed, of all people it was a historian, supposedly a keeper of memory, A. J. P. Taylor, who wrote, 'The German resistance movement is of no interest to the historian because it was politically impotent'. What Taylor never seems to have realised is something that many Germans of the younger generation tell us: that although it was the famous German economic miracle that enabled them to survive physically, nevertheless they would be unable to live with themselves as Germans, spiritually, were it not for the presence in their history of those members of the German resistance who chose to live by the spirit rather than submit to the forces of death.

A roll of honour celebrating those human beings who have redeemed our death-bearing situation would be a very long one indeed. But perhaps I may be permitted to cite for you one instance which I myself encountered personally, but which is little known.

In 1984 I was invited to the commemoration in Marzobotto, a community to the south of Bologna, of the massacre that had taken place there 40 years previously of some 2,000 citizens of Marzobotto. One of the abiding memories of my visit is that if ever one of the guests at the commemoration happened to speak of 'the massacre by the Germans', then one of the citizens of Marzobotto would politely correct them, explaining that it was not the Germans but the Nazis who had been responsible. The reason why the people of that community were always so careful to make that correction was because, on the day of the massacre, one young German soldier had refused to take part and had himself been shot in consequence. That young soldier, in his stark loneliness, had saved the good name of his nation.

Yes, as I said earlier, it is the shame of our day that so few of us are ever told about the thousands of witnesses of which the young German soldier was but one. But how can the younger generation learn when our very institutions of learning themselves give such little attention to those events? In how many of our universities, for instance, whether the ancient ones or the newly-burgeoning ones, are there courses – or even single lectures – on the story of these resisters against the forces of death? And since final examination papers represent the clearest signal to students of what is regarded as important, it is instructive to see how rarely these witnesses to the spirit appear in them.

Again, if we run over in our minds the number of volumes in our libraries, the number of lectures in our classrooms and the number of hours of study we devote to the works of death, think of how few are accorded to the symbols of life. Almost all history students, for example, devote many hours to that embodiment of death, Joseph Stalin. But how many who pass through our halls of learning are ever told of that moment in 1934 when Russia's great poet Osip Mandelstam was being interrogated by officers of the secret police, the NKVD, concerning his poem on Stalin, and Mandelstam unwaveringly recited his lines about Stalin:

> The Kremlin highlander is mentioned
> His fingers are fat like worms,
> His words hit hard like heavy weights
> His cockroach's huge moustaches laugh,
> And the tops of his boots shine brightly.[11]

What sort of priority is it which pays so much attention to the monstrous death-bearer but does not treasure that moment when the life-giving poet faced the death-bearer's minions?

One might, of course, respond that it may be necessary to study the martyrs in an age of apocalypse, but that they are not very relevant in a society such as ours where the temperature is so low and we are protected from the most extreme forms of suffering.

But that would be an unenlightened response. For just as Plato, in order to search out justice in the soul, projected it writ large on the screen of his *Republic*, so it is with us: we see the truth about the choices in our daily lives when we see them in the light of the martyrs, the witnesses to the spirit. Surely that was the lesson Sir Walter Moberly was hoping to teach us, particularly us university teachers, when he published his book *The Crisis in the University*[12] soon after the second world war? For he had been dismayed and alarmed at the failure of the German universities to inspire any considerable resistance to National Socialism. And he wanted us to scrutinise the patterns of behaviour and priorities in our own universities in order to discover whether they might not manifest a similar unreadiness when faced with a similar *Gleikschaltung*.

Put quite starkly: have we in British universities provided any considerable lead to resistance against the forces of death rampaging abroad throughout the earth during the past 50 years? Would it be unfair to say that the conflicts, for instance, in Northern Ireland, in Bosnia and the Middle East, as well as the struggle against nuclear proliferation and the arms trade, might almost have been taking place on another planet as far as our universities have been concerned? That failure to lead the resistance in such wider matters may well go some way to explain the supine fashion in which the universities have colluded in their own *Gleikschaltung* at the hands of successive governments. Have they not allowed themselves to be either bullied or seduced into a state of blindness which has left them incapable of seeing that it is the university itself which is now at stake?

Reflect for a moment on the significance of my old university's having accepted £3 million pounds from Rupert Murdoch in order to establish a Rupert Murdoch Chair of Communications, along with several research fellowships. Not surprisingly, university spokesmen assured us that the source of the money would not in any way influence the teaching from the chair established. Equally unsurprising, however, was the statement in the first professor's inaugural lecture that she wishes to emulate 'some Murdochian qualities ... above all, farsightedness, global vision, a capacity for goal-directed hard work, and a deep interest in the media'?[13] When I read those words I could hardly help noticing that the qualities attributed to Murdoch did not include a love of truth; nor, indeed, that a powerful claim for the qualities described as 'Murdochian' could be made in favour of Joseph Stalin.

And even though Stalin belongs in a different dimension from the proprietor of News International, the lessons which the great martyrs of resistance offer us when face to face with the former are equally valid when we are facing the latter. In dealing with all bullies and megalomaniacs, so Solzhenitsyn assures us from his own experience, 'You must not even grant them so much as the tip of your little finger. If you do so then you will never get free except at the price of cutting off your finger' – an observation which gives added meaning to the gospel injunction that if your right hand leads you into sin then you must cut it off if you wish to be free.

Having now pointed to some of the areas in which the struggle for life against death is taking place I would like to touch upon three issues which will, I hope, illustrate how each one of us is engaged in the struggle even though we may initially consider the scale of them to be beyond us, and that we are therefore exempt.

The first issue, in fact, is that of scale, in regard to which the key statement is the declaration of Mme Hautval, previously quoted, that 'All terrible deeds in this world are the result of small acts of cowardice'. To that declaration might be added the gloss that one root of such cowardice lies in giving in to the feeling that the events of one's own small world have no bearing upon the shape of events in the world as a whole. Whenever that feeling arises within us, we need to remember a truth complementary to Mme Hautval's statement: that is, all the great movements of healing in the world are the result of myriads of small acts of courage. An eloquent reminder of that truth is to be found in a letter written in his last illness by David Jones. One of his correspondents had likened David's experience of illness to the agony David had experienced at Mametz Wood during the epic battle of the Somme in 1916, as recorded in his poem *In Parenthesis*. David, in answer to his correspondent, wrote: 'Yes, Mametz again, but a bloody sight worse . . . Thinking for hours on end of all the trials, pain, miseries of the human race I am beginning to think that these "ordinary" accustomed things are more demanding of "bravery" or whatever the words [than bravery in battle].'[14]

The question of scale is equally crucial for a further issue which I touched upon earlier, and that is the need to remember that, though we may be a species for purposes of biological classification, we are a family in spirit. And one of the characteristics of a family is that each individual member is intrinsically precious. That is a truth more and more difficult to hang on to as images of mass-killings are flashed before our eyes every day. As one journalist has recorded:

> I saw the worst sights of my life in Rwanda, like the dead at the Church of Ntaramma. Dry-retching as I battled to take notes, I came away concerned for my mind, worried that I was learning a contempt for life through the discovery of the low value attached to it. A contempt which must eventually prove self-destructive. [So I] stumble on behind the Four Horsemen of the Apocalypse.

Another journalist reports, 'In Rwanda it was impossible to think of the killers as human at all', and impossible not to think of the victims 'as no more than rotting cabbages'.[15] And I myself have to say that if we fall into the habit of regarding ourselves as no more than one species among others, then there is no good reason for us to mourn the death of any individual so long as the species survives, nor any good reason why in certain circumstances we should not cull millions of human beings in much the same way, for instance, as we cull seals when they become too numerous. We could do it less violently, of course. By contrast, if we can learn to live by the spirit, as a family, then the life and death of any one member of the family will be treated as equally and uniquely significant as that of any other member of the family. And in the same spirit as the human family takes responsibility for the lives of its own members, it will also accept responsibility for preserving other species.

The final issue of scale raised by my talk and which I wish to highlight is the one emphasised by my imaginary extra-terrestrials – that is, the exponential acceleration in speed to which the human family has subjected itself, especially by accepting clock-time as the yardstick by which to shape our activities. How destructive it is for human beings to measure their life and work by the clock was instinctively felt by the French communards who took over Paris in 1870. Almost their first act was to go around the city shooting off the hands of the public clocks, on the grounds that the clock was their enemy, the instrument of their enslavement. But, of course, it was already too late because the clock had by that time got inside their heads, as it has ensconced itself in ours, so that most of us now believe as though by reflex that hours and minutes are just as much constituents of the universe as are the sun and the moon. Hence the widespread illusion that the more actions you cram into an hour, the more life you are enjoying – and the connected illusion that by increasing the quantity and intensity of stimuli you increase your enjoyment of life, when the truth is that you are more likely to become exhausted and finish up incapable of any joy whatsoever.

Fittingly it was the vice-president of the USA, Al Gore, who set his seal of approval on this illusion when he told his fellow-countrymen that they must get into the fast lane of the information super-highway or else they would be left behind. It was an unfortunate, if revealing, metaphor which he chose, since in the fast lane of a super-highway of exponentially increasing speed you are virtually certain either to get run over and squashed or else be first over into the abyss.

In fact the only people who can be confident about surviving are the ones left behind – the very people who, in the biblical story, are described as the remnant. The remnant (Hebrew *sheerith*) signifies that group of people which seems to be left behind by the events of history, and yet is the group in which is preserved the promise of a truly human life and which is the hope for the human family. To quote the prophet Micah:

> I shall restore the lost as a remnant
> and turn the outcasts into a mighty nation.
> The Lord will be their king on Mount Zion
> for ever from that time forward.[16]

Not unnaturally, upon reading these lines from Micah, one seeks to discern those groups of human beings who might qualify as the saving remnant. And when I attempted to do so, I came to a strange conclusion. In the light of my own experience I have to report that the groups who know best how to live in sacred time, how to celebrate and offer spontaneous welcome, are those for the mentally disabled in the L'Arche movement or communities of sufferers from Down's Syndrome. A similar conclusion was forced upon the psychiatrist Dr Piachaud after he had watched a play by Strachona, a Down's Syndrome theatre company. He said, 'As a species we have become so competitive that we are poised on the edge of self-destruction. These people teach us another way.'[17]

It is strange, at least initially, to conclude that essential humanity is safer in such communities of the mentally handicapped than in the hands of the self-important figures who flit across our television screens. So it may well be that anyone who chooses to join in the resistance against the forces of death upon the earth and be a witness to the spirit, which is life, has also to choose to go with them into the slow lane of life. There they will have time to give themselves to the humble, everyday tasks that David Jones spoke about, time to appreciate the uniqueness of every human being and the wonder of creation, fulfilling the dictum of Boris Pasternak: 'In an epoch of speed one needs to learn to think slowly'.

Yet suppose that someone is moved to take up resistance against the forces of death, what reason can they be given for believing that the resistance will be successful? The answer is, 'None'. It is a matter of faith which is inseparable from courage.

This issue used regularly to be brought up by my students when we were studying the Soviet Union. They would protest that there was no more point in a Soviet citizen trying to resist Bolshevik tyranny than there would be in trying to stop an avalanche with one's head. In answer I used to draw their attention to the epigraph which the prophetic Dostoevsky had set at the head of his great novel *The Brothers Karamazov*, an epigraph whose significance continues to puzzle many commentators. The epigraph reads, 'Unless the grain of wheat, falling to the ground dies, itself remaineth alone. But if it dies it brings forth much fruit.' Have not subsequent events shown that, as with ancient Israel so with the Soviet Union – it is the martyrs, those witnesses to the spirit, who are the seeds of Life, who in the end prove stronger than the forces of death?

Part II

7

Good Friday, 1950

(1951)

It was dark. Looking up from the floor towards the window I could feel, rather than see, the dawn breaking. But to try to sleep now was useless, even though the priest in the next cell had at last become quiet. All night long his groans had sounded through the wall between us, getting more like a mad nightmare as the night wore on and as their echo rang up from the floor on to my ears and nerves. Old priests and old nuns left lonely in their cells during years of trial; it is not often that one has the grace of being so close to them, so I had asked God to let me share the old priest's pain; and the night had been long. The darkness lay heavy upon me, shutting me in upon my own emptiness. Out of habit my mind twisted to escape from the emptiness, searching for the light shining in eyes which I loved, only to fall back upon itself, sinking into emptiness once more. No explanation was needed; today was the death of God; the day when the light of God's countenance revealed my sins, the sight of which caused Christ so much suffering that he had to shut his eyes. Today I should not look into the eyes I was searching for, since there was darkness over the earth. I closed my own eyes, for there was no light.

On each of my members Lent had left its mark; on my feet the mark of hard roads, in my head the ache of sleepless nights, while days of hunger were making my stomach squirm towards my backbone in search of food. If only I could fill myself with bread! Not until these last few days had I known that kind of hunger which possesses you so completely that every part of your body begins to ache, as though even your toes and eyes could eat if given the chance. I had learnt the difference between going hungry and fasting: that fasting is something which we organise, an experience which we can control with our minds and subdue it; when we are fasting under obedience we always know at the back of our minds that we *shall* eat at a certain hour in the future – if Lent occupies the foreground, we comfort ourselves with the thought of Easter, and the surrender is not complete. Going hungry, as beggars go hungry, is entirely different: they do not know when they will eat next; they cannot organise their experience, because hunger becomes the 'mastering-me God', the God who strikes relentlessly from moment to moment until the soul cries, 'then lull, then leave off'. Trying to learn what hunger means to a beggar by fasting has little more chance of success than trying to share the lot of the miserable worker by living for six months in the slums. The secret of the beggar's suffering, as of the worker's suffering, is that it cannot be given any form; the mind cannot fix itself round it to give it shape and significance; hunger and misery invade their persons like great waves pouring into every nook and cranny of their being, flooding their every member until the waters cover their souls. And there is no end to it – only the hardly, barely prayable prayer that seems to be no prayer at all.

Bread is the first thing. And it is a measure of our failure as Christians that we have forgotten first things, that we imagine ourselves living on a higher plane. But bread is also the last thing in this life, at any rate for those of us who love God. At the highest moment of our spiritual life, in the ecstasy of communion, we eat consecrated bread, and, like the apostles, we know Jesus Christ in the breaking of bread. Even the ancient Egyptians realised that no one would be justified after death unless they could say, 'I never allowed anyone to suffer hunger'; but many of us Christians have fallen below the level of Egyptian religion. It was with admiration, and not with horror, that a friend once told me of a priest so detached from creatures, so wholly given to God, that he would give alms to beggars with the words, 'I am not giving you this, my man, out of pity for you, but simply for love of God'. Did any words ever approach those words for sheer arrogance? As if he had ever seen God, he who had been created out of nothingness. As if anyone of all the millions of persons on this earth, even the most holy of them, had ever seen God, or even knew anything about God except what God himself teaches us when he gives us bread and beggars and misery.

How little I had known of all this until the last few days, when I had wandered past brightly lit cafés in which people were eating,

eating food, real food, not the imaginary food with which my mind had tried to satisfy my stomach's cravings. It was food that I could have reached out for and touched, substantial, not imaginary – food that would fill. After some time I could scarcely notice anything else. One day I was very kindly shown around a religious house, admiring the paintings and the architecture, wandering through the library and the lecture-rooms – but the only room which came to life was the refectory. Once we were inside, my guide's words began to sound like echoes from a remote world, slurring off into irrelevance in the face of what I could see lying on the refectory table. It was bread. My attention concentrated itself on one lump which was, perhaps, bigger than the others. Soon it began to grow even bigger, the voice beside me began to grow less and less, until, for a moment, the refectory contained only two things – me, hungry, and that enormous lump of bread. Then the voice began to register once more, everything in the refectory fell back into place – knives, glasses and plates, all of them called into existence again. A few minutes later I was standing in the bright sunshine of the street.

There are two classes of human beings – those who eat and those who do not eat. It was early one morning that this division asserted itself in my mind, while I was kneeling in front of the Blessed Sacrament making my preparation for Mass. Kneeling next to me was the priest who was to offer the sacrifice. Last night he had eaten; I had not eaten; and the joyless visage of Karl Marx came before my eyes when the priest, a few minutes later, began the offering. '*Introibo ad altare Dei.*' Marx certainly had got hold of something, even if he had twisted it. '*Confiteor Deo omnipotenti . . .*' – it was the priest's confession, and he was confessing to me. From the depths of my soul I forgave him, and then it was my turn. '*Confiteor . . .*' – I confessed to the priest and he forgave me, so that now we were both clean. We had been washed by Christ, the same washing with which he had washed the feet of his disciples before sharing together the paschal feast; the priest and I were now to share the very same feast. Within a few minutes, within the space of time between the annunciation and the ascension, I had become one of those who eat, for the priest had given me bread, and he was one with me in the breaking of bread. There are two classes of human beings – those who eat and those who do not eat.

But Holy Thursday was yesterday, and each minute of today was Good Friday. The past had gone; there was no future but only the eternal present, the emptiness inside me and the emptiness of the long, cold corridors down which I walked to the church. The church also was empty, the high roof and the long nave a vacant shell. Whether there were people inside the church I could not say, because it would still have been empty though there had been thousands thronging into it. God was not present in the tabernacle. God was not with his people; we had driven away his Son, so that there was no dwelling-place for him. God was not present. The dreadful truth remorselessly seized me, like a paralysis binding one part of me after another, winding itself first round my heart and then my arms, running down to my feet, and numbing my brain until I felt like choking. Desperately my mind tried to twist itself away from the Truth, away from the darkness towards some imaginary light, refusing to be pinned down with the Truth. It was useless trying to move, I thought, for wherever I moved I should still not find God. Then I remembered the altar of repose and looked across the church towards the quiet figures kneeling before the altar. They had found God in that corner, in that piece of bread, where I could also find him. I had started to rise from my knees when a hand gripped me and pushed me back again to the floor, where I knelt motionless. Now my mind was twisting less desperately, slowly being pinned down to the Truth with Truth, just lying there without struggling. Today I could not find God. But perhaps if I lay still in the darkness where he had left me, God could find me. A quick impulse of hope ran through me as I saw the priests come out and approach the altar, remembering how the Passion itself in earlier years had brought comfort enough for a lifetime. *Hodie mecum eris in paradiso.* Those were the words my mind had been searching for. I had first seen them under a picture of Christ crucified, years ago; a bomb had landed, and that picture had been the first thing I saw when I pulled myself out of the corner where I had been thrown. *Hodie mecum eris in paradiso.* Those were the words I would cling to. I would be Dismas. That's right. I would be the penitent thief, and Christ would look at me with his own eyes. He would speak those words with his own lips, and I should live.

Patiently now I listened to the priests reading the Passion, the turning of the pages being the only other sound to be heard. Complete stillness had settled upon the congregation; complete solitude descended upon me, for there was not one person here whom I knew. But I waited for the words in patience, until I heard the priest's voice: '*Stabant autem juxta Crucem*'. Then I realised the folly of clinging to comforts, the faithlessness in trying to reach out for God's gifts, as though we did not trust him to give them to us. What our Holy Mother the Church reads out to us on Good Friday is the Passion according to St John, in which there is no mention of Dismas and the promise he received, no mention of the words *Hodie mecum eris in paradiso*. To cast ourselves in the role of Dismas today is a mistake, at least, and probably much worse; it is presumption to cast ourselves in any role whatsoever, since in doing so we arrogate to ourselves an initiative which belongs to God. To choose any role for ourselves is to share in that sort of deceit which habitually speaks of 'the drama of the cross', a deceit which persuades us to look towards the next scene, the scene of Easter, when we are meant to be suffering, really suffering, at the foot of the cross. This is no play, but earnest.

Once more my mind stopped twisting and fell back into the darkness where there was no sign, no light from either heaven or earth. For an instant a loving hand touched me most tenderly at the words '*Mulier, ecce filius tuus*', and then all that was left in the silence was an echo, the echo of those same words. Not satisfied with the echo, however, my careering brain refused to let the echo sound for itself and started to pursue it, only to drown the echo in my own movements. Again I had refused to sit still, I had drowned the message in my own restlessness and noise. But God would speak to me again if only I would listen. *Mulier, ecce filius tuus*: surely this was the truth that God was trying to pierce me with today. How he was to do so I could never imagine, since God's gifts are beyond imagination, and before we can receive them our minds must be still, set in the habit of silence and darkness. I am a worm and no man; like the worm, I wriggle in an effort to escape, but God in his mercy holds me still in order to pin me to the wood on which he has pinned himself; if he did not pierce my heart and my brain, these rebellious members of mine would drag me away from this wood of life, and I would die the death.

Was I at last beginning to learn something about suffering? I doubted it, somehow, when I thought of how easily we are deceived as soon as suffering becomes something we think about or meditate on, instead of something we just suffer. There is only one way to learn about suffering, and that is through suffering, not through reading about it. How many people imagine that they are learning about spiritual life or suffering when all that they are doing is reading the latest book on the subject? They imagine that they have come to savour suffering because the subject has become associated in their minds with the fresh smell of Sheed and Ward books and the restfulness of evening, or even with the mysterious sounds of *Tenebrae*. Anyone who pretends to love suffering is crazy. Suffering is something that just happens to you and that you would give almost anything to avoid. True enough, we are glad to suffer for someone we love, but only because we love them and because we think that this will shorten the beloved's suffering – not because we love suffering. If we have acquired a love for suffering on earth, then we can expect a long time in purgatory – because there is no suffering in heaven.

By the time I had reached this conclusion there was an unholy noise going on inside my head; my mind had lured me away from the wood of life, and I was no longer still. Moreover, I would *not* remain still any longer. Images of a different world from all this suffering were now presenting themselves – not of a distant world either, but the one a hundred yards away: dusty roads shining in the sunlight with their streams of hikers and cyclists happy in their shirt-sleeves and their freedom, laughing at the motorists who forced them into the edge of the road, chattering to each other in their joy at being free to go where they wished. They were not pinned down. The temptation to run out into the open air, to look at the blue skies and lose myself in the noise of this unthinking people, rose up inside me like the wind of a storm, driving me off-balance until I had to grip the pew in front of me and hang on. After a few more seconds the temptation began to slacken, the storm had blown over, and a deep calm spread itself over the tense congregation and the stone pillars of the church. Motionless as those very pillars, I waited for the next storm, no longer fearful this time because no longer trusting in my own strength. Until recently I might even have imagined that it was I who had overcome the temptation, for this kind of struggle raged inside me almost every day, and I might have believed that years of hanging on against the wind had strengthened my roots in their grip upon virtue. In fact, one single glance at the cross had taught me that even though the fields shone green in the sun and the roads were bright with light, they would not have been shining for me. There was darkness over the face of the earth, darkness too thick for the rays of the sun or for any natural light. It was not so much that I had resisted the desire to escape to the roads and the warmth of life, but rather that they did not exist. Sometimes things cease to exist because they are not desired, and it was in the moment when I glanced at the cross that the sun, the roads and the fields were swept away.

Always after the storm of temptation we are left secure in some truth, the very same truth that has been sheltering us in spite of ourselves. This particular truth was all of a piece with the other truths that I had been learning during the past weeks, which were now knitting themselves together in me. Though, in fact, I had not 'learnt' these truths at all: they had been driven into me, slowly screwed into me as the dentist's drill presses into a tooth. One had come in through the pain in my feet, another through the gnawing in my stomach, and another through heartache – all pushing in through my body, occupying it, entering it so that they could be embodied.

Mastering me now was this one sure truth: each of us is in love with one person named Jesus Christ. It is all completely simple, the ultimate secret of everything that all human beings do at each moment of their lives. The reason why priests swing incense, why young people leave the freshness of fields and bury themselves in monasteries, the reason for everything, for solemn Holy Year ceremonies and the twisting of beads round an old man's finger – we are all in love with a person named Jesus Christ. And he is dead. He is dead, because that is he stretched out on the cross which the priests are carrying up to the altar.

Silently the congregation was filing out towards the altar rails, old women bending wrinkled heads over wrinkled hands, clear-skinned boys standing erect like soldiers on guard, kneeling in turn, shoulder to shoulder, waiting breathlessly for the one they loved. He came, carried on a cross for them to kiss his feet. He was dead. How can he be dead? My mind protested against the darkness, trying to thrust upwards to the light, searching for consolation in the truths of faith,

111

in the ready distinction between nature and person. But the truths were not working today; the truth was nailed down on that cross to which I was being dragged back, away from the mind's consoling operations, back to the stillness where the mind had stopped twisting. The question of whether he was God had become irrelevant by this time, just as pointless as in the moment years ago when I first believed; I had stood in an empty barrack-room gazing at the cross formed by the wooden supports, and slowly in the evening light I had said: 'I don't care whether you were just a human being, and not God. I don't care whether there is a life after death as you promise. Still I love you and will follow you, Jesus.' In that moment I had believed. But now all I knew was that I loved this human being; and he was dead. To have tried to leave the human level after this Lent would have meant betrayal. God's eyes had closed in pain, leaving us in darkness, abandoning us to hunger for bread; and we must hunger in our stomachs, in our hearts, and in our minds, empty of food and of human friends.

Moving from one end of the rail to the other the priests were working in unison, like navvies: the cross, then the kiss and the flick of the cloth, backwards and forwards in front of the people. I knelt at the end of the rail as the cross moved away from me, the cross, then the kiss and the flick of the cloth. As the cross came back there was nothing but the cross in my line of vision; the priests had sunk from sight, just as the voice of the priest in the refectory, days ago, had faded. Then I had been left gazing at bread; now I was left gazing at the body on the cross. I was alone in the world with that body. All movement in my mind had ceased. At last, after all these weeks of squirming and twisting, I was pierced to the spot where I was meant to be. And I recognised who it was they had laid upon the cross, hearing voices from down the years telling me, hearing the keening of an old woman in the night. Her wail had sounded down the deserted street, like the cry of a stricken animal; it had come out of the fog, swept into the warmth of the fireside and wrapped itself round our hearts, turning them to ice. Startled eyes looked at one another, yet no one spoke; those with hearts remain silent when a mother loses her child. Very deliberately she moved round the kitchen, her hand fixing surely on anything she wanted – the soap, the towel, the clean white shirt; it was as though the rest of the world had ceased to exist, leaving her alone with him, talking to him: 'I brought you into the world, son, and I'll see you out of it. I was with you at the beginning and I'm going to be with you at the end.'

The cross, then the kiss and the flick of the cloth; it had passed, and I was treading deliberately down the altar steps, my lips still shaped for the kiss I had given. Over the earth lay thick darkness; out of it sounded a voice, *'Mulier, ecce filius tuus'*, and I knew where I had been standing on Good Friday.

8

Stalinensis/*yurodivi*

(1969)

This is an essay that I have wanted to write for a long time. Perhaps not exactly this essay but one like it. In fact, I once did so, about 20 years ago. That essay was all about the rights of conscience: how our consciences are formed; and how to be Catholic means to be free. But the article was turned down by the editor of the journal in question because my remarks on conscience were 'meat being offered to babes who can only take milk'. If the Catholic 'babes' had been given such meat 20 years ago, perhaps they would not have suffered such pains from the diet which recent events have provided for them. Yet what saddened me most about the episode was the editor's assumption that anything written by a Catholic must in some sense be 'definitive'.

This notion that an article must be definitive leads to articles being mass-produced, all of the same form, and above all, identical in tone – very solemn, rather omniscient, final in their judgements, giving an air of finality even to their non-judgements, donning the judge's black cap even when pronouncing the accused not guilty. This means to say that writers are encouraged to pretend that one of their half-thoughts is a thesis, and two of their half-thoughts a whole book (a publisher once asked me to turn an article of 12 pages that I had published into a book of 140 pages, saying 'You needn't add anything of substance to it'; he produced a series of such books). The fact of the matter is that almost none of us has illuminations sufficient to occupy a book, and we deceive ourselves grievously if we imagine that there is anything under the sun upon which our opinion is definitive. But most of us, at some time, have ideas which we would gladly put forward as possibilities, suggestions, hints, approximations, in the hope that someone else may take them up, develop them, refine them, appropriate them, give them back. We bring out such ideas in a playful, comradely, trusting spirit, and they can only remain alive if they are received in the same spirit; they are sentenced to death once they are judged definitive.

It is one such idea that I wish to put forward now.

In the late summer of 1939 the bridge at Brest-Litovsk spanning the frontier between Germans and Russians was occupied at one end by NKVD men and at the other end by members of the Gestapo. One day the NKVD men marched a group of prisoners from their side of the bridge to the German side, handed them over to the Gestapo, with whom they checked their lists, and then went back. The prisoners were mainly Germans, who had sought asylum in the Soviet Union away from the Nazi regime, and who were now being returned as part of the Molotov-Ribbentrop pact. Similar exchanges were made at a later date, in the other direction, the Gestapo handing over prisoners to the NKVD.

That bridge at Brest-Litovsk in late 1939 has become in my mind a symbol of how easily and constantly and stupidly we mislead ourselves and others with labels. If you had asked many influential people in the West at that time whether the action of the Communist and/or Nazi regimes in handing over these political refugees was wrong, they would have replied 'Yes . . . but . . .' – and then, according to whether they were right or left wing they would have excused the actions of either the Nazi or the Communist regime: the same action was judged by the same people as different according to the label (Communist or Nazi) attached to the people performing the act.

So remove the labels. One way to do this is to imagine yourself for a moment to be a visitor from another planet who can see what human beings do to one another but cannot read their manifestos and commentaries. Such a visitor would have only a limited understanding of what was going on, but would be preserved from the illusion of labels. One would not be tempted, for instance, to regard the suffering of a prisoner in Katorga Camp as different from the sufferings of a prisoner in Dachau Camp simply because one was inflicted under the label of Communism and the other under the label of Nazism; one would also see quite clearly that the behaviour of the Gestapo is the same sort of behaviour as that of the NKVD men, and that those in authority who order such behaviour are the same kind of people, no matter what label they stamp upon their actions.

Now and again one needs to remove labels; it is a way of allowing the scales to fall from one's eyes. Just for a precious moment, one glimpses the human landscape with great clarity before the mist closes in again.

When trying to understand the last 50 years of European history, I usually find myself shrouded in such mists. I see signposts saying 'Russian Revolution', 'Treaty of Locarno', 'Yalta', 'Communism', 'cold war', 'spring-time in Prague', and so on, each of the posts having inscribed upon it millions of words explaining what such means. However, one signpost simply leads to another so that I can hardly see the landscape or any human beings, but only further mist and further signposts.

But then there emerged the bridge at Brest-Litovsk: the labels vanished; the scales fell away; for a moment there lay before me an area of the earth's surface centred on Brest-Litovsk and stretching out to a radius of 1,000 miles and a span of 50 years.

And what was there to see?

I saw 60 million human beings killed in this area, in this time, by their fellow human beings.

The second, and only other thing I saw, was a 'biological' mutation, the emergence of a new species, *Homo stalinensis*, the 'man of steel'.

Ever since that moment of illumination I have found myself back amidst the signposts, mystified still but now realising that the professional signposters keep fixing up their ideological labels ('The Christian Democratic Experiment', 'The Thaw', 'The Death of God', etc.) in order to make sure that people don't see the 60 million human beings killed or the appearance of *stalinensis*. And now I too am scribbling upon a post – but in order to retain what I saw when the scales fell away.

Scribble One. It is laughable to a point beyond belief that these people who have killed one another to the number of 60 million should be so brazen as to imagine that they can go off to Africa, Asia and Latin America in order to teach other people *how to live!* Surely the peoples of Africa, India and Latin America would be better advised to try to learn from the tiger, the elephant or the duck-billed platypus than from these monstrous beings who slaughter one another

116

on this scale. Similarly, any being faced with the choice of re-incarnation would surely choose to become a bear or a wolf rather than one of these monstrous characters?

Scribble Two. Killing on such a scale is bound to breed a new type of being out of those who survive. Modern war depends upon steel; the product of modern warfare is *stalinensis*.

Scribble Three. Notice how often the metaphor of steel is applied to human beings. The obvious instance is the choice of the name *Stalin*, 'man of steel', by Josef Vissarionovich Dzhugashvili. Similarly, Hitler spoke of himself as a magnet drawing to himself the steel elements out of the dung-heap of the German nation. Hitler also said that he wanted German youth to be like the steel which emerged from the Krupp armaments works: the most popular book in Germany during the 1920s was *In Stahlgewittern* (*In a Storm of Steel*) – in which Junger describes how he was 'tempered in a storm of steel' – the very same phrase that was used by the young Communist writer Ostrovsky as the title for his autobiographical novel *How the Steel was Tempered*, which the Soviet authorities made into a best-seller during the Purge period. Ostrovsky's second novel, predictably enough, was entitled *Born of the Storm* – that same storm as gave birth to the *Stahlheim*, the 'steel-helmeted ones', who were the shock troops of German nationalism. When Hitler and Mussolini embraced each other, their embrace was named '*The Pact of Steel*'. Not that the metaphor is always precisely of steel; but when one of Stalin's companions chose to become 'a hammer', *molotov*, he was claiming that he was made of the same material – though how that happened to a Scriabin remains a mystery. Of course one had encountered similar metaphors previously; we had an Iron Duke, and an Iron Chancellor, before the new men of Romania formed themselves into an Iron Guard. But the Iron Duke and the Iron Chancellor seemed so hard in contrast to the flesh around them – whereas the Iron Guard are part of an iron machine: the Romanian refugee shuttled between Nazis and Communists in *la vingt-cinquième heure* realised that he was not in the presence of humans at all but of monsters begotten upon women by machines – those machines, *apparati*, which turn out their *apparatchiki*, servants of the machine in Eastern Europe and Western Europe, those beings depicted in the drawings and sculpture of the Soviet artist Neizvestny, more or less human in shape but held together by nuts, bolts and levers.

'We Communists are people of a special type,' said Stalin at the funeral of Lenin. 'We are carved out of a special matter.' Hitler made exactly the same claim for the Nazis.

Scribble Four. Then it should show in their faces and not only in Neizvestny's art. It does.

One of the most tangible and painful changes which came about as a result of the revolutionary upheaval was the astounding transformation in the appearance of many men and women. A new type of man seemed to have emerged. There was none of the tolerance and kindness in him so characteristic of the prerevolutionary type of Russian . . . These new faces showed eyes firmly fixed on the external realities; sympathy and mercy for others, especially for those holding heretical views, became an unknown quality.[1]

We should have recognised what this new type was up to if, instead of learning to read labels and books, we had learnt to read faces: see again Leni Riefenstahl's film on the Nuremberg rally and watch the faces of Ley, Goering, Streicher, Hitler, as they come to the rostrum. Only the facially illiterate could fail to read them, and know that destruction lay ahead.

Or look again at the photographs of those who have ruled Eastern Europe for 20 years. You see there the result of a mutation: *stalinensis*. No wonder the Czechs kept hoping that destalinisation meant 'giving Communism a human face'. (Though how can you have a human face without a human heart? All you get is façade.)

Has the species *stalinensis* been observed in the West? On a number of occasions during the 1930s *stalinensis* was to be seen in Western Communist parties, but occurs nowadays more frequently amongst the *apparatchiki* of capitalist countries: they can be seen among NATO chiefs and defence ministers, for instance; there are several easily recognisable aspiring 'men of steel' in the upper echelons of the English Conservative Party; the portrait gallery of the American magazine *Time* features them regularly; saddest of all, they have begun to appear amidst the people who have suffered most from them, the people of Israel, by whom they are misnamed 'hawks'.

Scribble Five. Nevertheless, human nature (or God) is very fertile; so if the abyss of nothingness and darkness threatens us through the masks of steel worn by the faceless ones, at the same time the presence of humankind and God among us is guaranteed by a face – so long as there exists upon earth a face such as that of Chagall, darkness cannot swallow us entirely up. And there are other like faces: Martin Buber's; that of Elie Wiesel. One such face appeared earlier this year on television in a discussion between Jewish writers: some of them were spreading hawkish wings when the quiet Pyotr Rawicz, who had lived through Auschwitz, gently drew the steel splinters from their hearts.

All these faces reflect the Jewish Hasidic tradition, which arose and flourished in Russian lands and probably owes something to a strikingly similar Russian Christian tradition: tales of the Hasidim and the tales of the *yurodivi* could almost be interchanged. *Yurodstvo Khrista radi* (foolishness for Christ's sake) is illustrated in the story of the holy fool of Pskov, St Nicholas: when Ivan the Terrible came to him for a blessing, Nicholas offered the tsar raw meat, despite its being Lent. Ivan refused indignantly, saying, 'I am a Christian and do not eat meat during Lent'; to which the holy fool replied, 'No, but you drink Christian blood'. (There is a touch of *yurodstvo* in Father Berrigan, the American priest who poured blood into the filing system of the army recruitment office.)

The latest witness to this Russian tradition is Solzhenitsyn. Among the many characters in his writings who draw strength from this source is the aged Matryona in *Matryona's House*. The story ends:

> We all lived right beside her and never realised she was that very just one, without whom, according to the proverb, no village can stand.

> Nor any city.
> Nor any land whatsoever.

A fool for Christ is not a buffoon. Perhaps Valery Tarsis has not always realised this, but Sinyavsky has. And the incredibly balanced Solzhenitsyn has realised it so exactly that he drives Ivan the Stalinist to distraction – one such, the editor of *Pravda*, said of Solzhenitsyn, 'He is a psychologically unbalanced person, a schizophrenic'.

Scribble Six. Schizophrenia is also a label used in the West to stick upon those whose broken hearts remain an irreducible reminder to the steel ones that people of flesh have not yet been 'normalised' (as the Soviets say of Czechoslovakia) or *gleichgeschaltet* (as the Nazis used to say). This is what the psychiatrist R. D. Laing is getting at when he says that schizophrenia is one of the forms in which – often by means of quite ordinary people – the light begins to break through the cracks in our armour-plated minds.

The note of *yurodstvo* heard in Laing's work is also echoed by Gironella (Spain), Böll (Germany) and Mihajlov (Yugoslavia).

Gironella's novel, *The Cypresses Believe in God*, was more than the steel ones of the Falangist movement could stomach: the central character was not tough enough to be a Falangist hero; so the Falangists pursued Gironella with the same zeal as the Stalinists pursued Solzhenitsyn, driving him into that schizophrenic state of which he tries to make some sense in *Phantoms and Fugitives*.

Heinrich Böll has almost consciously been searching for *yurodstvo*; perhaps he detected a hint of it during his soldiering in Russia. Anyway, Hans Schnier, the narrator of *The Clown*, manages in his foolish way to highlight the inhumanity of Catholic marriage regulations; and Böll is constantly being denounced by the *apparatchiki* of the Church; but he does not go schizophrenic even when he is attacked in pastorals, probably because he wears open-necked shirts and is a devout bicyclist.

The directness of the holy fool is practised by the Yugoslav Dostoevsky scholar, Mihajlov, but perhaps without the same sure touch; his blundering reminds one of Prince Myschkin. But it is liberating to see him in Russia, blithely asking questions which no one else dare raise, explaining unabashed to such an establishment lion as Ehrenburg that his vision of life is abominable and beneath human dignity. Mihajlov collects the words of underground songs and prison-camp songs and stories, runs out of money and then goes back to Yugoslavia and publishes an almost comically candid account of what he saw and heard. For his troubles he is tried twice, being sentenced on the second occasion to four-and-a-half years imprisonment (less, one notes, than Father Berrigan!). From the prison he serenely continues to explain that only faith in immortality gives freedom and affords justification for life. The trouble with being a fool is that people consider you foolish.

Scribble Seven. The most human are regarded as fools. How can this be, for Christ's sake?

9

The eternal child

(1987)

I can still feel the soft warm touch of his skin as he gently put his left arm around my neck and shoulders and nestled against my right side. It was the night of Christmas 1944, and I was kneeling beside a pillar just as Mass was beginning in the crowded cathedral of Santa Cruz, which is situated in Mattancheri, an ancient section of Cochin, 'the Venice of South India'.

In a manner I was actually hiding behind the pillar, because upon entering the cathedral I had quickly taken in and instantly shunned the apartheid rule that was clearly being observed by the congregation. In one area of the cathedral there sat the few white-skinned worshippers – mainly British, I imagined. Then there came row upon row of Portugese-Indians or Anglo-Indians. Concerning them I had received a powerful word from my dark fisherman friends with whom I used to sit at night by the shore as they pulled away at their cantilevered nets. They said, 'Our place, master – India; your place master – Blighty; Anglo-Indian . . . where their place, master?' The poignancy of that question was underlined for me as I noticed that the darker-skinned Indians in the cathedral had placed themselves, for the time at least, a little lower than the Anglo-Indians.

Since this hierarchy seemed to leave no place for me I had chosen to kneel at the side, in the shadows, still feeling uncomfortable and rather tense, nevertheless, as some of the nearby Indians cast puzzled glances at this eccentric British soldier, kneeling in the wrong place. But now, in a twinkling, all that was to change for me when, to my astonishment, I felt this warm arm around my shoulders. I turned to discover who on earth it might be. And there, close to my own eyes, I saw the shining eyes of little Antony. So long as he was standing up and I was kneeling down we were on a level.

'You Catholic, master?' he asked. 'Yes, Antony,' I replied. 'I Catholic, master,' he smiled happily. He smiled even more when I pointed in wonder and delight to his gleaming white shirt and shorts.

Our mutual delight requires a word of explanation, a word to explain how it was really through dirt that Antony and I had become friends.

We first met one bright morning when I walked out of the bungalow in which our small unit was billeted and set off to cross the *maidan*. After two or three paces I was met by a cheerful urchin of some nine or ten years who stuck his hand out to beg a few annas. It was as grubby a hand as I had ever seen – though no grubbier than the rest of the boy, for every square inch of him and of his ragged shirt and battered shorts was thick with dust and grime.

In mock horror I opened my eyes wide, let out a deep sigh, took the boy by his filthy hand and led him to the public water-pump on the other side of the *maidan*. There I drew out of my pocket a whole rupee, held it up before his eyes, and then indicated that it was his if only he would stick his head under the water-pump. He needed no second bidding but grinned and did as I had requested. Then for several minutes I pumped away as the boy, Antony by name, enthusiastically splashed water over his head and face, his hands and his legs. It was not an immersion so total as to have satisfied a strict Baptist, but not far short. And certainly once Antony had introduced order into his hair with the comb I lent him, he looked for all the world like a new creation.

That was to be the beginning of an unusual friendship. For every time afterwards when Antony would see me on the *maidan*, even if he were 100 yards away, he would give a great delighted shout of 'Master!' He would then leap a couple of feet in the air, run to the water-pump and stick his head under the spout, waiting for the water to pour over his head and the money to pour from my pocket. Of course there was no way that we could sustain the rate of exchange fixed at the initiation ceremony – on a soldier's pay, that would have quickly driven me to sticking my own head under the pump in hopes of finding a benefactor. But we did arrive at a *modus vivendi*.

Soon I learnt more about Antony from the friendly stall-holders along the dusty street where a lively crowd of sacred cows and Christians and Hindus all used to jostle together. Antony, they told me, had come down from the hills beyond Alwaye because his family was too poor to keep him, and here in Mattancheri he could at least put bread in his mouth by running errands for the stall-holders and begging from whoever would give him a few annas.

Where did he live? That was a question I was able to answer for myself not long after Antony's 'baptism', when I was walking late one night down the empty, narrow street near our bungalow. It was dark with the thick darkness of the tropical night, and everywhere was silent except for the faint hum of a kerosene lamp in the one stall still open, where the local *dhursi* was sitting cross-legged at his sewing. As the *dhursi* and I whispered greetings to one another, I noticed a small figure propped against the door-post, almost hidden in the shadow cast by the kerosene lamp. It was Antony, totally abandoned to sleep as only the abandoned know how. And he was beautiful, the icon of the eternal child.

Antony lived all his days and nights on the street. When I saw him the next day, Christmas Day, after our meeting in church, his clothes were once more as grubby as ever. The gleaming shirt and shorts of last night had only been lent to him as a special treat for the Christmas Mass. After the Mass he had to return them.

Why, I ask myself, do I imagine that *Tablet* readers might be interested in such an everyday episode from a world that is gone? And, yet further, why does this memory become not less but more and more central to my own celebration of Christmas as the years go by?

The answer to this second question may well be quite simple, the same as that given by Alyosha Karamazov to the boys gathered at Ilyusha's stone:

My dear children . . . you must know that there is nothing higher and stronger and more wholesome and good for life in the future than some good memory, especially a memory of childhood. People talk to you a great deal about your education, but some good, sacred memory, preserved from childhood, is perhaps the best education. If a man carries many such memories with him into life he is safe to the end of his days, and if one has only one good memory left in one's heart, even that may be the means of saving us.

What is the danger from which I, and many others of my generation, need to be saved?

One of them is the insidious danger of bitterness. For when we returned to our own land at the end of the war, we truly did have a vision of a world in which the relations between persons and between peoples would be brotherly and sisterly, based upon a deep desire for justice and equality for all human beings. Instead of which, we learn with every fresh news bulletin of how the powerful in almost every nation on earth are using the power of their armaments, their wealth, their organs of propaganda and their control of law to ensure that they and their minions maintain their privileges – even though it means inflicting lies, hunger, sickness, ignorance and death itself upon those outside their privileged circle. Even in our own land, where during the war we were given a foretaste of what a joy it might be to live in a united, just and brotherly society, we can only gaze in disbelief as those in power, with breathtaking brazenness, lead the assault of the wealthy and privileged against the poor and marginalised in a legalised form of warfare.

Yet this betrayal of our hopes itself secretes the danger of an even worse betrayal on our own part: the danger that we ourselves should become bitter over it. For there is a dreadful finality about bitterness: if at the end of our lives we are bitter, then, no matter what great achievements we may have to our credit, we have colluded in final defeat. To stave off such defeat we have a golden word that comes from the pen of Robert Speaight in his biography of Hilaire Belloc. Referring to Belloc's contempt for the plutocrats of his time Speaight says, 'No doubt Belloc was right about the Edwardian plutocrats, but he should never have allowed them so much room in his mind'. Yet we all know how difficult it is to put Speaight's wise words into practice, and to prevent evil from occupying our minds whenever we raise the courage to face up to it. Perhaps, indeed, evil's trump-card is precisely to make us obsessional, so preoccupied by evil that we leave no room for anything else.

Which is why we need Christmas – so that the Child for whom there is no room in the world's inn may instead occupy our hearts, leaving no room there for evil. For, as Andrei Sinyavsky has written from his Soviet labour-camp, childhood is the invention of Christianity. And he continues,

Why were infants so important for the new era? Children had never been so much in evidence. Thoughts of the future become somehow interwoven with the idea of innocence . . . Now, for the first time, an infant became a symbolic figure – and his mother together with him: Mother and Child. And all fell prostrate before him, remaining as innocent as babes themselves.[1]

Here we have a child who is 'a constant reminder that in God the child is never extinct'.

With that last sentence Sinyavsky provides us with a clue to one of the truths about being human that is little observed, yet can never be contravened without disaster. The truth is that we have to carry the child within us safely through each stage of our growth – through childhood, adolescence, adulthood and old age, and even death itself – for if we lose the child within us we thereby lose the way into the Kingdom of Heaven.

Most vivid expression was given to this truth, strange as it may seem, by a Zen Buddhist, D. T. Suzuki. Only one day before he himself passed into death this 96-year-old sage wrote that we should 'aspire so to live that we can say along with Meister Eckhart that "Christ is born every minute in my soul" '.

So long as we cleave to these maxims of Eckhart, Sinyavsky and Speaight we are enabled to sustain without harm one of the afflictions of our media-ridden world that none of us can escape. I am referring to the note of falsity which one so often hears in the voices of the top-dogs, whether they be prime ministers or presidents, or moguls in business, show-business, parliament or trade unions. The grating pain caused by their 'easy speeches that comfort cruel men' may well tempt one to dismiss the speakers as hypocrites and pompous frauds. And no doubt some of them are. But, more important, the very falsity of voice is a sign that somewhere within the speaker is a child who feels lost – who is entombed beneath layer upon layer of falsity, each layer specially composed for a different voice, until the speaker no longer knows who he, or she, is. When we lose our own voice we are lost, no matter how 'successful' we may be. Yet, as Sinyavsky says, 'in God the child is never extinct'. And if we listen carefully, whether to others or to ourselves, we shall always hear below the falsity an echo of the sweet child who issued innocent from the hand of God.

How bitterness may be transformed into sweetness is woven into the traditions of Christmas by a story of the children of Israel. We learn in Exodus of how the exiled children of Israel were wandering through the wilderness of Shur and were without water for three days. Fortunately they then came upon an oasis. But unfortunately they could not drink the water because it was bitter – hence the name of the oasis, Marah (Hebrew for bitter). However, Moses called upon God, who drew his attention to some wood lying there and directed him to throw it upon the water. When Moses did so, the bitter water was turned sweet and the people were able to drink.

What was so special about the wood that it could transform the bitter into the sweet? The answer, according to the Church Fathers, is that the wood was the wood of the cross. And just as Moses cast the wood upon the water of Marah, so we are meant to take up the wood of the cross and cast ourselves with it upon the bitter ocean of this world so as to traverse it in sweetness.

The inspiration evidenced here in the Church Fathers was never to be lacking in the following centuries among the people of God, who in their turn were led to see that, not only was the cross hewn from the wood of the tree of life in paradise, but so also was the cradle where the Christ-child was laid in Bethlehem. The outburst of carols upon this theme, composed by anonymous folk of all lands, are in themselves an irrefutable argument for the truth of what they proclaim, for they sing of a joy that is pure and transparent, and is unshakeable on account of having transformed and not denied the bitterness of this world. It is the same note of pure joy which we hear in Bach's *Christmas Oratorio* where the composer's sure Christian instinct led him to use the Passion hymn *'Herzlich tut mich verlangen'* for both the first and the ultimate chorale.

Neither in Bach's *Christmas Oratorio* nor in our folk carols is there any note of sentimentality – sentimentality is superficial and saccharine, like Christmas in secular England. Nor was there any sentimentality or sugariness in the child who lodged in my heart at Christmas 1944. He was a waif and had nowhere to lay his head; but through it all he could laugh and be joyful. His laughter and joy, I do not doubt, has helped me to carry the child within throughout the years between. So once more this Christmas I shall be praying that Antony also, wherever he may be, remembers Christmas 1944 as one of those good, sacred memories from childhood of which Dostoevsky said that one, carried in our heart, may be the means of saving us.

10

Hitting the buffers

(1992)

My life was going along as it has done for years, each day filled with interesting events such as occur in a round of lecture engagements, travel, study and writing, as well as in corresponding with people and institutions in many parts of the globe. Then, almost without warning, my life hit the buffers and came to a full stop.

That metaphor of buffers is the most exact way of describing what happened, because it registers the sense that for me there was no way forward. When reflected upon, it further registers the fact that the horizontal dimensions of my life had simply vanished. As a result, when I now heard people speaking to me of something planned, say, for 'next Thursday', it meant nothing whatsoever to me. 'Next Thursday' might as well have been light years away, as far as I was concerned – just as, for that matter, 'last Thursday' seemed to be ages ago – even, indeed, as did yesterday.

That symbolism of the horizontal dimension was familiar to me from having read a book, *Symbolism and Belief* by Edwyn Bevan, 50 years ago. In his book Bevan invokes the horizontal as a symbol for the immanence of God and, correspondingly, treats the vertical as symbolising the transcendence of God.

In any case, I was left devoid of any foothold in the horizontal dimension along which we human beings for most of the time trundle, distracting ourselves, as well as finding pleasure and satisfaction, in work, busyness, gossip, friends, parties, food and entertainment.

It seems to me that Teilhard de Chardin was describing a similar experience when he wrote, ' . . . the path faded from beneath my steps; I found a bottomless abyss at my feet, and out of it came –

arising I know not from where – the current which I dare to call *My* life . . .'

After encountering those words by Teilhard de Chardin I naturally hoped that for me also a current would arise from the abyss which I would likewise be able to call *My* life. However, I soon had to recognise that my own case was more desperate than his in so far as I had lost my balance in life. Hence all my energies were being consumed in preventing myself from over-balancing – over the edge into the abyss. As if to underline my predicament, moreover, I injured my ankle so badly at the time that even physically I felt I had lost my foothold. So I could scarcely hobble – one more symptom of my lost equilibrium.

A further factor in my predicament was that, whereas Teilhard de Chardin lived as a member of a religious order and was willy-nilly being incorporated into the horizontal dimension of communal meals and devotions, and was constantly drawn into the play of a variety of human fellowship, I was living a distinctly isolated life. So the experience of those three months has made me acutely aware of the far-reaching truth of the statement in Genesis, attributed to God, that it is not good for man to be alone. Human company is a precondition of a healthy life for all human beings except the rare hermit. I kept recalling, for instance, how the Aran islanders had known this to be true when the original figure for *The Playboy of the Western World* came over to them from Connemara. Contrary to the impression conveyed by J. M. Synge, they were making sure that the depressed young man was surrounded by pleasant company every evening. They entertained him with stories, songs and dancing in the attempt to ensure that he was never left alone in his depression.

Since I was in the position of neither Teilhard nor of the Playboy, I was faced with two tasks. First, to learn something of how to live a life situated almost entirely in the vertical dimension; and second, to find a way back into the horizontal dimension.

Fortunately I knew, at least from reading, of a goodly company of people who had lived to the extreme in the vertical dimension. Indeed, an incident had occurred many years before which had led me to coin a phrase that I felt applied precisely to those who had managed to live in the vertical dimension. It was an occasion when I felt I had to visit a man who was in the last stage of a crippling disease. I dreaded the depression that I anticipated would descend upon me as a result of the visit. In the event, I came away from my dying friend's house in a completely different mood from the mood in which I had entered. Because, in the words that then formulated themselves in my mind, I had witnessed 'a triumph of the Spirit'.

It is worth recording that my friend was not an overtly religious man. Yet the memory of him, I have to say, has lately been a powerful help at a time when many of the works of the professional religious – which came to me via newspapers, books, radio and television – failed to touch me. That was because the words of those religious professionals rolled on and on and ever on the horizontal level, witness to their unruffled confidence that engagements scheduled for next Thursday would actually take place – as, indeed, would their plans for next year and even for the following year. Neither buffers nor any abyss, nothing from above or below – nothing from the vertical dimension would be allowed to interfere with their plans.

From what source, then, might a word of encouragement be found for someone such as me, seemingly petrified in the vertical dimension? From somewhere in the depths of my unconscious (the unconscious being a channel of the Holy Spirit or a 'Cloud of Unknowing') I was guided towards the witness of fellow human beings who had been caught in situations where there was to be no 'next Thursday', much less 'next year', and for whom the only dimension now left was the vertical. Here is one such:

Dear parents: I must give you bad news. I have been condemned to death. I and Gustave G. We did not sign up for the SS and so they condemned me to death. You wrote to me, indeed, that I should not join the SS; my comrade, Gustave G., did not sign up either. Both of us would rather die than stain our consciences with such deeds of horror. I know what the SS has to do. Oh, my dear parents, difficult as it is for me and for you, forgive me and pray for me. If I were to be killed in the war while my conscience was bad, that too would be sad for you. Many more parents will lose their children. Many SS men will get killed too. I thank you for everything you have done for my good since my childhood; forgive me, pray for me.[1]

131

Those are the words of a farm-boy from the Sudetenland and were written by him on 8 February 1944.

I read them first some 35 years ago, and I have read them so often since that I can almost repeat them by heart. And every time I do so, I am filled with wonder that a farm-boy should have been able so simply and serenely to have surrendered his life in the name of truth, when many in Church and State who were highly educated and highly placed were found wanting.

The book in which the farm-boy's letter was published, *Dying We Live*, contains many such precious testimonials, all of them memorable in their wonderfully different ways. Consider, for instance, one short extract from a letter to his wife of Helmuth, Count von Moltke, on the eve of his execution by Hitler's henchmen:

Dear heart, your very precious letter has just arrived. The first letter, dear heart, in which you have not understood my mood nor my situation. No, I do not occupy myself with God or with my death. He is unspeakably gracious in coming to me and occupying himself with me. Is this arrogant? Perhaps.

Dying We Live provides us with more than 50 such witnesses to the truth that the Spirit is stronger than death. That truth is vital for us to grasp if we are not to be defeated by depression or despair, whether that depression is caused by the unredeemed behaviour of the human family or whether we despair at the futility of our personal lives which seem doomed to the nothingness of death – assuming, as a prominent zoologist has said, that human beings are nothing more than temporary machines by means of which genes survive.

Not that the serenity of our witnesses *proves* that death is not the end. Such proof is no more possible than it is possible for a frog at the bottom of a 100-foot well to know whether there is anything beyond the rim of the well 100 feet above. But what our witnesses do show is the Spirit alive and at work in them, testifying to the triumph of Jesus. For just as, in the strict sense, one can never prove beyond doubt that there is life beyond death, so one can never in that strict sense prove anything about the life of Jesus, not even his crucifixion. But through the Holy Spirit one is made aware that the martyrs celebrated in *Dying We Live* were granted a serenity and faith which they display through their conformity to the cross of Jesus.

For, as Edith Stein says in her farewell letter, 'The only way . . . is by feeling the whole weight of the cross . . . From the depths of my heart I have said: *Ave crux, spes unica.'*

But when Edith Stein proclaims that our only hope is to greet the cross, she is not saying that the cross offers a ticket to heaven for each of us as individuals. She who was at that time on the journey to Auschwitz was offering herself in union, in communion, with her people, the Jews. In so doing she points to the way in which sufferers can make some sense of their suffering – by allowing it to draw them into the lives of other sufferers.

The way she points is particularly crucial for those who are suffering depression. Because whereas certain forms of suffering – those endured for the sake of justice, for instance – have obvious meaning and usefulness, depression seems to have no meaning or usefulness whatsoever. It is at this point that the depressed person suffering from a sense of uselessness may overcome despair by recognising that there is an economy of suffering which has been made necessary if the wicked, destructive history of the human family is to be redeemed. Anyone with the slightest sense of justice, observing the undeserved and pointless suffering of our brothers and sisters in, say, Somalia or Iraq or East Timor, will wish to put their mite into the economy of suffering, sharing the burden with them.

Such a wish cannot be genuine if it only arises in one as an idea, however edifying; it must spring from a level deeper than consciousness – from the heart, in fact, which is the point at which God in the person of the Holy Spirit re-orientates the depressed one so that her condition no longer seems pointless. It may well be, indeed, that depression often results from the fact that one's conscious is at odds with one's unconscious. And healing takes place when one's conscious is realigned with one's unconscious, and there opens a channel for life once more to gush up. This is the moment at which a prayer of Symeon the New Theologian addressing the Holy Spirit is most apt:

> Come, for you are yourself the desire within me;
> Come, for you are my breath and my life.

In response to that invocation, the Holy Spirit doubtless leads each one of us back to the horizontal dimension, to the struggle and warmth of the human family, in a way that is unique to each person. I myself was led in a most unexpected direction, at the time not knowing whether, or why, or even whether there was a way at all – until I had arrived.

On the wall to the right of my desk is fixed a notice-board which over the years has become covered, not with notices, but with photographs or sketches of the faces of holy people, in all of whom the Spirit has triumphed through adversity: Maximilian Kolbe; Black Elk; my friend Sadhu Ittyavirah; and a dozen more. As I sat at my desk in the depths of one long night, I was prompted to take up a pencil and a large sheet of blank paper. On it I drew one vertical and two horizontal lines, thereby dividing the sheet into six panels. Then, one by one, I took down the pictures of six of my holy friends and began slowly and painstakingly to try to sketch their faces in pencil.

Sitting at my desk for hour upon hour, I tried again and again to catch the spirit reflected in the eyes and on the lips and chin and, indeed, on every feature of dearly beloved St Seraphim of Sarov, and of the infinitely tender Edith Stein. Next came Ramana Maharshi of the radiant glance, followed by my dear friend Thubten Yeshe, the Tibetan Buddhist with his cheerful smile ... Clumsy as my efforts were, they proved to be a means of healing. For what I had constructed in the presence of the saints was the frame for that Eastern symbol of wholeness and holiness, a mandala. But where was the central figure which is essential for a true mandala?

The answer came when I was reminded of the orthodox teaching that the Holy Spirit, as person, remains unimagined, unmanifested, hidden; and will not be manifested as person until the restoration of all things. In that moment his image will be revealed as the whole company of the saints taken together, all those who have been deified by the action of the Spirit.

Such a mandala, we have been taught in recent years, is a revelation of the unconscious mind. If so, it seems that my mandala with its missing centre was telling me once again to heed the words of St Seraphim: 'The whole aim of the Christian life is to acquire the Holy Spirit'.

11

The ascent of love

(1993)

Since all human beings are aware that they had a beginning and will have an end, all of us feel a need to work out some story which has both a beginning and an end, and that helps to make sense of our life. For although abstract statements of principle may prove useful to us on occasion, it is only a story that can give meaning to our whole life.

Naturally the story gets modified with the passage of the years, as we come upon loose ends and inconsistencies which we need to tie up and straighten out. What is more, since the essence of being human is to be part of the human family which extends through time and space, our personal story can never be complete until the human family itself comes to an end.

Moreover, human beings also know that they are connected through every atom of their being with the whole of the universe. And therein lies the rub. Because it is difficult, even perhaps impossible, to work out a convincing story for ourselves personally and for the human family unless we have a credible story for the whole of that creation in which we live, move, and have our being.

Yet it is undeniable that the created world is so seriously flawed as to render it seemingly impossible for us to make sense of it. Such is the infinity of rough-hewn ends in creation that it appears inconceivable they could ever be fitted together.

Even as regards the story of the human family, such events as Auschwitz and Hiroshima are proof enough for many people that there is no golden thread of meaning to it. But at least those events can be traced to the free choice of human beings rather than to any fundamental flaw in the rest of creation. What is one to say of earthquakes, famine, plague, deformities in every form of life, and all those other catastrophes which lawyers and insurers describe as 'acts of God'? Such events appear to be beyond incorporation into any story whatsoever – which is why we generally avert our eyes from them. Only rarely are human beings prepared to confront the seeming absurdity of earthquakes, floods, hurricanes, ghastly deformities, and the like.

Fortunately for Christians there is one of our apostles who, for all his infuriating temperament, was ever prepared to confront difficulties head-on. And he has left us a classic statement in his own response to the deep flaws in creation. I am referring, of course, to St Paul, and in particular to the passage in Chapter 8 of his letter to the Romans which runs:

> For I reckon that the sufferings we now endure bear no comparison with the glory, as yet unrevealed, which is in store for us. The created universe is waiting with eager expectation for God's sons to be revealed. It was made subject to frustration, not of its own choice but by the will of him who subjected it, yet with the hope that the universe itself is to be freed from the shackles of mortality and is to enter upon the glorious liberty of the children of God.[1]

It is symptomatic, perhaps, of how reluctant we are to follow St Paul's example of facing difficulties that, out of all the many commentators who reverently quote that passage and the apostle's subsequent hymn to the Spirit, there are only a few who call our attention to the kernel of his response: 'the created universe . . . was made subject to frustration, not of its own choice but by the will of him who subjected it'.

Evidently, according to Paul, 'frustration' accompanied creation, was a condition of creation. Since *mataiotes* – the Greek word of the original text translated as 'frustration' – is not restrictive in what it denotes, it allows our minds a certain amount of play in our search for the truth enshrined in Paul's statement. Sometimes, for example, the word is translated as 'vanity', and sometimes as 'emptiness'.

It was, in the first instance, the translation 'emptiness' – a key word in the Buddhist tradition – which set me thinking how close the word *mataiotes* might be to the word *dukkha* in Buddhism. And then I was reminded of a conversation I had once had with a Buddhist friend who was trying to convey to me the meaning of *dukkha* by way of an image.

My friend said that a good way to imagine *dukkha* is to envisage a perfectly round wooden spindle, perfectly centred within a hollow and perfectly round tube. In nirvana the spindle turns perfectly, and therefore never strikes against the sides of the tube. There is therefore no friction. But in our present life we are not perfectly centred. And so, as we move, we are constantly banging against the sides of the tube, thus producing friction which then gives rise to a feeling of vanity and emptiness.

After hearing my friend's explanation, it may have been the fricative echo of 'frustration' and 'friction' which led me to bring together the Greek word *mataiotes* and the Pali word *dukkha*. However that may be, it prompted me to try to incorporate their meanings into an account of creation somewhat as follows.

If all that is were to be in the perfect condition of the spindle within the hollow tube, then the spindle would turn eternally. So there would be no time. And there would likewise be no thing, other than the spindle and the hollow tube. Nothing new would ever emerge because nothing *other* would ever emerge. For anything other to emerge, there has to be friction. So it is not the case that an other is created, and then subsequently friction occurs which carries with it the danger of frustration and emptiness and a deeply flawed universe. Rather, friction is itself an aspect of creation; and so every act of creation is fraught with danger. Do we not all learn in our childhood, for instance, of how 'early man' learnt to rub wood against wood? By means of that friction energy was produced in the form of fire; and fire, like every other effect of the creative act (including the great artistic creations of mankind) can be both beneficial and destructive.

The above brief reflection on a subordinate clause in St Paul's letter to the Romans has enabled me to work out for myself a story of the created universe by the truth of which I can live. The vocabulary of the story is anthropomorphic – unashamedly so since I am *anthropos*. Indeed, my story is childish – how could it be otherwise, since in face of the universe I am no more than a child?

To begin with, I think of God, who is love, as longing to create others into whom he can pour love, so that they also may become love by participating freely in the freely offered love of God. But otherness, and the potentiality for freedom that goes with it, are not to be achieved in an instant. They take time, aeons upon aeons of time.

In fact the first form taken by the energy released at creation is the extremely sluggish form of *matter*. Out of all creation, matter is the least 'other' and therefore the least 'free'. And, for the same reason, it is the lowest form of the reflections of God. Matter is rightly described as 'blind', because it takes billions of years and it generates endless destruction before it develops a capacity for accommodating that higher form of otherness and freedom which is *life*.

The energy which is life takes infinitely more forms than does matter – myriads, in fact, ranging from creatures which are scarcely distinguishable from matter to creatures which enjoy a high degree of otherness. These latter are even capable of themselves introducing newness into the world by such acts as building nests and dwelling-places, and learning to live by social rules. But, as we know, they are also capable of extreme forms of destruction, mercilessly inflicting pain and death upon other living beings.

Then suddenly creation witnesses an intense burst of energy, as a result of which a creature appears who is so far other and free as to be ready to destroy not only his own life but even the lives of his own children still in the womb and, possibly, the whole human family – even all life upon the earth. Indeed man, at his worst, can wreak destruction out of sheer malice, the uttermost denial of love. And yet this same creature has a capacity for freedom and otherness so deep as freely to surrender life for love of others. Whenever that happens, this creature perfectly reflects the love with which God created the universe, and thereby responds perfectly to God's longing for an other capable of sharing in the divine nature. Now we not only see matter and life, but also the presence of *spirit*.

Unsophisticated though my story may be, it is precious to me because, among much else, it impresses upon me the patience of God who is prepared to wait billions of years for a response of love from his creation. God, the wholly other, waits for a creature so far advanced in otherness as to be able to love purely – no longer using others as instruments, as means for his own purposes. One difficulty in accepting the story I have sketched is that, in our sluggish moments, when we are not alive to the miracle of spirit, we are tempted to murmur to ourselves that the age-long groaning of creation was too high a price to pay for our present condition. But is our murmuring not due to our failure to recognise that love is not commensurable with time?

Think, for example, of someone you have loved who is now dead. And imagine that a higher being says to you, 'I can guarantee that you will see your beloved again, but you will have to wait 30,000 years. Will you wait?' Anyone who knows love will unhesitatingly say, 'Yes'. 'Will you wait a million years?' Again the answer is 'Yes'. Love has no end.

But the most precious gift contained in the story of creation, one that only reveals itself when the story is meditated upon night and day, is that we human beings are not the products of some blind, impersonal configuration of forces, but have been longed for by God since before the foundation of the world. We are not valued just as members of a species; for each of us is loved by God as a unique person with an intensely personal love, and each has been endowed with a capacity to respond to God with a unique, personal love. Nor does that intense personal love separate us one whit from any other fragment of creation. For, once we start to live our story and not merely tell it, then all of us may say truthfully, with Dante:

> Now my desire and will,
> like a wheel that spins with even motion,
> are revolved by the Love
> that moves the sun and the other stars.

12

A wandering scholar

(1994)

Christmas-tide of 1947 stands in my memory as the moment of my coming to birth as a European.

Of course I had dreamed of Europe throughout the years when I was studying French and German, fascinated by Péguy, Alain Fournier, Hans Carossa, Stefan Zweig, and numerous other writers. But after the dream-time there comes the birth, and that took place in the library of Blackfriars, Oxford, during Advent of 1947.

After completing my final examinations, and in order to escape the post-mortems, I settled into Blackfriars library, even though it was chilling to the bone. Maybe, indeed, it was the stark chill that directed me towards the article which was to shape my life. Because the title of the article, '*Von der Heimatlosigkeit Gottes*' ('On the homelessness of God'), symbolised for me the cold and hunger which millions of homeless Europeans were enduring that Christmas-time.

The meditation announced by the title proved to be every bit as striking as the title itself. So much so that even now, at a distance of 46 years, I can still recite the words of some of the sentences. Thus, 'The Son of Man came for us to know once more and never forget that we were born for happiness and not for sorrow, that all pain belongs to the fading countenance of this world, that all joys are a type of the coming kingdom'.

Perhaps it is not surprising that I can remember those words since they are the result of my painful struggle to translate the beautiful German of the original, a struggle which then occupied me for the rest of the term.

Yet the pain was mitigated by the fact that I had already fallen in love, via cold print, with the writer of the article, who was blessed with the truly German name of Ida Friederike Görres. In my mind's

140

eye she was a classically tall, blonde, graceful German beauty whose appearance matched her fascinating prose-style and the imaginative sweep of her meditation.

In the event, the manuscript of my translation went into the pending tray of my friend Father Conrad Pepler, and the name Ida Friederike Görres faded a little from my mind – until the day I called on Tom Burns, then of Burns and Oates, *en route* for Germany. He gave me the address of a writer with whom he had lost contact and to whom he wished to send greetings. Her name was Ida Friederike Görres.

It was a name that I was frequently to hear invoked almost from the first moment I arrived at my host's home in Münster, Westphalia (a city nearly totally destroyed by the Royal Air Force). Indeed, some might even say the person bearing the name was notorious.

For she it was whose book on St Thérèse of Lisieux, *The Hidden Face*, had provoked sharp criticism for having removed the veil that a misguided form of devotion had cast over the saint. Even more rage had been aroused by her 'Letter on the Church' published in the *Frankfurter Hefte*. In that passionate 'Letter', worthy of Leon Bloy, Ida had denounced the mediocrity of the German Catholic Church, and of the clergy in particular. In answer (or so it seemed), a pastoral letter from the German bishops had in turn denounced this fierce female critic. Then that pastoral (so I was told) itself gave rise to a blessing from the pope on the editors of the *Frankfurter Hefte*, a blessing engineered by Ida's aristocratic friends in Rome.

Already, then, within a few days I had begun to sense how it must have felt to have been a wandering scholar in the Middle Ages, bewildered by the controversies he had fallen into.

Also like a wandering scholar I had no money to speak of, and so I depended on the hospitality of the Germans – even though they themselves were living at rock-bottom. And yet, as I moved from one place to another, I never lacked for a warm corner in some house or monastery at night. Once it was in the home of a Catholic worker family in the Ruhrgebiet; at another time in the Dominican house of Walberberg; and later on I was welcomed into the mansion of the Herders, the family at the helm of a publishing house in Freiburg. All that was tacitly asked of me was that I should be content with a meagre diet of potato soup, black bread and *bohnen-kaffee* –

and, most of all, share a desire to work for the revival of European culture, so fractured by the war.

And everywhere I travelled I was filled with gratitude for the evidence that the Europe I had dreamed of had not been destroyed. The heroic story, for example, of Nikolaus Gross and Bernhard Letterhaus was lovingly retailed to me by Catholic workers in the Ruhrgebiet: Gross and Letterhaus, leaders of the Catholic workers, had died with great dignity at the hands of Hitler's executioners. And from the same source I was instructed in the meaning of *Mitbestimmungsrecht*, that principle for bringing harmony into industrial relations which both British trade unionists and employers were later to spurn.

No more than two days later I was taken to Cologne, to a suburban house in which the Carmelite sisters from Lindenthal had found temporary refuge after their convent had been severely damaged by the RAF. There, by virtue of the sort of luck that sometimes accompanies a wandering scholar, I received from the hands of the prioress, Sister Renata, a copy of her biography of Edith Stein fresh from the press. Within a few hours I had read the book and become devoted to that philosopher-saint about whom Sister Renata had spoken to us with such love. I carried the precious volume back to England and urged Frank Sheed to publish a translation, which he did gladly.

Oddly enough, what I remember most vividly about that visit is the scenario when Sister Renata discovered that there were no ash-trays for us. 'No ash-trays for these two gentlemen!', she exclaimed to the extern sister in mock indignation. 'What sort of a Carmel is it that has no ash-trays?' I felt that the spirit of Avila was alive and well in Cologne.

By the time I left Cologne, I had worked out that Ida Görres and her 'Letter' might serve as a sort of litmus paper to alert me at any moment as to the sort of person I was dealing with. So I was encouraged at the next stage of the journey by the response of Wilhelm Neuss, a priest in Bonn, who in the 1930s had courageously published a refutation of the *Mythus des XX Jahrhunderts* by Rosenberg, Hitler's ideologist. When I broached with him the question of whether Ida Görres's strictures upon the clergy were justified, Neuss nodded his head and slowly replied, '*Ja! So sind wir. So sind wir.*'

The hours I spent with Neuss were memorable for many reasons, but none more so than the incident he recounted, which stands still so clearly in my mind as a witness to traditional European culture. Neuss's training as a historian had brought him into friendship with another historian of the Rhineland, a Jew – the author of *England and the Continent in the Eighth Century* – Wilhelm Levison. In the late 1930s Levison had decided he must leave Germany on account of the persecution of the Jews. And on the day of his departure Neuss accompanied him to the railway station in Bonn, not only out of friendship but also as a demonstration of solidarity with his friend. While they were waiting for the train, those two old scholars did not speak to one another about the sadness of parting, or about politics, but about their plans for historical research. 'In fact,' Neuss said to me, 'the last words I heard from Levison as he leaned out of the carriage window, waving goodbye, were "Don't forget to publish the *Acta* of Sts So-and-so"' (So-and-so being Rhineland saints of the early Middle Ages). That scene remains as a wonderful cameo of European humanism.

What I could not then have anticipated, of course, as I travelled on to Stuttgart-Degerloch, the Görres home, was that God had a laugh on me in store. Because when I stood somewhat nervously on the Görres' threshold I was naturally enough expecting to be greeted by that embodiment of Teutonic beauty who, in my imaginings, had written *Von der Heimatlosigkeit Gottes*. Instead of which I was faced with a short, rather thick-set, bespectacled woman with straight, black hair drawn into a bun, and the sturdy legs characteristic of certain Japanese. I would not have been so astonished had I known that she was a Coudenhove-Kalergi, the daughter of an Austrian diplomat and a Japanese princess. But God had the laugh on me because, as I was soon to recognise, the one he had created was infinitely preferable to the creature of my imagination.

That moment on the threshold of the Görres home was referred to ever afterwards by Ida as '*unsere Blitzbegegnung*' (our lightning meeting), meaning that we hit it off in an instant. She was to become my *anmchara* (soul-friend) until she died. For me that *Blitzbegegnung* was lightning in a further sense: the whole European landscape was lit up for me under her guidance, and I developed a sense of its rich variety of regional cultures – Swabian and Bohemian, Rhineland and Slovak, Romanesque and Baroque.

And she was shrewd enough to edge me into circles that I could not have entered on my own – such as a right-wing aristocratic group, where I encountered a dotty and occasionally sinister side of Europe. I think, for example, of an aristocratic Jesuit to whom I expressed my admiration for his fellow Jesuit, Alfred Delp, who had been executed for being a member of the von Moltke circle. My interlocutor agreed that Delp was a fine man; but he added that his death at that time may have been providential. 'What do you mean?' I enquired. '*Er war ein wenig links*' (he was a bit left-wing), came the dumbfounding reply.

But even such unhappy encounters were grist to my mill when, at Father Conrad Pepler's request, I edited an issue of *Blackfriars* on the condition of the Christian Church in Germany (November 1949). Through that undertaking I made contacts which led me, in the following three or four years, to translate several works of philosophy and theology – as well as to write for *Wort und Wahrheit, Herder-Korrespondenz* and *Documents-Documente.*

The last of these, to which I was introduced by a lively French Jesuit, Jean du Rivau, was devised so as to provide readers in France and Germany with the identical documentation of events, in the hope of nurturing their mutual understanding. I was delighted to take part in the enterprise since by this time I had already made a pilgrimage to France. My pilgrimage had been to the grave at Avon of Père Jacques de Jésus, the Carmelite hero of Mauthausen concentration camp. And in the course of hitch-hiking across France I had discovered that there also, as in Germany, nothing was asked of me except words of hope in exchange for the like hospitality – though in France the coffee was better.

My experience was typified by the seminary for priest-workers in Lisieux. There I found a company of hardy young men – some of them ex-soldiers, including two Germans – who received me with easy comradeship. But the extent of the large-heartedness that was to be found in that company only became clear to me later. It came about because I had mentioned to the superior of the seminary that I was interested in the story of Barbe Acarie, but could not obtain a copy of her biography. He listened carefully. Then some weeks later the book arrived on my door-step in Scotland – I might keep it, he said, so long as I had a use for it.

The season of my French journey being Lent, I was suitably hungry and tired by the time I arrived on Maundy Thursday at the Dominican house of studies, *Le Saulchoir*. I quickly perked up, however, when I found myself almost immediately sitting in the garden at the feet of Père Congar, along with a dozen other young men from various countries who were engaged in a passionate discussion of just about every cultural and political issue that Europe was then facing.

And I felt my wanderer's luck was still holding later, when I discovered that I had been allotted a room next to that of Congar! After supper one evening he was to come and talk with me for a couple of hours. By the time he left the room I was ready for sleep; but as I drifted off I could hear the tap-tap of the typewriter next door. The great man was busy on yet another book.

I met other Frenchmen during those weeks whom I think of as great; and one, Jean de Menasce, became a dear friend. But what stands out most vividly in my memory as a flash of pure French *esprit* was an incident that took place on my return journey through Paris.

It was a Sunday afternoon, and I was visiting Nôtre Dame for the first time. I spent an hour or so rather dreamily in one of the chapels, until I became aware that a sermon was being preached from the cathedral's main pulpit. Going over to stand beside one of the pillars, I realised that the preacher was the Jesuit, Père Riquet, famous as a survivor of Dachau. He was addressing the issue of suffering by way of the story of Job. I sensed that his sermon was nearing its end when he began to describe how Job had challenged God to give an answer to suffering. '*Et Dieu,*' he said, '*n'avait pas de réponse*' – and then, after a long pause, ' . . . *mais après six siecles Dieu a donné sa réponse . . .*' – another pause, ' . . . *sa réponse, c'était Jésus Christ – au nom du Père, du Fils et du Saint Esprit, Amen.*' And with a great sign of the cross he came down from the pulpit. Sublime French theatre at the service of the Word.

I hope the reader may now realise why I am so saddened to hear government ministers these days, who purport to represent us, who declare that the reason for Britain to 'go into Europe' is because 'it is in our own self-interest', or who say, for example, that 'Britain has no interests in the Balkans'. For those ministers, Britain's interest in Europe means money, whereas for us in the immediate post-war period it meant sharing our cultures, our hopes and our very lives with one another.

Nevertheless, I can still take comfort from some lines which I wrote in 1951 after watching some children in Germany playing in the rubble of their city:

> But the captain of commerce will not have the last word, for you still find 'the city full of boys and girls playing in the streets thereof'. And in the last day they shall laugh, these children of the rubble, when they walk the streets of the New Jerusalem, playing before the face of God.

Part III

13

Scientia cordis

(1975)

It was an incident which led me to write what follows. I was talking
to a friend of mine, a well-known philosopher, who expressed some
concern about the direction that his philosophical thinking was
taking. Because, he said, it was beginning to get closer all the time
to the sort of conclusions expressed by his pious Hasidic ancestors.
And this was worrying him, because he thought that maybe he was
losing his touch and therefore falling back into ancestral patterns of
thought. I asked him whether his was the only explanation, or even
the most likely one. 'Why are you so surprised that you are coming
closer to your ancestors? You try honestly enough running your
fingers along the timber of reality and reporting what you find; the
longer you go on, the closer your findings coincide with the reports
of your ancestors who were also trying honestly to feel out the
grain of reality. So why should you be surprised? Should it not be a
confirmation for you, and a source of comfort? Unless you think that
originality means displaying your own personality rather than finding
the origin of our being?'

Once my friend saw his concern from the right angle it became a
source of joy to him; and a similar change of perspective may produce
like joy among all of us when we start comparing our findings not
only with those of our own immediate ancestors, but with the
different sacred traditions to be found among the rest of mankind
over the face of the earth. The fact, for instance, that Christianity is
nowadays set in the context of world religions has caused concern to
many Christians, as if this somehow threatened the originality of
their Christian faith. Whereas on second thoughts they may well
realise, like my friend did, that contact with other sacred traditions
assures them that they have not been out of touch with reality all the

time they have been feeling for its grain in virtue of their Christian living.

Certainly a striking feature of many of the great spiritual adventurers of this century has been the way in which, having lost their bearings within their own traditions, they have sought them in some other – and have almost gone over to that tradition, only to discover their bearings once more within their own. One thinks especially in this context of Louis Massignon (1883–1962), the great French Arabist, who had drifted away from the practice of his traditional Catholic faith, but was so impressed by the religious fervour of the ordinary Muslims whom he met in Morocco and Mesopotamia that he was converted, not to Islam but in a sense through Islam, back to the Catholic faith. After he died, a Muslim authority astonishingly said of him, 'He was a true Christian and a true Muslim'.[1] Noteworthy also is the fact that towards the end of his life, journeying through the Far East, Massignon found himself at home among Hindus, Buddhists and Shintoists. Equally striking is the case of Franz Rosenzweig (1886–1929), who moved away from his ancestral Jewish faith and towards Christianity – so much so that in 1913 he decided to become a Christian. But wishing to enter Christianity like its founder, not as a 'pagan' but as a Jew, he aimed to 'go through' Judaism to Christianity. Which is why he went to the synagogue on the Day of Atonement, 1913. He was converted back to Judaism on that very day, and in subsequent years became one of the most powerful spokesmen for twentieth-century Judaism.

It cannot be said of Rosenzweig, however, as it can of Massignon, that by almost going over to the other religion he acquired an admiration and special understanding for it; he could still say 'we have crucified Christ and, believe me, would do it again every time, we alone in the whole world'.[2] But his friend Martin Buber (1878–1965) throughout his life felt the attraction of his 'elder brother Jesus', and on his deathbed was able to say to a visitor, 'Mr Thomson, I want you to know that I believe that I have known the presence of Christ'.[3] He had some wonderfully perceptive things to say about Christianity and its relationship with Judaism. He said, for instance, that the Epistles of St John are Judaism at its highest, and that Christianity was 'the first Hasidic movement' among the Jews, but at the same time, 'If you want to accept Christ and the New Testament, the maxims of the Epistles are not enough. You must also believe in the Virgin Birth and in the Resurrection of Christ from the dead'; because 'The Christian is the incomparably daring man, who affirms in an unredeemed world that its redemption has been accomplished'.[4] And like Massignon, Buber became enriched not only by his dialogue with Christianity but also through his appreciation of the Far East of Hinduism, of Chinese thought and of Zen Buddhism. Yet these contacts enabled him to become ever more truly a son of Israel.

Buber's contacts with Hinduism were prompted by Mahatma Gandhi (1869–1948), with whom he corresponded, and who is a striking illustration of our theme; for in many respects it was through his devotion to Christ that the Hindu Gandhi came to a new and deeper love for Hinduism. It is an exaggeration to say that the religion of Gandhi 'is just this – a Christian foundation covered by a transparent screen of Hindu creepers'[5] – but no one can follow Gandhi's *Experiments with Truth* and not recognise that Christ came to fill his heart more and more the longer he lived. In the early days there was his daily reading of the New Testament where he found the teaching on *ahimsa* (non-violence), and there was his endless singing of the hymn 'Lead, kindly light'. In later years, especially after his pilgrimage in 1931 to the crucifix in the Sistine Chapel, the cross grew more central for him and his favourite hymn became 'When I survey the wondrous cross'. On the walls of his room at Sevagram there was no other decoration but a picture of Christ, and yet he no longer thought of going over to Christianity, as he had done in earlier years. Indeed, he described himself as a Christian, a Jew and a Buddhist, and yet in his last moments, struck down by a fellow Hindu, he called upon the name of Rama, the heroic Hindu god.[6]

Less obvious than in Gandhi, more in accordance with the enigmatic character of Zen Buddhism, is the example given by D. T. Suzuki (1870–1966), the Buddhist scholar, who first made direct contact with Christianity when he was only 15. The Christians he met in those days did not inspire him, but over the years he did find inspiration in the writings of the German mystic, Meister Eckhardt, though it is typical of Suzuki that he should not have revealed the depths of it until the last moments of his long life. On the very last day before he died, in writing an introduction to *A Flower Does Not Talk*, Suzuki penned these words: 'Let us not forget that Zen always aspires to make us see directly into Reality itself, that is, be Reality itself so that we can say along with Meister Eckhardt that "Christ is born every minute in my soul".'[7] There are not many Christians who can say that Christ is born every minute in their souls, as Suzuki did, and yet Suzuki's every word and gesture reveal him to have been a Zen Buddhist.

Massignon, Rosenzweig, Buber, Gandhi, Suzuki – these are only a few of the men who have approached close to other religions and been strengthened in, or rediscovered, their own. There are many others. One thinks, for example, of Sir John Woodroffe (1865–1936), the British judge, who was the editor and translator of many Hindu classics, and of the French expert on Chinese culture, Albert de Pouvourville, both of whom were led back to Catholicism by their studies. But there are also others who did eventually journey onwards into the other religion. Some of these, such as Narayan Vaman Tilak (1861–1919), acknowledge their debt to their own tradition: in homage to Tukaram, the Bhakti poet of the seventeenth century, Tilak exclaimed: 'Over the bridge of Tukaram's poetry I came to Christ'. Others, such as Verrier Elwin (1902–64), the Anglican missionary in India who became a Hindu, speak harshly of the tradition in which they were bred.

But, even when those journeying between religions speak harshly of certain traditions, so long as they are sincerely searching, then what they say nearly always catches at least the characteristic views of that religion and, when seen the other way around, like a photographic negative, may also throw into prominence its characteristic virtues. When, for instance, the spokesman for India's untouchables, Dr Ambedkar (1893–1956), was searching for the religion in the light of which he might lead his people out of their bondage, he considered whether Christianity might be that light. But he decided that it was not, because his experience of Christian missionaries in India convinced him that, in practice, Christianity was hardly more than a branch of Western imperialism; and so he became a Buddhist instead. Even though Christians might feel that Dr Ambedkar had given a most negative impression of Christianity, nevertheless this very negative throws into prominence the Christian truth that not everyone who cries 'Lord, Lord' is fit for the kingdom, but only those who give bread to the hungry and drink to the thirsty; and Dr Ambedkar and his oppressed people had not found many such among the Christians they had encountered. So they chose Buddhism.

But to others, Buddhism itself, far from being liberating, is a seductive illusion. Nikolai Fyodorov (1827–1900), the Russian thinker, says that Buddhism is 'the professional disease of the learned class', and is the last stage in the process of degeneration symbolised by the modern university.[8] Nor has the Jewish thinker Ignaz Maybaum anything better to say of Buddhism: for him it seems that dialogue with Buddhism is impossible because the smile of the Buddha is 'a cold disinterested smile, outwardly friendly but in truth cruel' – the representation of 'Asiatic nihilism', to which the only radical antithesis is prophetic Judaism.[9] A very instructive negative view, this time of Hinduism, is to be found in a letter of C. S. Lewis (1898–1963) to Bede Griffiths, when he says, 'Your Hindus certainly sound delightful. But what do they *deny*? That has always been my trouble with Indians – to find any proposition they would find false. But truth must surely involve exclusion?'[10] This remark of Lewis' is instructive because what he is saying seems so different when seen from the Hindu side of the negative. To the Hindu, it has often seemed that Christians can only affirm God's goodness by denying the Devil; that they need the springboard of hatred for someone as a means of affirming their love for another; that when they declare peace it is by means of violence – all of which mental habits are symptoms of the dualism inherent in C. S. Lewis' remark.

What C. S. Lewis, Ignaz Maybaum and Nikolai Fyodorov have in common, which leads them to make these negative judgements, is that they regard the other traditions about which they are speaking as a threat; and their statements are intended to ward off these others and keep them at a distance. This feature is characteristic of all theoreticians, and distinguishes them from the people we spoke of at the beginning, who are rather spiritual adventurers reaching out to feel the grain of reality wherever their contacts may take them. And it is one of the most encouraging features of our present age that these spiritual adventurers know one another, in the Hebrew meaning of the word 'know' – that is, to embrace lovingly. One thinks, for example, of the interconfessional kibbutz at Quiryat Jeharim, near

Jerusalem, where Jews, Christians and Muslims have been brought to live together under the inspiration of a Dominican priest, Father Bruno Hassar.[11] Or one thinks of the Ittoen community, near Kyoto in Japan, begun by Tenko-San whose conversion was prompted by *My Religion*, a book by the Christian writer Tolstoy. Ittoen is a community where the Buddhist and Christian and Hindu traditions are observed in an edifying manner.[12] Conversely, there are the communities for experiencing Zen established by Christians: the one by the side of the rive Akikawa under the direction of the German Jesuit Lasalle, now a naturalised Japanese, and the other at So-An where a Japanese Dominican, Shigeto Oshida, is the Zen master.[13] While a Catholic nun, Sister Shraddhananda Bahin, has spent the last few years in the Hindu ashram founded by Vinoba Bhave at Paunar in the Central Provinces;[14] and high up on the Ganges the Belgian-born Abhishikhtananda pursues his vocation as a Christian hermit in an area peopled by Hindu *sannyasis*.

A coat of many colours is being woven by the coming together of men and women from such very different traditions. After the second world war a young Romanian intellectual joined in the *hesychast* revival in that country, a movement of silent unceasing prayer. He later received the Russian Orthodox title of *starets* (spiritual elder), before being invited, on account of his deep knowledge of Hindu spirituality, to spend two years in the holy city of Benares. Since which date he has helped to found an Orthodox monastery in Beirut.[15] Meanwhile the most original sketch of an Indian Christian theology has come from a priest whose father was Hindu and mother Spanish, and who himself spends some months of each year at an Indian, and some at an American, university.[16]

The spirit in which these men and women are coming together – coming to know one another in the sense of 'embracing lovingly' – is as far removed as possible from the spirit in which exponents of comparative religion have often conducted their studies. These men and women seem to have a real distaste for making comparisons; just as it is a fundamental principle of spiritual life not to make comparisons between individuals, because every person is beyond measure, so it is invidious to make comparisons between the traditional religions. There is something distasteful at the mere thought of such comparisons, because these religions have nourished millions of people and enabled them to grow to their full stature as human beings. When food is set before one by a host, one does not give a lecture listing the merits of this dish as opposed to that – even less does one look for the book of recipes. Rather one thanks God and one's host before tasting and eating.

Eating together, sharing one's food, is the most profound symbol of harmony and trust among human beings – though the moment has not yet arrived when all, without exception, can sit down together at the common meal. To try to insist upon our right to do so at this particular moment of time would be brash and unhelpful. None the less we do wish, in some way, to share in the food of other peoples. What other position, then, is available for us than that of the Syro-Phoenician woman spoken of in the gospels? When Jesus said, ' "It is not meet to take the children's bread, and to cast it to dogs", the woman replied, "Truth, Lord, yet the dogs eat of the crumbs which fall from their masters' table".'[17]

The Syro-Phoenician woman's identification of herself with a little dog seeking to nourish itself on the crumbs that fall from the master's table is an appropriate one for those who seek to come close to the traditional masters of the spiritual search. To begin with, the ones sitting at the rich table can hardly object to those who do not belong there taking the crumbs and nourishing themselves upon them. Such little dogs are truly fulfilling Jesus' injunction to 'gather up the fragments that remain that nothing be lost'.[18] Moreover, there is a lot of truth in the old German quip, *Man ist was man isst*, a man is what he eats, not only in the obvious physical sense but even more in the spiritual sense: if we feed on flattery we become inflated; if we feed on bitter thoughts we become bitter; and if we feed on truth we become true. When, therefore, we nourish ourselves even upon the crumbs from any tradition, we actually become members of that tradition. When the Muslim authority said of Louis Massignon that he was a true Muslim he was speaking correctly: Massignon had gathered up the fragments of Muslim spiritual life and taken their substance into him in a fashion that few avowed Muslims themselves have managed; that substance became his substance – which is not to deny, of course, that he was a Christian, for he also fed on Christ.

How else than in terms of the little dog can one account for the fact that almost everyone looking for Christ-life in the twentieth-century world turns toward the life of Mahatma Gandhi rather than towards the careers of many official or self-appointed defenders of Christianity? Gandhi was a man who collected up the fragments of Christ that the West had thrown under the table; he fed upon them; they were his daily bread through his study of the New Testament and his devotions to Christ. Only by taking the term 'Christian' in a very strained sense could one deny Gandhi's own claim to be a Christian.

From what has been said already it is clear that spiritual seekers are not content with examining merely the external features of other traditions or their statements of belief, but rather they penetrate to the very heart of them, they find that by which those in the tradition live. And they share in it, without taking it upon themselves to make comparisons, knowing that one can only compare what lies on the surface. They share in the worship and prayers, the pilgrimages and festivals; they rejoice with the others at their feasts and mourn with them at their funerals. One of the most moving accounts of such a quest is to be found in *Hindu and Christian in Vrindaban* by the German Catholic Klaus Klostermaier, who spent two years in Vrindaban, the playground of Krishna. The seeker, he says,

. . . will not want to have anything more to do with academic dalliance or a science of comparative religion, behaving as if it stood above all religions. He will also not want to know anything more of a certain kind of theology that works 'without presuppositions' and pleases itself in manipulating definitions and formulas and forgets about man, who is the main concern. He will be more and more pulled into what is called 'spirituality': the real life of the mind. I wanted to see a famous man in Benares, a sagacious philosopher, feared by many as a merciless critic of Christian theology. I had my own reasons for paying him a visit. He was polite, invited me for tea and then mounted the attack. I let him talk his fill, without saying a word myself. Then I began to talk about the things I had begun to understand within the dialogue – quite positively Christian. We got into a sincere, good, deep discussion. He had intended to send me away after ten minutes. When I left after two hours, he had tears in his eyes: 'If we insisted on our theologies – you as a Christian, I as a Hindu – we should be fighting each other. We have found one another because we probed more deeply, towards spirituality.'[19]

In the light of this statement by Klostermaier we catch a glimpse of how one might penetrate to the heart of other spiritual traditions and achieve a real *scientia cordis*, a science of the heart, on which all of them converge. They converge for the very good reason that they are all in contact, in one manner or another, with the same reality. It is such a *scientia cordis* which I wish to say something about for the rest of this writing.

The primary thing to notice is that the *scientia cordis* is, in the proper sense of the word, a science. This may at first glance seem a surprising statement, since matters of the heart are often thought of as emotional and subjective, and so hardly susceptible of agreement. But if one looks more closely, one sees that there is more agreement among the practitioners of this science than among the practitioners of any other. Whereas, for instance, among the authorities on physics there is disagreement upon such fundamental questions as whether there is an ether or not, and whereas there is disagreement among biologists as to whether we are more influenced by nature or nurture, the rest of this discussion will show, I hope, that the authorities in the *scientia cordis* are in substantial agreement on all fundamental issues.

It is said of Jesus, in the gospels, that he spoke as one having authority. Which does not mean to say, of course, that he spoke as if he had a piece of paper or a seal or a sword from someone to say that he was to be obeyed. In spiritual life the second-hand is of no worth whatsoever; here the only person who speaks with authority is the one who has experienced what is being talked about. And any other form of authority in social or political life derives whatever validity it may have from its connection, however remote, with someone who at some time has spoken with authority. So long as the people at large still continue to make the connection in their minds between the person now brandishing seals or tokens of authority and someone who at some time really spoke with authority, then there is always a chance that the people will obey, because in effect they are obeying the original speaker. But once that connection is broken in their minds, then so is their obedience.

Because the pure form of authority, of which other forms are simply shadows, is spiritual. And spiritual authority means having the character to command obedience. The truth of this definition becomes clear as soon as we think of the three words 'character', 'command' and 'obedience'. Because 'character' signifies not something borrowed or put on for the occasion, but *what* a person has in substance come to be over the years, the set of human being that one has established in oneself. To 'command' means to leave no choice but to obey; and its application here becomes intelligible when we bear in mind the roots of the word 'obedience', because this word has its roots in the Latin word for hearing. So when we say that a spiritual authority has the character to command obedience, we are pointing to the fact that such a character compels others to listen, to give it a hearing; such a voice is compelling, you have no choice but to listen. Of course you may in the end refuse to act in accordance with what the spiritual authority has said; that freedom must always remain in any transaction of the spirit – as opposed to the political realm, say, where power can in the end force people to conform. The element of compulsion with a spiritual authority consists in the fact that you have no choice but to hear in your heart, even though you may then harden your heart against such words and try to dismiss them.

Two events that I observed may serve as illustrations. I had the opportunity several years ago, at the time of student 'troubles', to see how differently two sorts of authorities responded to the crisis. In the first university, the authorities had over the years failed to say any compelling words to their students at the times when students needed them; they had issued plenty of orders, to which students had been forced to conform if they chose not to be punished. But when the crisis came, many students now proved to be less frightened of punishment than of losing their self-respect. So they chose not to conform; and once this happened it was revealed that no one in the university had the character to command obedience. In other words, there was no authority.

At the second university, the pressure upon the students from outside political forces to organise a revolt was much more intense. But in this case the central person was of different mettle; he was in the habit of issuing virtually no orders at any time, and when the crisis came he did not break this habit. But when a great mass-protest meeting of students was held, and speaker after speaker strode to the rostrum to harangue the students, this man stood quietly in the crowd. Then, as the speeches followed one after another, you could feel the attention of the crowd moving towards this man and centring upon him. Eventually he was asked to speak, because he had the character to *command* a hearing. He did not speak very lucidly or brilliantly, and certainly the students did not immediately do what he proposed; but in the deeper sense of the word they *were* obeying him, and somewhat later were even doing what he proposed. He was an authority.

The second illustration comes from the year 1950, in Edinburgh. Martin Buber was about to visit the university, and a group of university lecturers was discussing the prospect with amusement; they belonged to the tough-minded school of linguistic analysis, and were saying that they had never been struck by the 'Buberonic plague' but they would go along to the meeting nevertheless, for the fun of it. When they returned from the meeting their attitude was changed. Previously they had only encountered people who spoke with words, but in Buber they had met a man who spoke with authority, the authority of having lived what he was saying. They were chastened, having been brought face to face with a character who commanded obedience.

This, therefore, is the primary thing to notice about the *scientia cordis*: it is science. And the next thing to note is that in no sense is it a branch of psychology. Psychology, like all positive sciences, attempts to analyse the object of its study as if it were a fixed, given thing whose future is in principle totally predictable, provided the scientist can exhaustively analyse all its parts. But the heart is the seat of aspiration, of prayer; and even an agnostic such as Iris Murdoch, for instance, is glad to acknowledge that human beings who pray live in an added dimension, beyond the reach of those who do not pray. It is more exact to say not that they live in an added dimension, but that they plunge into a dimension which alters every single thing about them. Their whole being then is transformed by aspiration, and cannot be analysed and predicted – because the aspiration, the prayer, is an affirmation that renewal is possible, that there is genuine

159

newness in the world, that not everything can be reduced to what was given in the past.

This distinction is common to all cultures. They all distinguish between aspects of the human being, partial aspects (which are subject to fixed laws and therefore susceptible to study by psychology) and the whole human being (symbolised by the heart or the centre as the seat of prayer), which is beyond the reach of immutable laws. The Jarai people of Vietnam, for instance, are a people at the centre of whose culture are gongs: gongs are used to symbolise the most solemn and joyous moments of Jarai life. Therefore, when they wish to make the distinction referred to above, they will sometimes say of a person who does seemingly wicked things that his wicked deeds are the result, say, of his bad liver, but that nevertheless he makes the right sound – his gong, so to speak, is sound. Or it may happen the other way round, that a person always does correct things but does not give off a right sound.[20] The Jarai here seem to be expressing, in terms of hearing, what Saint-Exupéry expressed in terms of vision: '*On ne voit bien qu'avec le coeur. L'essentiel est invisible pour les yeux.*' ('One does not see well except with one's heart; what is essential is invisible to the eyes.')[21]

That invisible which is essential was evoked by a Hindu when Aelred Graham asked him whether there is 'any place in Hinduism for what Christians call faith, a kind of belief in an unseen without any real knowledge of it?' The Hindu replied:

> There is *sraddha*. For example, when I talk to you I must have faith in what I say; you must have faith that I am worth talking to. *Srad* means 'heart'; *dha* means 'to put into': 'that which you have firmly put into your heart'.[22] *Sraddha* is faith. But in Hinduism, as one might expect, there are many ways of expressing this truth, as for instance by dancing; for the place of Shiva's dance, *Chidambaram*, the Centre of the Universe, is within the heart.[23]

Japanese Buddhists make a similar distinction when they speak of two 'I's. One of these 'I's is the 'I' that is susceptible to study by psychology, which strives to satisfy its desires, talks about itself and observes its own reactions, displays itself and is eminently visible. It is known as *shoga*, and has to perish if the other 'I' is to be properly born. This latter, known as *taiga*, refers to the whole human being when that human being is entirely taken up in aspiration and prayer.[24] And the distinction between them is perfectly symbolised by the Latin translation in the Vulgate Bible from the Hebrew Song of Songs where the lover assures his beloved, '*Ego dormio, sed vigilat cor meum*'[25] – 'My ego has gone to sleep but my heart is keeping watch'. The sense of which is that if the heart is not to be hindered in its deepest aspirations, then the ego – that partial self which is always watching itself and composing a role for itself to play – must disappear.

The fact that the *scientia cordis* is a science of the heart, of the human being in aspiration, also implies that it contains a further dimension than any of the positive sciences such, for instance, as psychology. Because positive science tries to formulate immutable laws about what *is*, psychology too attempts to freeze human beings in terms of laws about needs and demands that can be specified – but the aspirations of the heart always go beyond what can be specified in such laws; and it is these aspirations which keep the heart in motion and prevent it from being frozen into immobility. Positive science, by confining itself to what *is* and not to what *ought* to be, always runs the danger of becoming sterile; for as Goethe put it, 'Treat a man as he is and he will become worse; treat him as he ought to be (or as he aspires to be) and he will become better' – for our aspirations are the most real part of us.

For this reason, also, the characteristic medium for stating the *scientia cordis* is not the principle or law characteristic of the positive sciences. The essential point about the principle or law formula is that it leaves the situation unchanged, and it leaves both the person formulating the law and the one hearing the law in a state of detachment: there is nothing that anyone ought to do as a result of the formulation; everyone can still say, 'So what?' By contrast, both the person stating the science of the heart and the person to whom it is stated have to be moved by it, since it is concerned with human beings in aspiration and prayer; and unless they are quickened in their aspirations, then the statement has proved empty. Hence the characteristic medium of the *scientia cordis* is neither a principle nor a law but a story – a story that will move the heart.

And this is what we find among all the authorities of this science, that they do their teaching by stories that will touch the hearts of their listeners. Almost all the incidents and stories in the New Testament, for instance, are of this kind. An obvious instance is the parable of the good Samaritan. In answer to the question, 'Who is my neighbour?', it would have been quite easy for Christ to have given a definition embodying some principle or some law which would have satisfied the questioner by leaving him in his fixed condition of detachment. Instead, Christ tells a story about a man on the way from Jerusalem to Jericho, which in no time involves the questioner in the man's fate and touches his heart. No one can remain unmoved by the story – or ever forget it, because the heart has a good memory.

Nor is such story-telling peculiar to the New Testament, for it is an essential part of all the traditions that we are invoking. One finds it among the Sufis of Islam, among the Jewish Hasidim; the Buddhist Scriptures are full of such stories; while it is no exaggeration to say that the mass of Indians have been educated by the *puranas*, those ancient stories that acquired their savour as they were transmitted throughout India between the fifth and the eighteenth centuries.[26] For it is another feature of these stories that they have gathered richness over the centuries by passing through the hearts of the labouring people; they never smack of the detached observer spinning out some isolated thoughts, but are always redolent of the soil, the dust of the roads, the sweat of work and the laughter of the festival. This was what Vinoba Bahve had in mind when he said that, in so far as he had been able to move people in his Boodhan campaign, it was through recognising the peasant as his guru, his teacher, who taught him by popular stories.[27]

But of all these traditions, none has attached so much importance to story-telling as the Hasidic movement within Judaism. This movement began in the poor Jewish communities of Eastern Europe during the eighteenth century under the impulse of the Baal Shem Tov (1700–60), a man of great learning who nevertheless earned his living often in menial trades – he was at one time an innkeeper, for instance. It was in many respects a protest on the part of the wretched, ill-housed, badly fed Jews of the ghettos against the dry, cold, cerebral teaching of the rabbis who worked out their formulas and commented on their laws, remote in the isolation of their studies, detached from the sufferings of the common people. For the God-seekers of the ghettos, rabbinic teaching was 'teaching without heart' – and so they themselves, over the course of the years, built up a tradition of telling

162

stories that moved the hearts of the pious who had come to listen to them.

Perhaps this feature of Hasidism is best illustrated by the story from the third generation of the movement. Some of the younger Hasidim had been talking about what it must have been like in the early days, when they remembered that nearby was a very aged cripple who had actually known the Baal Shem. So they went to the crippled old man and asked him to describe to them how the Baal Shem used to tell a story. Which the old man began to do; and as he warmed to his tale, he spoke of how the Baal Shem's words were not simply words but also deeds, so that if, for instance, the Baal Shem were telling a story about dancing, his hearers would finish up dancing – at which point the crippled man's limbs were loosened and he began to dance. That was how the Baal Shem told a story.[28]

A story should not merely be *about* what happened; it should itself *be* a happening. And this is why the Hasidim were not in favour of writing down their stories in books; because once it is down there in black and white, then anyone can pick it up, in however cold a spirit, and take it away to read in isolation. In which case it is almost impossible for the story to be itself a happening, for truth can only travel from one person to another along the path of warmth and personal affection.

And even though the Hasidic attitude towards impersonal articles may seem exaggerated, the intuition behind it receives confirmation from a wonderfully good man in Japan, a Shin Buddhist. His name was Saichi and his trade was to make *geta*, a type of wooden shoe traditionally worn by Japanese. Saichi used to warn that modern articles of production were not accompanied by joy in their making and so they brought no joy. But Saichi's hand-made *geta* were made with joy, and so carried joy wherever they went, as many people can testify who wore Saichi's *geta*.[29]

The reason why story-telling is the appropriate medium for the *scientia cordis*, then, is that in matters of aspiration the motto is that very motto which Cardinal Newman took for his own – *cor ad cor loquitor*, 'heart speaketh to heart' – and it is only along the path of such speech that dancing and joy and truth can travel. Mere statements of principle leave us unmoved because, to adapt W. B. Yeats' phrase, they have been conceived in the brain and only touch our own brains, whereas we only *believe* those thoughts which have been conceived in the heart.[30] What is said can find echo in one's own heart because it has already struck home in someone else's – and then it does not come from outside at all, like an order, but comes from within, like a prayer or aspiration of one's own. This was well described by Vinoba Bahve who was telling once about the effect on him of Gandhi when he first went to learn from him: Vinoba says that Gandhi's voice 'seemed to come up from the centre of my own being instead of striking at my ears'.[31]

The following pages will attempt to show how the echoes from within the spiritual traditions of humankind come up from the centre of the other traditions and harmonise marvellously with them into what anyone listening will recognise to be a true *scientia cordis*. So far we have been speaking *about* it, but now we can apply ourselves to making a sketch of this science-which-moves, and test in somewhat more detail the stages through which a human being moves in accordance with the science.

It was once pointed out to St Seraphim, the Russian saint (1759–1833), that certain people who strive for holiness really become transformed, while others, who seem to begin with the same dispositions, make hardly any progress at all. And he was asked, why is this? He replied simply, 'Just determination' – thus echoing the words of the Italian saint, Thomas Aquinas (1225–74), who once said 'If you want to be a saint then the first thing is to *want* to be a saint'. These pithy answers are necessary reminders of how easy it is to deceive one's self in these matters – to mistake whim for real longing – because the area of spirituality, along with the area of sexuality, is the classic place for illusions.

Because they are so aware of the danger of illusions about the spiritual journey, Zen Buddhists are quite fierce in their determination to dispel any such illusions. At one time anyone wishing to enter a Zen monastery, for instance, might have to sit silent and cross-legged for hours, or a day, or even several days, waiting for a Zen master to take notice of him and allow him to enter. Nowadays at Ittoen he is much more likely to be ordered to perform *Takuhatsu*, that is, going into a district and offering to perform selfless service, working without expecting any reward whether in food or drink or shelter. Performing *Takuhatso*,

. . . the novice may very well become depressed. The sun does not take compassion on him, nor does it delay its setting until he has obtained work. Darkness and hunger close in upon him. He has neither rice-ball nor lodging. He has only loneliness. Life has at last become very serious. He should not try to escape but swallow the experience to the very dregs. What should he do? Neither trying to think things out, nor any philosophy will help him one iota. He is utterly ashamed, utterly helpless. All his conceit is dead. There is only one road open. He turns to prayer. This at last is true self-discipline [– and not illusion].[32]

How exacting this scrutiny might prove is told by D. T. Suzuki, who was later to become such a famous Zen scholar. As a young man he made the long and uncomfortable journey to a temple called Kokutaji near Takaoka, and then, in his own words,

I arrived without introduction, but the monks were quite willing to take me in. They told me the Roshi was away, but that I could do *zazen* in a room in the temple if I liked. They told me how to sit and how to breathe and then left me alone in a little room telling me to go on like that. After a day or two of this the Roshi came back and I was taken to see him. Of course at that time I really knew nothing of Zen and had no idea of correct etiquette in *sanzen*. I was just told to come and see the Roshi, so I went, holding my copy of the *Orategama*.[33]

Most of the *Orategama* is written in fairly easy language, but there are some difficult Zen terms in it which I could not understand, so I asked the Roshi the meaning of these words. He turned on me angrily and said, 'Why do you ask me a stupid question like that?' I was sent back to my room without any instruction and told simply to go on sitting cross-legged. I was left quite alone. It was the first time I had ever been away from home and soon I grew lonely and homesick, and missed my mother very much. So after four or five days I left the temple and went back to my mother again.[34]

Doubtless this treatment sounds harsh – though it is no harsher than telling a rich young man, supposedly in search of the Kingdom, to sell all he has and give it to the poor[35] – but it helped to strip young

Suzuki of illusions and to discover the root of determination that was within him.

Part of the reason for extreme severity at this stage of the science lies in the great danger of the undertaking. Once a person is launched upon such a journey there is no turning back; one has to journey further and further towards reality and leave the comfortable world of illusion ever further behind. If one tries to turn back once one is launched, there is no possibility of one's ever again finding the old comfortable illusions; instead one will fall further and further. This truth has been expressed in many stories. We remember, for instance, the story of the man who decided to build a house, but instead of building it upon rock, so that it would stand the ravages of time and the weather, he light-heartedly built it upon sand; and, as a result, when a storm came the sands proved an illusory foundation and the house fell down; it was a great fall. Or the story of the house that was swept empty only to let in seven devils where previously there had only been one.[36]

Unless one is prepared to go the whole way, unless one is whole-hearted, it would be better never to set out on this journey. Because wisdom, the true science, will never come to dwell in the heart against its wish. One must desire it and desire it with a whole heart.

You learn one day that on the other side of the river lies a *swami* about whom marvellous things are spoken. At all costs you must get his blessing. So you set off. There is the river. You can't ford it, and to try to swim would be too dangerous. But on the bank you notice a ferryman with a boat. You ask him to take you to the other side.

'Gladly,' he replies, 'But first of all you must get rid of your luggage. I only take men, not their belongings.'

'But it is not possible to leave my luggage. How can I manage without my belongings? I have in it my food for the journey, my blanket for the night. I have flowers and fruit to offer to the *swami*. And I have my holy books, which I read each day. After all, my luggage is not so heavy; come on, ferryman, be reasonable! Take me as I am, with what I am carrying. I will pay you for it.'

'Please yourself,' says the ferryman, 'Take it or leave it. Without luggage I will take you. If you stick to your luggage I shall leave you

here. Which do you want, the blessing of the *swami* or your old bits
and pieces?'

So the luggage is thrown away, one crosses and one receives the
blessing of God.

> What the *guru* awaits from you
> is you
> Not what you have brought
> passing through the market.[37]

But even when material possessions have been left behind, the quality
of wholeness is not always achieved; nor is the peculiar quality that
is wholeness of heart even recognised. A Zen story makes it recognisable:

After Bankei had passed away, a blind man who lived near the
master's temple told a friend: 'Since I am blind, I cannot watch a
person's face, so I must judge his character by the sound of his
voice. Ordinarily when I hear someone congratulate another upon
his happiness or success, I also hear a secret note of envy. When
condolence is expressed for the misfortune of another, I hear
pleasure and satisfaction, as if the one condoling was really glad
there was something left to gain in his own world.

In all my experience, however, Bankei's voice was always sincere.
Whenever he expressed happiness, I heard nothing but happiness,
and whenever he expressed sorrow, sorrow was all I heard.'[38]

Nothing so surely prevents this wholeness as the habit of looking at
one's self, because in order to do so, part of one's self must become
split from another part in order to look at it; so neither part can be
the whole. In illustration of which there is a story of ancient India:

Once there was a young fellow named Yajudatta. He was a very
handsome youth, so he would look in a mirror every morning to
see his image reflected, and he would smile at his own image. One
morning his face was not reflected in the mirror. He was really
surprised and upset, and he thought that his head was lost. He
looked for his head everywhere, but he couldn't find it anywhere.
Finally he came to realise that the head for which he was searching
was nothing but the head doing the searching. The careless fellow

167

had looked at the rear of the mirror, and naturally his head was not reflected . . . He had been looking for his head with his head. So the more he looked for his head externally, the more he went contrawise.[39]

The ability of the eye to see is dependent upon its inability to see itself.[40] A truth which Rabbi Mendel illustrated very gently when the Hasidim were devotedly gathering to hear him:

It was the day before the New Year and people from all over had come to Voiki and gathered in the House of Study. Some were seated at the tables, studying. Others who had not been able to find a place for the night were lying on the floor with their heads on knapsacks, for many of them had come on foot. Just then Rabbi Mendel entered, but the noise those at the tables made was so great that no one noticed him. First he looked at those who were studying, and then at those lying on the floor. 'The way these folk sleep', he said, 'pleases me more than the way those others are studying.'[41]

The ability of the heart to become whole is dependent on its ability to let go not only of belongings but also of those parts of itself that it has picked up in the market, or the House of Study, which are unwilling to go on the journey.

But there is unanimity among the authorities of the *scientia cordis* that those encrusted parts of the heart will only be got rid of by a shock sufficient to knock them off. If there is to be enlightenment, there has to be an awakening – and if the sleeper is in a very deep sleep only a shock will do, especially if one is dreaming that one is already awake and enlightened.

Sometimes a fairly gentle shock will be sufficient. It is related of the Russian Orthodox *starets* Ambrose that he was one day deep in conversation with a peasant who was telling him his troubles, when in burst a nobleman who had grown impatient waiting outside while the peasant was rambling on about his cows and crops. 'I wish to see the *starets* Ambrose', he said. At this Ambrose slowly drew himself up to his considerable height and faced the nobleman, silently turned to the right so that the nobleman could see his profile and ran his hand down the outline of himself from his head to his generous belly;

then he turned right again so that the nobleman was staring at his back; finally he turned to face the nobleman and said, 'Now you have seen the *starets* Ambrose', before once more sitting down and resuming his conversation with the peasant.[42]

As with all such happenings, just as with jokes, if explanation is necessary it is also superfluous; but one cannot help being reminded of Saint-Exupéry's words, 'One only sees properly with one's heart. What is essential is invisible to the eyes.'

Rather more shocking was the behaviour of the Russian woman Pelagia (1809–84). She was a *yuroditsa*, or 'fool for Christ', attached to a nunnery where there was dissension, and the worldly party within the nunnery was being supported by the Bishop of Nizhni Novgorod. In 1860 this bishop visited the nunnery and, by a combination of smooth words and veiled threats, overbore the just group within the community. Afterwards, travelling back in his carriage on the road to Nizhni Novgorod, he saw Pelagia sitting under a hedge by the roadside and knowing her reputation for holiness, as well as her firm opposition to his behaviour, he went up to her and unctuously greeted her. At which she promptly gave him a clout on the cheek. The bishop, however, had read his New Testament and knew that there were certain rules about how to respond to such circumstances, so he turned the other cheek to Pelagia. But she simply said, 'One is enough for you'. Pelagia was a real Zen practitioner, trying to awaken the bishop out of his dream of concepts and rules into reality.[43]

In fact the whole Russian Orthodox tradition of 'fools for Christ' is strikingly similar both to the Hasidic and to the Zen tradition. Take, for example, the story of an earlier fool for Christ (*yurodivi*), Nicholas of Pskov. In 1570 Tsar Ivan the Terrible had been terrorising the land, and when he came to Pskov the frightened inhabitants received him with great awe and deference. But when the tsar came to Nicholas to receive his blessing the holy fool offered him instead a lump of raw meat. The astonished tsar refused indignantly, saying, 'I am a Christian and do not eat meat during Lent'. To which the holy fool replied, 'But don't you drink Christian blood?'[44]

At a different level, but of similar structure, is the story of the cup of tea. A Japanese master who lived during the Meiji era (1868–1912), whose name was Nan-in, one day received a university professor who came to enquire about Zen.

Nan-in served tea. He poured his visitor's cup full, and then kept pouring. The professor watched the overflow until he could no longer restrain himself. 'It is overfull. No more will go in!'

'Like this cup,' Nan-in said, 'you are full of your own opinions and speculations. How can I show you Zen unless you first empty your cup?'[45]

So keen are the Zen masters on ensuring this awakening that they have a special word for the means by which it may be provoked: they call it *koan*. Any event may serve as a *koan*, such as the fall of a petal or the rod seen by the prophet Jeremiah; or a story may serve; but over the years the Zen masters devised a series of *koans* for teaching purposes. Such as, Zen is like a man hanging in a tree by his teeth over a precipice. His hands grasp no branch, his feet rest on no limb, and under the tree another person asks him: 'Why did Bodhidharma come to China from India?' If the man in the tree does not answer, he fails; and if he does answer, he falls and loses his life. Now what shall he do?

Such *koans* are given by Zen masters to their students for them to chew on every hour of the day and night, day in and day out, year in and year out, until the moment when awakening comes to them. The student must chew on the same *koan* until his teeth fall out, because the master has carefully chosen the particular *koan* which is suited to bringing that particular student to awakening. If one were to attempt to define a *koan* one might say that it is a way of teaching you that reality is beyond your grasp; and if you are under the illusion that you do comprehend it, then the constant attempt to squeeze meaning out of a *koan*, though it may not enable you to solve the *koan* (perhaps a *koan*, like reality, is not soluble?), will nevertheless force your hand to open, and then your mind and heart will open towards the reality which you were trying to squeeze into your hand. Reality is not something you grasp, but something you plunge into.

And the Zen masters are not slow to recognise the *koans* of other traditions. Abbot Zenkei Shibayama, for instance, tells us that Christ's enigmatic saying, 'Before Abraham, I am', can be a Zen *koan*; it makes us realise the limitations of our discriminating intellect and finally drives us to despair of it.[46] But the most striking example of such recognition is given by another Japanese, a member of the Ittoen community, Makoto Ohashi:

> Although my Congregationalist uncle failed to impress me with Christianity in my boyhood, I have since heard about the Gospels and found myself strongly drawn towards Jesus Christ. I feel very close to the breathing of Christ during his last moments on the Cross. It stirs me more than many lectures or sermons. I picture him killed on the Cross, all alone surrounded by scornful and contemptuous people. Very few, I think, appreciate the bliss he must have experienced when all were against him.

Makoto Ohashi goes on to say that the crucifixion is therefore the supreme *koan*, because 'the need for self-noughting or dying to self has been known for thousands of years. It is the one great *koan* that all truth-seekers have tried to answer'.[47]

But as Makoto Ohashi says, to die to self is easy to talk about and understand intellectually, but to live it as a reality is far from easy, and the attempt to do so has been the one great *koan* of his 30 years in the Ittoen community. What he says, indeed, is true not only of himself and the Zen tradition, but also of all the teaching of the *scientia cordis* – that it is an attempt to move from what is to what ought to be, from vain words to fulfilled deeds, because it is only someone who does the truth who comes to the light of the awakening. Most of our lives, though we say we wish to plunge into reality, we are like a man hesitating to plunge into the ocean; who walks along the sands wondering whether *this* is the appropriate point, and then climbs on to some rocks wondering whether *that* might not be the best, and then he gets into a boat, thinking that maybe it would be easier from a boat.

Such a person may then go on to read pamphlets and books on whether the sand, or the rocks, or the boat is the best point from which to enter into the reality of the ocean. One may even progress to writing pamphlets and books oneself, and taking part in seminars on it. But one still remains outside the reality of it, addicted now to the illusion that one will one day take the plunge. The masters of the spiritual adventure have all had something to say of a person in this state of addiction. Sakyamuni Buddha said: 'The man who talks much of his teaching but does not practice it himself is like a cowman counting another's cattle'; or again: 'like beautiful flowers, full of colour but without scent are the well-chosen words of the man who does not act accordingly'.[48] The Zen masters say that such a person is like a man who imagines he can nourish himself with a meal painted on rice paper, while St Isaac the Syrian (600) says almost the same thing: 'A word not made good by action is like an artist who makes pictures of water on walls, yet cannot quench his thirst with it'.[49]

The fact is that the point of entry into reality, out of illusion, is of little importance. Once plunged into the ocean of reality, a person is moving amidst reality, no matter how she got there; whereas, until she enters in, she is moving amidst illusions, no matter how seductive they may be. And a *koan*, whether it is a word or an event or a spiritual authority, gets us to carry out the most difficult task of all, that of making some start, no matter what. As, for instance, happened to the Russian peasant from Tambov province, Simeon Ivanovich Antonov (1866–1938), when he heard the gospel words, 'Love your enemies'. These words were spoken by one who was an authority in the science of the heart, and the words seemed to rise up out of Simeon's own heart, commanding obedience. From that moment onwards he chewed upon the words day in and day out, year in and year out, just as a Zen master orders his disciple to do. Simeon did not drop the *koan* to seek others with which to compare it; he knew intuitively that one truth is enough, one way of plunging into the ocean is enough – it is foolish to keep getting out again and trying other ways of entering into reality – because you might not find your way in another time. One truth is enough to live by, and collecting truths can become soul-destroying, because it inevitably means that one collects more truths than one needs; and any truth left lying about idle in the heart spreads infection that can be deadly.[50]

Always bearing in his heart the words, 'Love your enemies', Simeon was led further and further from Tambov province; and he proved correct the Hindu proverb which says that if you will take one step towards God then he will take ten steps towards you, for God came to him on Mount Athos in Greece and transformed him into the *starets* Silouan. Not that Silouan, having plunged into reality, was able to abandon his *koan* because on God's holy mountain he was now in the midst of theologians; on the contrary, he discovered that collectors

172

of theological truths are even more deadly than collectors of other truths, because 'a theology which is not put into practice is the theology of demons', and some of his fellow monks, especially the learned ones, spoke ill of him and gave him every opportunity to fulfil the command 'Love your enemies'. This he continued to do until his last breath; until in virtue of that one truth faithfully realised the sinful peasant Simeon was transformed into a holy man. Not by comparing many truths but by living one.[51]

Though the transformation may take a lifetime, the moment of entering into reality is a moment of liberation and enlightenment accompanied by unexpected joy. The classic story of it is given in the life of Sakyamuni Buddha. He had spent many years searching, until that evening of the Full Moon of May; seated in the lotus position at the foot of the *bodhi* tree he passed, as he had passed a thousand times before, into deep meditation; then as the moon rose he saw the evening star and was enlightened, exclaiming, 'Wonderful, wonderful, wonderful'. And that cry of praise from the lips of Sakyamuni Buddha has been echoed throughout the world and down the centuries – less resoundingly, no doubt, than on that evening, but striking the same note all the same.

It is related of 'The Great Fool Ryokan', for instance, who lived in a remote part of Japan about the year 1800, that one day he came back to his mountain hermitage only to find that all of his few belongings, bowls and dishes, had been stolen. He instantly composed a haiku poem:

> The moon out of the window!
> Left by the thief unstolen.[52]

Another version of the tale speaks of the hermit's hut having been burnt down, whereupon he composed a haiku:

> My storehouse having
> burnt down
> Nothing obscures the view
> Of the bright moon.[53]

No matter which version one takes, the joy is the same at discovering that, when one has lost everything to which one was attached, one enters the whole reality, for the first time seeing the evening star and the moon.

Most like Ryokan among Western saints is St Francis of Assisi (1182–1226), who describes similarly how it is through poverty and the experience of rejection that one comes to perfect joy. He tells Brother Leo that when the two of them arrive at Santa Maria degli Angeli, soaked by the rain and frozen by the cold and befouled by mud and afflicted by hunger, and they knock at the door, if the doorkeeper refuses to believe that they are friars and shuts them out in the cold and if they think charitably of the door-keeper, then they will find perfect joy. And if they continue to knock when night falls and the doorkeeper comes out with a knotty club and seizes them by their cowls and throws them on the ground in the snow and beats them with his club, if they then bear these things patiently they will have perfect joy.[54]

And seven centuries later, in the Indian province of Bihar, the Hindu holy man Vinoba Bahve (1895–1982), undergoing almost the same experience received the same enlightenment. At Deoghar he tried to visit the famous temple of Shiva in company with some of the local 'untouchables', but the priests of the temple were furious at this breach of caste and began assaulting them. Vinoba said:

I was meditating reverently on a hymn in praise of Shiva, so that when this sudden and unexpected assault started, I experienced a feeling of comfort. And those of my companions who were badly battered tell me that they too suffered no anger within them. Still in this happy state of mind, I turned back, but as we were going away our attackers became more zealous. My companions tried to cordon me off and shield me from the blows that were aimed directly at me. Yet just at the end of this sacrificial rite I also was not without my taste of it. I remembered how Mahatma Gandhi was subjected to a similar assault at this very place of pilgrimage. And I felt honoured to be blessed in the same way.[55]

Meanwhile, among the Hasidim we have the story of Rabbi Zusya of Hanipol (d. 1800), who used to travel throughout the country collecting money to ransom prisoners.

He came to a tavern at a time when the innkeeper was not at

home. He went through the rooms, according to custom, and in one saw a large cage with all kinds of birds. And Zuzya saw that the caged creatures wanted to fly through the spaces of the world and be free birds again. He burned with pity for them and said to himself: 'Here you are, Zusya, walking your feet off to ransom prisoners. But what greater ransoming of prisoners can there be than to free these birds from their prison?' Then he opened the cage, and the birds flew out into freedom.

When the innkeeper returned and saw the empty cage, he was very angry, and asked the people in the house who had done this to him. They answered: 'A man is loitering about here and he looks like a fool. No one but he can have done this thing.' The innkeeper shouted at Zusya: 'You fool! How could you have the impudence to rob me of my birds and make worthless the good money I paid for them?' Zusya replied: 'You have often read and repeated these words in the Psalms: "His tender mercies are over all his works".'

Then the innkeeper beat him until his hand grew tired and finally threw him out of the house.

And Zusya went his way serenely.[56]

The Franciscan note of joy which is audible in these stories, in the rejection of Francis, Vinoba and Zusya, for instance, is a note of folly in the ears of those who live by calculation. Indeed, Zusya was known as 'Zusya the fool', which is not surprising since so many of the authorities for the science of the heart acquired the same title. We have already mentioned the *yurodivi* (fools for Christ) of the Russian Orthodox tradition, and we find their like also in the Chinese tradition, especially among the Taoists. Lao Tzu, for instance, on meeting Confucius, is supposed to have said: 'If endowed with a rich supply of inward virtue, the superior man has the outward appearance of a fool'.[57] And on a later occasion he observed, 'Every man under heaven says that our Way is greatly like folly. But it is just because it is great that it seems like folly. As for things that do not seem like folly – well, there can be no question about *their* smallness.'[58] And his teaching was put into practice by none more wholeheartedly than the 'happy idiots', Han-shan and Shih-te, those joyously carefree poet-recluses of the Chinese T'ang dynasty.[59]

This current of folly passed from China to Japan, where Tenko-San tells us:

We should regard ourselves as fools, always seeking to learn from others. Ittoen may be described as a school where one learns to act as a poor man and a fool. Had I been a clever man I might have lived a very different life. But being quite uneducated, all I could do was to enquire into my own faults.[60]

The current has produced a group of such simpletons among the Shin Buddhists who are given the name *myokonin*.[61] The name itself is derived from the *myogo*, meaning a sort of intuition that does not work on our senses and intellect – which are relative – but works on that part of our being which extends beyond the senses and the intellect and which in this present writing has been called the 'heart'. The behaviour of such *myokonin* is illustrated by the story of one of them who was told that some boys had climbed up the precious apple tree in his garden and were stealing his apples. On hearing this, he rushed out of the house and got a ladder which he quietly placed against the apple tree and then stole away unnoticed. Astonished at such crazy behaviour, his informant asked him what on earth he was doing; at which the *myokonin* said that he had put the ladder there so that the boys would not fall when they came to climb down.[62] But the outstanding person of this sort was Ryokan, the Great Fool, who did not have, or did not care for, any social status or ecclesiastical rank, and lived alone in a mountain sanctuary. He loved playing with the village children. Everybody found it easier to be good in his presence.[63]

We have already spoken of this current of holy foolishness as flowing from China to Japan but it originated, like so many other religious traditions, in India with the perception of the world as *lila*, the play of God. As Swami Vivekananda has said:

This world is a superstition. We are hypnotised into believing that it is real. The process of salvation is the process of de-hypnotisation. This universe is just the play of the Lord – that is all. It is all just for fun. There can be no reason for his doing anything. Know the Lord if you would understand his play. Be his play fellow and He will tell you all.[64]

'When you begin Zen, mountains are just mountains and lakes are just lakes, but when you get into Zen then mountains are no longer mountains and lakes are no longer lakes' – because the science of the heart is a science which moves, and takes one out of this world into an 'other world', a world whose geography is different from this one and where the human being has a different anatomy through having an 'other heart'. In the presence of those who inhabit that other world, the whole environment of this world changes. In the words of D. T. Suzuki:

> Another doctrine generally held by Indian thinkers or religious leaders is that when one attains spiritual perfection the place where he is situated, or his environment, changes with him. That is, when a person attains enlightenment – moral perfection – the environment in which he finds himself also changes according to his subjectivity. When Amida attained enlightenment, therefore, his environment changed in the same way he himself did. The country or realm, wherever he was, changed with him and became a place conducive for other people to attain enlightenment. Other people who come to that country, which is called the Pure Land, will attain enlightenment without struggling against odds or against undesirable circumstances.[65]

It was said of the holy fool Ryokan that 'quarrels and other annoying incidents which sometimes darken our daily lives cleared up if he happened to appear in the midst of them'.[66] And in our own day Ramana Marashi has said, 'Even one's environment does not happen by accident. The Guru creates the conditions necessary for one's quest.'[67]

This change of the environment in the presence of certain people is reported time and again. Thus Dr Ainslie Meares has recently described a 134-year-old Yogi saint whom he met:

> This man was completely different from any other man I have seen. It seemed that some invisible aura surrounded him. And when you were in his presence, the calm of it was all through you. Peace came, and body and mind were at ease. There was naturalness, and a feeling of unity with things about.[68]

And similar witness has been given to the effect of Mother Theresa of Calcutta: people have been looking at some dirty street in Calcutta flanked by old shacks and crowded with half-starving, disease-ridden, aimless-looking creatures in gloomy despair, and then along came Mother Theresa – and not only is she herself a source of light, but everyone else in the street and all the things there seem to become illumined from within, as though an inner source of radiance within all things had been set flowing.[69]

But the classical illustration of the environment changing is given in the conversation between Motovilov and St Seraphim which took place in November 1831 beside the river Savovka, while snow lay on the ground and was falling thickly. In the course of their conversation Motovilov was led deeper and deeper into the Holy Spirit by St Seraphim until he glanced at Seraphim's face and, in his own words,

> There came over me a yet greater awe. Imagine the face of one who speaks with you, surrounded by the sun in the dazzling brightness of noon. His lips move, his eyes change expression, he speaks. Someone holds you by the shoulders with invisible hands. Yet you see neither his form nor yourself. One blinding light shines for yards away, irradiating the snow on the ground, on the elder and me.

Motovilov then goes on to describe how he experienced a peace and tranquillity in his soul that no words could express, as well as unaccustomed delight and unwonted joy – and a beautiful fragrance, far more beautiful than that of the expensive perfumes of Kazan. And despite the falling snow they were wonderfully warm all through, although the snow did not melt on them.[70]

It is interesting to notice that Motovilov refers to the beautiful smell that he experienced, because a comforting smell often seems to serve as an indication of someone living in a world other than that of worldly illusions. Which is only to be expected, because people tend to smell of the substance that they live off; people who feed off fish have a fishy smell, meat-eaters smell of meat; people who feed on power have a sour smell; and so it is only to be expected that those who feed on the substance of the 'other' world should have a different smell. Perhaps this explains why, in his later years, it was noticed that Tolstoy gave off a distinctive smell. V. F. Bulgakov says: 'It seems to me that Tolstoy has a kind of very strong church smell compounded of cypress, the sacristy and communion bread'.[71] Oddly enough Tolstoy himself must have noticed the same thing about the holy idiot who inspired the figure of Platon Karatayev in *War and Peace* (the peasant who opened up the other world to Pierre Bezukhov), because he speaks on two occasions of the peculiarly comforting smell that Platon Karatayev exuded.[72]

In fact, all the perceptions through the senses are different in the other world. As a Hasidic rabbi once said to me, 'Bread which you eat in communion with your brothers tastes different from the same bread eaten in isolation', and, 'To the man who is growing in holiness bread itself begins to taste differently'. Testimony to this other-worldly taste is again given by friends of St Seraphim: the onion which he gave to Natalia Evgraphova, for instance, tasted as no other had done; Praskovya Ivanovna said the same about some raspberries which he once gave her; and Dr Vasili Sadowski says that he had never tasted crusts such as Seraphim once gave him as a gift from the Mother of God.[73]

Again, in the matter of hearing, the Taoists say that if we fail to pursue the science of the heart, 'We then lose both our spiritual light and our faculty for hearing the voices of silence, and we can no longer taste the "Savour of the Tao" – we are incapable of listening to the "stringless lute" '.[74]

That the senses record different impressions in the 'other' world is hardly surprising, since that other world has been discovered by a change of heart – and the heart, as we have seen, is our organ of perception. Now that poisons of egotism, envy, lust and ambition have been eliminated from the bloodstream of the authorities in this science, the heart has been changed – that is, the organ of perception – and so, consequently, have the perceptions themselves. And not only the sense-perceptions but also the intellectual perceptions. To quote the case of St Seraphim again. One day he was speaking to Antony of Vysako-gorsk about a troubled person who had come to him; Antony said, 'Father, the soul is open to you as a face in a mirror. You said everything to this man without having even heard what he wanted. I saw it myself. Your mind is clean, and nothing in the heart is hidden from you.' To this Seraphim replied, 'Not a word, my joy. The heart is open to God alone . . .' – but 'The first thought in my mind is for me the will of God. I speak, not knowing what is on the other's soul, but believing that God instructs me for that man's good. On occasions I am told some circumstances and think about it, as if I alone could decide it without the help of God. Then I always blunder.'[75]

St Seraphim is here saying that if he acts according to the promptings of his changed heart then his words course along the paths of the other world, in accordance with a geography that is not of this world; and so they find their way unerringly to the heart of the person to whom he is speaking. But if he consults the map that he carries in his head, which is based on the geography of this world, then his words go astray and never reach the heart of the person he is addressing. This explains why the authorities in this science say things that are surprising to common sense, and which point the way to a different geography that you could never have thought of for yourself. Take, for example, the story of Zusya the fool of Hanipol.

One day some rabbis were discussing the problem that has exercised men from the beginning, that of how to reconcile the goodness of God with all the suffering there is in the world. Like all their predecessors they were unable, by taking thought, to resolve the dilemma confronting them. Finally one of them said, 'Why don't we go and ask Zusya? He has had to suffer so much and yet he is always serene and joyful. All his life he has had to endure a painful illness, his children have gone off and his wife is for ever nagging him. He must have some answer.' So they set off on the journey to Zusya's house and when eventually they got there they found him smoking his pipe. Then they put to him their problem, of how to reconcile God's goodness with human suffering. And he replied, 'What suffering?'[76]

A similar group of questioners were surprised by an equally unexpected reply from the medieval Russian saint, Nil Sorskij (1433–1508). A problem that had much exercised medieval theologians had been that of explaining how it is that anyone who has received the divine touch, or had some vision of God, can then move back into everyday forms of perception, without being wrapped up in God. Following the geography or mechanics of the theologians' world, it was impossible to envisage why this should happen. When they asked Nil Sorskij why, he simply answered, 'God allows it to happen so that they shall have more time for their friends'.[77] As with Nil Sorskij and Zusya the questioners are pointed outside their own closed world, so it is with the answer which a later Russian thinker, Nikolai Fyodorov, gave to the question of whether Christ is really present in the sacrament of the Eucharist. Many people have wracked their brains over this issue, and many people have been killed for answering one way or the other. But Fyodorov replied, 'The question of whether Christ is really present in the Eucharist will be able to be answered in the affirmative when the Eucharist is not simply a rite performed in churches but the regulating principle of everyday life'.[78] That Fyodorov was able to give such a liberating answer was due to his not living in a world frozen into the positivist 'what is', but was living in another world revealed by the science which changes things, penetrating to the heart of the matter and of humanity.

There are many witnesses from the authorities of this science to the way that in the other world, which they have moved into, people penetrate into one another. They are no longer like a series of billiard balls which never penetrate one another but simply make external contacts, banging into one another then cannoning off, unaffected by one another's fate. On the contrary, the further a person moves into the other world the more one finds that one's personal destiny is the destiny of Everyman.

The authorities speak of this interpretation of human beings with one another in different idioms. The most familiar to Christians is that by which people are described as members one of another, in an image derived from the human body and the interdependence of its members. Kegon Buddhists use an equally beautiful image – the image of a great web which is to be pictured as extending throughout the universe, its vertical lines representing time, its horizontal ones representing space. Wherever the threads of this vast net cross one another there is to be seen a crystal bead symbolising a single existence. Each of these crystal beads reflects on its bright surface not only every other bead in the vast net but also every other reflection – countless, endless reflections, each in a sense independent, and yet all bound together in a single related totality.[79]

This tremendous sense of interdependence lies at the back of the Jewish mystical tradition as recorded in the Kabbala. There one finds a constant insistence that the fate of the whole human family is in the balance every moment, and is so delicately balanced that it depends for each one of us on our throwing our weight on to the side of goodness rather than of evil. Everything that is done by the individual or the community in the mundane sphere is reflected in the upper region, i.e., the higher reality which shines through human acts. The impulse which originates from a good deed guides the flow of blessing which springs from abundance of life in the upper realm into the secret channels leading into the lower and outer world.[80]

But perhaps the most memorable expression among the Jews of this sense of human interdependence occurs not at the philosophical level but in their legend of the 36 just men.[81] Already in the Old Testament we find the saying that the just man is the foundation of the world. But by the eighteenth century this simple saying has been enriched by passing through Islamic and Christian aspirations until it has become a whole network of stories. According to these, the continued existence of the world depends on there being in it 36 just men, who are hidden. They themselves do not know they are just, nor does anyone else, and they are hidden from one another.[82] Lately another story about them has come to us from the pen of Elie Wiesel. He tells us that a year or two ago he visited the town of Siget which used to be Hungarian in the time when he was a child, before the second world war; in those days, before Wiesel and his family and his neighbours were transported to the death-camp at Auschwitz, the town was almost entirely Jewish; now there are no Jews there and the town itself has been transferred to Romania.

Naturally Wiesel found the place eerie, a ghost-town, because although the streets and buildings were very much the same, the people were quite different and none of the faces his memory prompted him to expect appeared before his eyes. In his desire to establish some sense of coherence with the past, he wandered out of the centre of the town to where the Jewish cemetery stands, all forlorn and overgrown now, totally neglected. Dejected and isolated he stood by a grave and said a *kadish* for the dead, then suddenly he heard someone behind him, and a voice saying, 'There are not many who come here these days'. He turned and saw standing there a rough-looking, middle-aged man with a kindly face. After Wiesel had explained who he was, and what he was doing there, the stranger replied that he was the *shochet* of the Jewish community, the ritual slaughterer. It surprised Wiesel to learn that there were still Jews in the vicinity who would need a *shochet*. Actually, the man explained, there were indeed very few Jews left. After the war virtually all those who had escaped the death-transports had left the country and emigrated to Israel. His own wife and children had gone. But there were some few dozen old Jews for whom it was not possible to leave and who, if he had gone, would have been left without a *shochet*; and so he had postponed his going to Israel until there were none of these old Jews left. 'How,' he said without any sense of being noble, 'how could you leave Jews without a *shochet*?'

Wiesel comments that in this simple, unpretentious *shochet* he felt he had met one of the 36 just men, the hidden ones upon whom the existence of the world at any moment depends.[83] As, of course, he had – because every person you encounter may be one of those upon whom the continued existence of the world depends; every person may be what the Welsh tradition describes as 'one of the secret princes'.

It is significant, moreover, that the *lamedvovnik*, as the hidden ones are called, should appear at the moment that Wiesel was saying a *kadish*, in remembrance of the dead, because the more one penetrates into the other world the more one is aware not only of the interdependence of the living with one another, but also of their interdependence with the dead. It is at the moment when the dead come to life that the living also come to life. Few have expressed this so vividly as that Christian in the heart of Hinduism, Jules Monchanin, in the words he spoke to that Christian in the heart of Islam, Louis Massignon:

When we have converted all the living in the whole world to becoming Christians after our fashion (so incomplete) there remain all the dead of India for me and of Islam for you. And in so far as we shall not have understood this all-powerful intercession for all the dead which alone permits the convergence to be brought about between the different religious traditions of humanity from their origin up to the Judge of the Judgement, the Christ with hands pierced by his Justice, in so far we shall not have fulfilled the vocation which God has engraved in our hearts, the universal vocation.[84]

And the Catholics Monchanin and Massignon find a powerful advocate for their longing in the Russian Orthodox thinker Nikolai Fyodorov. Fyodorov grieved with unparalleled grief for the dead, for those to whom the judgement of death had already happened, the majority of the human family, the fathers, grandfathers, forefathers. For this reason he was angered by the positivist theory of progress, with its heartless attitude towards the past generations and its building the welfare of posterity upon the corpses and suffering of the ancestors. 'Progress', he said, 'transforms our fathers and forefathers into accused prisoners, and gives judgement and dominion over them into the hands of their sons and descendants.' And he added that all those who in the nineteenth century rejected the cult of the fathers thereby deprived themselves of the right to be called the sons of man. They became prodigal sons who, if ever they awaken out of their stupor, will, like the prodigal son in the gospel, ask to be regarded as a slave and not a son. Through becoming disrelated to the dead they have lost their communion with the living. For Fyodorov all true religion is cult of the dead, and Christianity 'is the union of the living for the resurrection of the dead' – that is, the combination of those eating and drinking for the return of the absent ones to the meal of love; and the only way to repay the ancestors is for all the living to unite in the communion task of restoring the dead to life.[85]

There is yet another consequence of penetrating into the other world which the authorities are aware of, besides the interdependence of the living with one another and then with all the dead. This is the increasing harmony of the spiritual adventurer with the whole of creation, including the animal and vegetable worlds. All readers of the Old Testament are familiar with the numerous songs to be found there in praise of creation, especially with the song of the three children cast into the fiery furnace:

All ye works of the Lord: praise and exalt him above all forever . . . Ye sun and moon, bless ye the Lord: praise and exalt him above all for ever . . . Ye dews and hoar frosts, bless ye the Lord: praise and exalt him above all for ever.[87]

... and so on. And in our own century we have had some notable examples of holy people who knew how to join in the hymn of praise that all creation raised to the Creator. In 1920, for instance, there died the most recently canonised Greek saint, Nectarius, who on the island of Egina had gathered around him a community of nuns whom he was able to teach to hear the song of the trees. And not far away there lived Father Joseph, who is the most skilful grafter of trees and who owes his skill to his ability to distinguish between the songs of the different saplings and trees, and so knows which graft will harmonise with which main stem. Father Joseph says that anyone who listens carefully enough can hear the circulation of the sap in the tree.[87]

Nectarius and Father Joseph are of the same lineage as St Anthony of the desert, St Francis of Assisi and St Seraphim of Sarov, all of whom formed friendship with the beasts, with wolves and bears and flies and birds, as though once they had found the centre of their own being, then they had also found the Centre of the universe where there is room for all without fear and without murder.

Witness to this truth comes to us from ancient China where the unorthodox Buddhist monk Chikung

... loved the poor, simple peasant folk, and he also loved nature. Every tree was a brother to him and every bird or squirrel was his child. It is said that even the fishes rose to greet him when he approached a pond or stream. He believed that everything in nature had its own mode of existence and its own consciousness, and that he could establish an intelligible contact with it.[88]

And from more recent times we have the witness of a learned professor from Ceylon who visited the Shivapuri Baba in 1930. One striking memory of his visit was the sudden arrival from the depths of the forest of a full-grown leopard, which entered as a domestic cat might have done, to sit beside the Shivapuri Baba. The professor was unable to master a moment of terror, but the Shivapuri Baba explained that those who live for many years in complete solitude in the forest – as he had done earlier in life – become so friendly with wild animals that no fear is felt on either side.[89]

It seems that a Hasidic story about human beings applies also to the beasts. A rabbi was once travelling along a road in his trap when he saw one of his Hasidim walking by the road-side. He called to the Hasid to get on to the trap and have a lift with him but the Hasid replied, 'I would like to, but I can't, because there isn't enough room up there'. To which the rabbi replied, 'Well, let us love one another more, and then there will be room for all of us'. Because St Francis, St Seraphim and St Nectarius were so full of love, they had room for all the living and the dead and the brute beasts themselves who smelt no fear or danger in their presence and so came into their hearts, to the Centre.

It will be seen, also, that by going into that 'other world' the spiritual adventurers do not, in the end, lose this one. On the contrary, the more surely they come to know the geography of that world of the heart, the more exactly they know the geography of this world of point to point reasoning – not laboriously and by taking thought, but simply and intuitively. As has been said of St Seraphim, in that world his heart was trained to hear the primordial Word. When the ebb set in, and human life was once more spread out before his mind's eye as a concrete network of ordinary facts, the fabric of particular human lives appeared before him with its particular design; the pattern that every one of these lives should follow was obvious to him. One's mistakes – intentional and unintentional, in the present, past and future – stood out as clearly discernible blotches and tangles. They disfigured the particular pattern of divine purpose.[90]

Or, as the Zen Buddhists so epigrammatically put it, 'Before you begin Zen, mountains are mountains and lakes are lakes; when you get into Zen, mountains are no longer mountains and lakes are no longer lakes; but when you come to enlightenment, then mountains are once more mountains and lakes are once more lakes'.

As we come to the end of this sketch of the journey undertaken in the science of the heart, we refer again to what we said at the beginning about spiritual adventurers who go searching in remote places and then find their centre within their own spiritual tradition. The story goes that there was once a rabbi in Cracow, Isaac son of Yekel, who dreamed one night that there was a great treasure under the bridge at Prague. So he set off for Prague, but when he got there found that there was a heavy guard on the bridge – because this was in the days when the Habsburgs ruled in those parts. For a week the rabbi hung around the area of the bridge looking for his opportunity to examine beneath it, but the opportunity never came. And eventually the sergeant in charge of the guard, becoming suspicious, approached him and asked him what he was up to. The rabbi had no other choice but to explain that he had had a dream about there being a treasure under that very bridge. And when the sergeant heard the story he burst into uncontrollable laughter. Once he had stopped laughing he said, 'How crazy can you get? Suppose everybody went off after their dreams? Why, I once dreamed that there was treasure hidden in a house in Cracow. And it was in the house of a man called Isaac, son of Yekel, but do you think I was going to go off to Cracow because of that dream? In any case, half of Cracow is called Isaac son of Yekel.' So the Rabbi Isaac returned to Cracow.[91]

And so it is with the Christian who undertakes this spiritual journey. Returning to one's own tradition, one discovers treasure there which one had never seen before because one had not trained oneself to see with the heart. This is not to go back on what was said earlier about the vanity of comparing different religious traditions to the advantage of one or another of them. It is rather that, just as, say, Louis Massignon's own Christianity was immeasurably enriched through his feeding at the table of Islam, any treasures we now discover in our own tradition through our joining in the science of the heart we owe, not to our own cleverness, but to authorities in that science – Hasidim, Hindus, Muslims, Zen Buddhists, fools for Christ, *Myokonin*, and others.

For example, it is no reflection on the Buddhist tradition to say that, when you have journeyed through some of it and come out again, as it were into the sunlight, to see the Christian tradition again, then there is one Christian teaching which you see as you had never done before. That is the teaching of the goodness of creation, a teaching derived from Judaism (which is another lesson, by the way – that of how deeply Christianity is rooted in Judaism). Because as you steep yourself more and more in the Buddhist atmosphere, you begin to be more and more aware of the need for compassion in the world, for this world is so suffused with pain, borne by all sentient creatures, that you begin to understand why it would seem to be the greatest good to be liberated from this world and to put it behind one for ever. And then, when you are in danger of being overwhelmed by this atmosphere, you remember the ringing affirmation of the first

187

chapter of the book of Genesis, 'In the beginning God created the heavens and the earth', with the repeated affirmation, 'And God saw that it was good' – ending with the cry of triumph, 'And God saw everything that he had made, and behold, it was very good'. For the first time, in a breathtaking fashion, you begin to realise what is meant by the goodness of creation, a goodness deep down in things, rooted so deep down that no evil and pain can in the end uproot it or blot it out; because always, no matter what happens, goodness will once more appear. The source of goodness is infinite.

Similarly with the Christian who has been delighted and refreshed at the Hindu sources, especially with the myths of Krishna and Rama, both of whom are described as *avatars* of God – 'incarnations', as the word is usually translated. One day one learns that:

> The commonly accepted translation of *avatâra* by 'incarnation' is misleading, because Krishna and Rama are not described as having really suffered and died. In the *avatâra* God does not, as for Christians in Christ, become really man; he only appears in human form and remains, behind and beyond this earthly appearance, purely divine and unaffected by human vicissitudes.[92]

And the Christian begins to realise how much she herself has in the past been temperamentally a Hindu, thinking of Jesus as a manifestation of God, but not really man. One may realise also that one has thought of Christ as some sort of 'guru' who, in accordance with Indian tradition, abstains from food and sex and laughter and who, the more he rises above human weaknesses and the accidents of life, so the more he is considered to be a master and superior. Then one discovers that Hindus themselves, especially the Indian peasantry, are greatly drawn to the divine man who laughs, eats, takes wine, is no ascetic – for Christ is no ascetic in Indian eyes – who is truly man and does not deny his humanity. And so through the longings and aspirations of the Indian peasantry the Christian is enabled to see, for the first time, how astonishing and world-changing is the incarnation – what it actually means to say that God emptied himself, became man and was crucified, without ceasing to be God. And he is no ascetic, but a warm human being.[93]

Once the Christian begins to realise what the incarnation means, especially what it meant for that warm human being to undergo such suffering and pain, one readily understands why Muslims, who revere Jesus as a prophet, simply refuse to believe that he can have been crucified. The Muslims in this respect are revealed to be so different from the Hindus, because it is to Muslims blasphemous for a human being to claim to be God, or even united with God, so deep is their awareness of God's transcendence. The Hindus, however, are so aware of God's immanence that they have no difficulty in believing that God can take the shape of many creatures, but that God should actually suffer the crucifixion is 'the one great *koan* that all truth-seekers have tried to answer'.[94] The Muslim mind cannot grasp it; the Hindu mind cannot grasp it; nor can the Buddhist mind; nor the Jewish mind. Nor can the Christian mind. At the same time none of them can keep away from it, because their hearts are set upon it, and the Christian at least knows now that her heart will break upon it. For the first time, perhaps, she no longer thinks it an exaggeration on Pascal's part to say, 'Jesus Christ will be in agony until the end of time'.

So far, our returning Christian has been finding her treasures mainly in the light of what she has learnt from Buddhism, Islam and Hinduism. But as the truths of creation, incarnation and crucifixion bring her ever closer to her own home, so she is brought ever closer to her Jewish heritage and her Jewish brethren. And few Jews have helped Christians to see so clearly what is involved in Christian faith as Martin Buber. Like the rest of his fellow Jews, Buber awaited the coming of the Messiah – and found it just as difficult to believe that the Messiah had come as Buddhists do to believe that there is creation and it is good. And for much the same reason, Buber used often to tell the story of the rabbi in Jerusalem to whom it was announced that the Messiah had come. The rabbi calmly looked out of the window, gazed around and said that to him nothing seemed to have changed. Indeed, nothing does seem to have changed, and so how can Christians maintain that the Messiah has come and the redemption of humankind been accomplished? This is what leads Buber to say that 'the Christian is the incomparably daring man, who affirms in an unredeemed world that its redemption has been accomplished'.[95] How many Christians had realised beforehand that they were themselves incomparably daring, signs that the redemption of the world has been accomplished?

As the returning Christian discovers these various treasures, she now begins to see *every* aspect of her traditional faith in a new light. Even what at one time seemed remote doctrine, such as the Trinity, begins to have a new meaning after she has acquired some experience in the science of the heart. Because one of the crucial questions recurring in that science is, how can persons be united without being swallowed up in one another? This question arises in any spiritual tradition which reaches out in love towards a personal God, and does not simply seek knowledge of some impersonal, absolute principle.

In Islam, for instance, the essence of God is regarded as absolute unity, inaccessible to humanity. Which means that there is an absolute separation between what is divine and what is human, between God and his creature. However the great Muslim mystic, al-Hallaj (AD 858–922), teaches that it is Satan who has established this separation, through treating God as an 'idea' which is therefore inaccessible to humanity because incapable of responding, in dialogue. But the essence of love is participation, and al-Hallaj was so much in love with God that he felt himself united to God and proclaimed that he was. For this he was crucified by his fellow Muslims, who were bound to see in his claim a mad attempt to usurp God's essence. How could they do otherwise, since their God allows no distinction into persons which permits there to be union without absorption?[96]

In Hinduism the question arose in a different fashion. It could hardly arise throughout the long centuries when Hindu seekers conceived of their search as one for knowledge which would allow them to recognise the soul as one with the eternal, impersonal Absolute. But as soon as the upsurge of warm devotion in the Hindu seekers enables them to reach, in love, towards a personal God, then they find little difficulty in accepting the union of God with the soul – but far more difficulty in acknowledging that the loving soul is not absorbed beyond distinction in, say, Siva. It is difficult for them to see, without the aid of Trinitarian teaching, that as love between persons increases, not only do they become more united but they are also more clearly distinguished from one another as persons.

In the light of such courageous strivings for science of the heart in other spiritual traditions, the Christian may begin to see that Christian love 'does not wish to abolish the distance from man to God or Christ; it intends on the contrary to deepen this infinite distance between persons because this distance is the very breathing-space of a more infinite love'.[97]

14

Jews and Eastern religions

(1980)

I

The present discussion arises out of a curious circumstance. It is that the author has in recent years found himself, a Christian, called upon to help young Jews try to answer the agonising question, 'What is it to be a Jew?' What brings this circumstance about is that I have been teaching religious studies in the University of California where a very large percentage of the students are Jewish, but only a minute proportion of them are in any sense observant or firmly rooted in Jewish tradition. And whereas for their parents, a zealous attachment to the cause of the state of Israel obviously serves to assuage their sense of guilt for not being observant, no such panacea will satisfy many of the younger generations. They feel that they must search more deeply for spiritual truth, and must find it either in elements of the Jewish tradition which have been obscured for them or else in other traditions altogether.

It is now commonly recognised what an enormous number of Jewish men and women, especially the young, take the second option, and either attach themselves to the Jews for Jesus movement or else to one or other of the Eastern religions that have lately moved into the USA, and especially into California. While there can hardly be any very reliable statistics concerning this issue, no one who moves in educated American-Jewish circles can have any doubt that this statement is substantially true. Already one hears many Yiddish stories about, say, the conference called to promote dialogue between Zen Buddhists, Sufis and Hindus when it turned out that the three spokesmen for these Eastern teachings were all Jews. And certainly it has been my own experience that whenever I have gone to address such groups they have always included a disproportionate number of Jewish seekers.

The sad thing is that these young Jewish people seem to find little help or understanding from their own elders or their rabbis. Let me give one instance. I had a very gifted Jewish student who wished to become a rabbi, and for whom I wrote a strong letter of recommendation to a rabbinical college. When he returned from his interview he was rather dejected. I asked him why, and he replied that he did not think he would be admitted to the college because of his practice of the Japanese martial art of aikido. In aikido it is customary at the beginning of a session for the class to bow towards a picture of the originator of aikido as a mark of respect. The examining panel of rabbis had been most disturbed when they learned that my student had joined in this custom, because they equated it with 'bowing down to vanity and nothingness' and 'praying to a god that cannot help' – against which, of course, a pious Jew defends himself three times a day. My student was really taken aback by what he regarded as the obscurantism of his examiners, and he tried to explain to them that his intention in bowing had simply been to show courtesy towards the aikido instructor: he was no more indulging in idolatry than were the other students in the class, most of whom did not worship anything or anybody, much less idols. This explanation did nothing to mollify the examiners, however, who replied that his invoking of 'intention' showed he was on the slippery slope, since the crucial determinant of the nature of an act is not the intention but the act itself. Not unnaturally this reply provoked my student and me to speculate on some of the logical consequences of such a position – as, for example, proving that a person would be guilty of idolatry if when passing a statue of the Buddha one was seized with an arthritic pain and one's body doubled up into the form of a perfect prostration. But that, of course, did not much console the young man.

What distressed him particularly was that his potential mentors seemed to have no idea that the presence of Eastern religion is raising the question, 'What is it to be a Jew?' in a new form that is proving more deeply disturbing to Jews than the same question has been in the past. In the past, it has not been difficult for Jews to bounce this question, so to speak, off the Christians and Muslims around them and to receive back a rather comforting answer. Over the centuries both Christians and Muslims have exhibited such devilish hostility towards Jews that it has seemed fairly simple and reasonable to deal with the issue of Jewish identity by saying that Jews, being the object of devilish hostility, are clearly the objects of divine favour. The presence of the unworthy gentile guarantees the identity of the Jew or, as one writer puts it, '*Es gibt Juden weil es nicht-Juden gibt*' ('There are Jews because there are non-Jews').

That some people saw this to be an inadequate answer many years ago is clear from the words of Rabbi Mendel, who said: 'If I am I, simply because I am I, and thou art thou, simply because thou art thou; then I am I and thou art thou. But if I am I because thou art thou, and thou art thou because I am I, then I am not I and thou art not thou.'

However, it seems to me that many Jews have been content with the inadequate answer, in spite of Rabbi Mendel; but the inadequacy of it becomes frighteningly clear when one is no longer confronting traditionally hostile and contemptible Christians and Muslims, but is brought face to face instead with a Hindu or a Buddhist or a Taoist. For if your being a Jew depends upon the hostility of the non-Jew, then you are in a sad position when you try to bounce the question of your identity back off a Hindu, a Buddhist or a Taoist who has never done you any harm and shows no signs whatever of hostility towards you.

II

I have seen this situation in reality when young Jews have faced adherents of Eastern religions, particularly Buddhism. As the young Jew is explaining his position to the Buddhist, the Buddhist just gazes at him in wide-eyed astonishment: as you (the Jew) look into the Buddhist's eyes you see what he sees – and he sees that you are worshipping a tribal god who commanded you to make bloody conquests and who demands fanatical devotion to a complicated series of laws, in reward for which you will be the object of his exclusive choice. Now if you have been brought up on the *Lotus Sutra*, the *Bhagavad Gita* or the *Tao Te Ching*, then this is a most strange god that is being worshipped. And when this reflection from the eyes of other people comes back to you, it proves a very unnerving experience. It is unnerving in this sense: if in the past your identity has depended upon the hostility of other people, then that hostility has been acting as a sort of drug for you – it has enabled you to carry on. As the deputy mayor of Jerusalem, André Chouraqui, once said, 'Contemporary Jewish thought continues to nourish itself on drugs which enabled it to survive at the time of the Exile'. The withdrawal of such drugs, as I have said, can prove extremely unnerving.

In this situation one or two students turn back to Orthodoxy. They put on *tefillin*, become strict about kosher food and about sabbath observance and they take as their guide the thinker Soloveitchik. A most powerful thinker, Soloveitchik is also very strict and rigid. When the Rainbow Group for inter-faith dialogue was begun in Jerusalem, the Jewish chairman stood up at the very first meeting to announce that he had received a telegram from Soloveitchik saying that there must be no dialogue between Jews and non-Jews for fear that Jews might be converted. And although I can but admire the power of Soloveitchik's mind as I read his study *The Lonely Man of Faith*, nevertheless I find myself echoing the words of the French observer as he watched the charge of the Light Brigade in the Crimea: '*C'est magnifique, mais ce n'est pas la guerre*'. Soloveitchik's stance and the way he works out his adherence to Orthodoxy are in a way magnificent, but they are not related to the needs of our age. And for 99 per cent of our students he is no help. As one of them put it to me after I had invited an Orthodox rabbi to speak to my class, 'I am not about to put my head back into that bag'.

Seeing, therefore, that Jewish students in California appeared to receive little help in these matters from their elders, it occurred to me that some help might be forthcoming in the centre of the Jewish world, Jerusalem, and the Holy Land around it. Especially it struck me that one might be able to persuade the conservatives to adopt a less negative attitude towards Eastern religions if they could accept that the historical roots of Judaism and Hinduism are very close; because researchers in the last few years have revealed to us how close the connections were between the Hellenistic world, of which Judaea was a part, and that of India. Enormous quantities of coins have been found, for instance, showing that trading relations between these two areas were very vigorous. And, of course, we have the cultural artefacts from the area to the north-west of India which display a marvellous fusing of Buddhist and Greek culture, especially in Ghandhara sculpture with its beautiful statues of the Buddha that are so reminiscent of Greek representations of Apollo.

Unfortunately, despite this sort of evidence, very little written evidence has survived which might enable us to trace the interconnection of ideas. We do get a story of a Hebrew flute-girl whose playing inspired Thomas the Apostle when he went to evangelise South India. And there is also a Talmudic sage of rather minor importance who was known as Rabbi Judah the Indian, who was a convert to Judaism. But in general there is very little written evidence to show what contacts, if any, Jewish and Hindu sages enjoyed during those days. And that is why one or two scholars nowadays are beginning to look not so much at the possible historical connections as at the thematic affinity between Judaism and the Brahminic tradition. For on the face of it, there are striking similarities between Brahminic and Jewish legislation on religious matters, especially in the concern for ritual purity and for purity of descent, above all in the priestly caste. But such research has not yet been taken very far.

I did hope to find some signs that Jewish communities in the East had acted as conduits bringing Eastern ideas into Israel, particularly since I had myself come to know the Jewish community in Cochin, India, when I was stationed there during the second world war. However, the Cochin Jews seem to have remained in their ghetto for 18 centuries. They simply sealed themselves off; and the only effect of Hinduism upon them, as upon virtually everyone who goes to India, was that they became strictly caste-minded, with their synagogue for whites being separated from their synagogue for blacks. But the Cochin Jews back in Israel have, in any case, had a hard time and have really brought nothing of India back into what we might call central or metropolitan Judaism.

For Chinese Judaism the net result has not been any more significant, but at least from Kaifeng there has been preserved for us a most charming picture of relations between a Chinese rabbi and his Taoist neighbours that could well serve as a model for contemporary dialogue. The picture comes from the pen of Peter Goullart who writes of his visit to a Taoist monastery:

When I entered the abbot's study in the flickering light of tapers and oil-lamps, a majestic figure rose out of the shadows from a long chair to greet me. It was so unexpected, so unusual and so out of this world that I involuntarily stepped back. I remembered paintings and pictures in old Bibles depicting the old Patriarch Abraham himself. Tall and extremely dignified, the old man had a powerful and noble face of slightly Semitic cast, framed in white hair, while his grey beard fell down to his ankles. His eyes were keen, alert and like those of a young man. On his left hand he wore a signet ring with a finely cut peridot, and on his right wrist a broad and massive gold bangle. In his flowing robe with wide sleeves and peculiar cap he indeed resembled a patriarch from the Old Testament. As I shook his hand the Taoist abbot intoned, 'Meet my good friend, Rabbi Wong Levy, the leader of the Chinese Jewish community in Kaifeng'. The rabbi also spoke, to my surprise, in a guttural old-fashioned English confirming the abbot's words. I had read of some Jews being in China since time immemorial, but I could never imagine that I would meet their head under such circumstances, and above all, at a Taoist monastery. Rabbi Wong spoke most enthusiastically about his friendship with Abbot Chushen and the Taoists in general. It appeared that such happy relationships between the leaders of the two religions had existed for ages – he thought that Taoism was nearest to Judaism despite the wide diversity in theological doctrine and practices. He considered the belief in Tao to be identical to the belief in one God, notwithstanding terminology. He informed me that the present Jewish colony in Kai Feng was quite small and was gradually disappearing.

Goullart writes that later:

Rabbi Wong said, 'I almost wish that I could be a Taoist monk myself, but I am too old, and I am a Jew. Truly the Taoists of the Lungmen creed are the quintessence of all that is best in Taoism; they are the true Taoists. Faithful followers of the great Lao Tse. The cleverest, most intelligent and most educated men comprise their saints. Nowadays, especially with all the unhappiness and turmoil growing in the world, due to mankind's departure from the ways of Tao, most of the intelligent men seek to retire to quiet monasteries with their beautiful and serene existence. However, this is regrettable, for if all the best brains of this country become hermits, the inferior men are left to govern the people.'[1]

What an attractive vignette! And how typically Jewish the 'Taoist rabbi' remains in his suspicion of the solitary life! Unfortunately there does not seem to have been any influence from China enriching metropolitan Judaism; and eventually the Kaifeng Jewish community itself died out.[2]

There is no evidence, then, of Eastern Jewry influencing Judaism, something only to be expected when one remembers how resolutely Israel faces towards the West. This comes out in all sorts of incidental ways, as you may notice, for instance, if you read the enlightened Norman Bentwich's book about the role of the Hebrew University of Jerusalem. He refers to it specifically as a bridge between East and West, but by this he more or less means between Asia Minor and the USA, and never so much as mentions what I and most other people mean by the East. Similarly his brother Joseph Bentwich published a selection of texts from Eastern religions in Hebrew over 20 years ago – but although only 2,000 copies were printed, the edition has still not sold out. And, interestingly enough, he himself has never had any personal contact with the practices of Eastern religion, having learned whatever he knows from books. I also discovered that there are virtually no translations of such books into Hebrew. The booksellers in Israel whom I questioned about the matter assured me that there was hardly any interest in them.

But there is one intriguing exception to this depressingly blank account from Israel, and that is the founder of the state of Israel – none other than Ben Gurion himself. For Ben Gurion became very friendly with U Thant, the Burmese secretary general of the UN, and in December 1961, went to visit him in Burma, where he was so impressed by the clear-mindedness of the Burmese Buddhists (which comes from the stilling of the heart inculcated by Buddhism) that he went and made a retreat in a Buddhist monastery. Afterwards he said that he had found the retreat so helpful in clearing his mind and stilling his heart as to declare, 'I have come to the conclusion that I am really a Buddhist, but I happen to have been born a Jew'. But what is perhaps most significant about this incident is that when

I have mentioned it to Israeli friends, even some who were close to Ben Gurion, they have always laughed rather indulgently about it, as if to say, 'Oh well, the old man used to say lots of strange things', and they obviously did not take the episode seriously.

Hence, in the light of my experience in Israel, one might be tempted to sum up the situation in the words which several people have more or less spoken in response to my enquiries. When I asked, 'What do modern Jewish thinkers think about Eastern religions?' I was virtually told, 'We don't think about Eastern religions any more than we think about Jesus'. Well, on the face of it that reply sounds to be final, but perhaps it is worth noting how the issue of Eastern religions is linked with the issue of Jesus. Because there is just enough excess of protest in those words to make one suspicious. Apart from anything else, it is just not true that modern Jews don't think about Jesus – especially those in Israel. The latter are frequently confronted with Christian pilgrims and Christian pilgrim places, and if you look at the official Israeli guidebooks to such places you will see that they inevitably refer to the events of Jesus' life in a way that Jews would never have done 30 years ago. They refer to Jesus' place of birth, the place of temptation, the place of transfiguration, and so on. Probably it is truer, therefore, to say, with one modern Jewish thinker, 'When any Jew reads the Messianic prophecies in the Scriptures, deep in his heart he thinks of Jesus. But that is not a brief that you would hand over to your opponents' lawyer.'

This echo from deep in the heart of a Jewish thinker encourages me to believe that there is more to be said than a mere 'We don't think about Eastern religions any more than we think about Jesus'. And it prompted me to suggest a schema of Jewish development during the past 200 years which is both more accurate and gives one more hope for the future.

III

According to this schema Jews have been pushed into making a decision about what it means to be a Jew ever since that fateful day in 1763 when Moses Mendelssohn went through the Berlin city-gate hitherto forbidden to Jews, and thereby forced Jews to face the demands of enlightenment and modernity. Jews have responded to these demands in a variety of ways. Those of the extreme left have come to regard their Jewish heritage as totally devoid of any divine significance; many of them abhor the attempt to endow Jewish history with divine significance as a form of obscurantism from which they wish to dissociate themselves: a Jew is a member of the Jewish people just as an Englishman is a member of the English people, neither more nor less. If one is living in Israel, one's first loyalty is towards Israel: if one is living in England, one's first loyalty is towards England. Such Jews have nothing to say to the young Jews who are launched on the spiritual quest.

Those of the extreme right are the Orthodox Jews who never really wanted to leave their totally Orthodox ghettos and who, in effect, carry the ghetto around them wherever they may be. Their desire is to turn Israel into a huge Jewish ghetto from which the gentiles will be excluded. Their message seems totally irrelevant to the vast majority of Israelis and, of course, the Orthodox have virtually nothing to say to young Californian Jews who have been touched by Eastern religions – except to warn them not to indulge in such 'idolatry'. That, at least, was the message from the Sephardic chief rabbi to the people of Israel in March 1977, when he told them that meditation was forbidden to Jews because it was associated with pagan worship. The very words he used made it clear that he had almost no acquaintance with what he was talking about, and so they carried little weight.

But between these two extremes of right and left, the majority of Jews have been struggling valiantly to come to terms with their position as Jews in the world changed by enlightenment and emancipation. Whether they are labelled Reform Jews or Liberal or Progressive or Conservative, all of them have been trying to answer the same questions. Two of these questions are: first, what does it mean to be a Jew in face of the fact of Jesus? Second, what does it mean to be a Jew in the face of gentiles? And now, so I suggest, some of them are being driven to answer the further question: what is it to be a Jew confronted by Eastern religions?

In regard to the first question there can be no doubt that a tremendous change has taken place in Jewish consciousness during the last two centuries: after 18 centuries during which he was simply 'that man', because even his name was unmentionable on the lips of a faithful Jew, Jesus is back on the agenda of what it is to be a Jew. It is anachronistic for a high Jewish authority to declare 'Judaism knows nothing of Jesus, cannot and does not wish to know: for Judaism the question does not exist'.[3] The increasing number of lives of Jesus written by Jews such as Klausner, Asch, Flusser, Aron, Vermes, and the studies by Buber, Pinchas a Lapide, Sandmel and many others, show that, as one of them has said, 'Our brother who was dead has been restored to us'. Indeed, some of these writers go so far in trying to bring Jesus back into Judaism that they seem to be denying him any place among the gentiles, as if to say that he was, after all, only a Jewish rabbi or only a Jewish prophet.

However that may be, there can be no doubt that the central tradition of Judaism has now broadened beyond the ghetto tradition and is coming to reckoning with Jesus. As part of the same broadening of consciousness, Jewish thinkers have been faced with the issue of the gentiles. In some ways this issue has proved more intractable than the reckoning with Jesus, because the contemporary Jewish attitude towards it is rooted in attitudes that had already hardened in the millenium before the birth of Jesus.

The hardness of that attitude can sometimes strike even those of us gentiles who have long been familiar with the Jewish tradition. It is now 40 years since I first began to find nurture in the tales of the Hasidim, but it is still possible for them to surprise me by the attitude towards the go'im that one can encounter there. As, for instance, in the story of the old Jewish widow who lived in Galicia, and who was so poor and alone that she was in danger of starving to death. Then along came a kind Polish peasant who chopped wood for her, drew water for her, lit the fire and brought her food. Every week he did this for her for many months. But the widow, although grateful for the services he rendered her, would weep and moan about them at night as she was saying her prayers, lamenting that such great mitzvot were being performed not by a Jew but by a goi. (She does not know, as the reader does, that her benefactor is really a rabbi disguised as a Polish peasant.) However, she eventually discovers the truth of the matter when the Polish peasant is revealed to be a rabbi. She rejoices, because the mitzvot will be reckoned to a Jew and not to a goi; and so, after all, the story does have a happy ending. Even now, when I read that story, the ending strikes me, a *goi*, like a slap in the face.

The slap is a salutary reminder that traditionally Judaism has very little place for the gentile. Judah L. Benor, in the journal *Petahim*, has summed the situation up very well. He says that traditional Jewish sources, especially in their final codification, the *Shulhan 'Arukh*, 'commonly show an attitude of hatred and contempt for the non-Jew'. In the Bible we find 'Thou shalt not avenge nor bear any grudge against the children of my people, but thou shalt love thy neighbour as thyself'. Benor comments: 'Towards the gentile you may take revenge and you may bear a grudge'. And again, 'Thou shalt not lend upon usury unto thy brother, but unto a stranger thou mayest lend upon usury'. A characteristic attitude is expressed in permission to violate the sabbath in order to save life, but this applies only to the life of a Jew. If there is doubt as to whether the person in danger is a Jew or a gentile, then the saving of life takes precedence. If there is no doubt that it is a gentile who is in danger, then one may not violate the sabbath on this account. These and many other instances cited by Benor[4] support the contention of Raphael Loewe that there is very little in the Jewish tradition that has encouraged any practical application of universalistic thinking by Jews – 'It has countenanced it, where necessary, as a means of obviating undue Jewish communal sacrifice or hardship'.[5]

And precisely because the tradition itself has been so constricted and constricting in regard to the gentiles, one admires all the more those Jewish thinkers who have managed in some way to find elements within the tradition which open up prospects for a more positive attitude. The two most notable such thinkers that I know of are the nineteenth-century Italian rabbi Elie Benamozegh (d. 1900), and the twentieth-century philosopher S. H. Bergman. Each of these, in his own way, has offered a vision of Israel's election which sees that election as essentially connected with the salvation of all the peoples of the earth and not just the Jews – indeed, if the Jews arrogate that election to themselves they are frustrating the Messianic endeavour. Of course the thought of Benamozegh and Bergman has not yet penetrated into general Jewish consciousness, which at the moment is probably more accurately presented in the banner which greets the visitor to Safed: 'Jews, love your fellow-Jews'. But it is their thought which is on the way to becoming the cultural tradition.

Yet the next step in the process of Judaism's opening up is the most disturbing of all. This is not just a matter of how a Jew judges Jesus – you can find yourself a comfortable answer to that, as we have seen. Similarly, when faced with Christianity and Islam, you can assure yourself that they are no more than degenerate misrepresentations of the elder faith of Judaism. But it becomes much less easy when you have to face the question, 'What does it mean to be a Jew in face of the great religions of the East?' Because unless you are going to give yourself the Orthodox answer and dismiss them as 'idolatry' – if, in other words, you are going to take seriously your belief that God is somehow the God of all people, who acts throughout all human history, and does not act merely through the destiny of one elect people – then inevitably you have to give some account of your own faith before the bar, so to speak, of the great world religions. For in our days the great world religions are inexorably brought together to form a bar before which all our religions have to appear. Each religion is there called upon to propound a *theologia religionum*, or theology of religions, in which it not only states its own claims but also gives a reckoning of the claims of the other great religions. And any religion which merely cries 'Idolatry' when faced with other religions will be laughed out of court as having no place among the great religions, as being a fossilised relic of a Stone Age tribal cult.

Now this demand for such a *theologia religionum* has been most clearly formulated by the Jewish thinker, Professor Werblowsky, in his book *Beyond Tradition and Modernity*. As you read the book you find him expounding the answers which, as far as he can see, have been given by the various religions before the bar of world religion. And the answer he attributes to Christianity, Hinduism, Buddhism and Islam are judged very severely; so that after hearing those judgements the reader awaits eagerly the *theologia religionum* of the Jewish tradition to which Professor Werblowsky adheres – but the reader waits in vain, for on behalf of Judaism he has nothing to say. Not a word. After all that he has said already, one realises that we have here come to *einer neuralgischer Punkt*; the very silence indicates a touchy spot. It is touchy, presumably, because Jewish thinkers in general have not yet managed to formulate a *theologia religionum* of their own.

Clearly this point is a crucial one for our young Jewish seekers who have journeyed into the world religions; and so it is worth our while to call their attention to certain Jewish thinkers who have made at least some pronouncements on the subject.

IV

As was to be expected, it was from the body of learned Central European Jews that there came the first responses to that influx of Eastern ideas into the West which occurred in the nineteenth century. One such response, indeed, is to be found in the book which many regard as a classic restatement for the modern world of what it means to be a Jew, *The Star of Redemption*, by Franz Rosenzweig – and a very sharp response it is. Rosenzweig writes so scathingly about Eastern religions (as, in truth, he does about Islam) that one realises he never met any worthy representatives of those religions in person. He says such things as, 'Never has the sound of divine freedom penetrated the taut circle of the Brahmin' – and he speaks of those who adhere to the Brahmin tradition as 'fleeing from the face of the living God into the mists of abstraction', 'retrogressing into the elemental', being absorbed 'as is the self, and every self, by the Brahmin's silence of the sea'. He speaks of those who adhere to Buddha and Lao-tze as having 'concealed themselves in the sound-proof chambers of Nirvana and Tao'.[6] Nor do we find any more sympathetic understanding of the East in one of Rosenzweig's younger intellectual successors, Ignaz Maybaum, who called upon both Christians and Muslims to join forces against the Eastern influx, speaking of the smile of the Buddha as 'a cold, disinterested smile, outwardly friendly but in truth cruel', the representation of 'Asiatic nihilism', to which the only radical antithesis is 'prophetic Judaism'.[7]

So that first encounter of modern Jewish thinkers with Eastern religions has to be reckoned a distinct failure in understanding. But a more serious encounter was going on at the same time in the studies of Martin Buber. During the years between 1900 and 1916 Buber busied himself, as did many another Central European, such as Hermann Hesse, with the study of the classical Eastern texts – in translation of course. The books and essays which Buber published during these years reveal a most positive attitude towards Eastern teachings. What is more, Buber learned that by the Western incursion into Asia and by its destruction of oriental cultures, 'The world is about to lose something irreplaceably precious'. Not only that, but he believed that only one European nation had the spirit to avert such a catastrophe, which was the German nation; and that within the German nation one group had a special calling to act as a bridge between the East and the West, and that group was German Jewry.[8] Even though he was soon to turn away from what he termed the 'mysticism' of the East towards the 'existential' world of his famous book *I and Thou*, Buber continued nevertheless to accord great respect to Eastern traditions: in his late work *Eclipse of God*, he speaks of Buddha's relation to the 'Unborn, Unoriginated, Uncreated' as itself an I–Thou relationship in which one sees 'unmistakable religious reality'; and in a letter of 1953 to Will Herberg he passionately defends his thesis that Eastern cultures are based upon a 'religious principle' that is from Heaven.[9]

Throughout that earlier period, however, Buber had no contact with living spokesmen for Eastern religions, which makes his first such contact so significant and revealing. This occurred in June 1921 when the Indian sage Rabindranath Tagore was making a lecture-tour and Buber went to hear him in Darmstadt. Suspicious of the heady enthusiasm aroused by Tagore, Buber characteristically put his finger on a crux in any Jewish–Hindu dialogue. He wrote in a letter:

> Tagore himself is a nice, childlike, remarkable figure with a beauti-fully touching faith that is completely inadequate for us. He is unacquainted with our burden and imagines he can make it light for us by demonstrating how lightly he lives – but we, even as we smile into those most childlike eyes, can never forget for one moment that we must not cast aside for one moment the slightest scrap of the full weight of our burden but have to ascend with it into the heights or plunge with it into the depths.[10]

Five years later Buber was able to spend some time in conversation with Tagore at the home of Professor Winternitz, where once again Tagore was urging that the Jews of Palestine should cast off a burden, this time the burden of machines and cannons. And once more Buber's reply was 'We cannot say, "Come, let us cast all this off!"'

The growth of technology and the industrialisation of society are irreversible processes.'[11]

The other spokesman for the Indian tradition with whom Buber became engaged was Mahatma Gandhi, and it is significant that Buber's initial admiration for Gandhi became more and more tinged with irritation over precisely the same issue that had divided him from Tagore, the issue of casting off a burden. In 1938 Gandhi published an article criticising the Jewish nation's reaction to Hitler's persecution, and questioning Jewish claims upon land in Palestine. In effect Gandhi was recommending to Jews both in Germany and Palestine the way of *satyagrah*, the way of renunciation, that Hindus had practised in face of the British in India. Not unreasonably, Buber, in his *Two Letters to Gandhi*, protested against Gandhi's unreality in comparing the British to the Nazis, also in failing to see that Jews had a historical mission placed upon them of hallowing the very soil of the Holy Land through their occupations.

V

How central this issue is for Jews in the face of Eastern religions was brought home to me vividly two years ago, when it came up in a class that I was teaching. In an attempt to convey to the class Buber's sense that Jews have a burden to bear within history and within marriage to the land, I read out to them Buber's comments about Tagore and Gandhi and thereby provoked a most passionate and sustained confrontation between the Jews in my class and those students who subscribed to Eastern traditions. In a highly abbreviated and somewhat stylised form, the discussion ran rather as follows, started by the Easterners, who said:

Of course, if you insist on laying that burden upon yourselves, if you really don't want to be liberated from it, then you will be crushed under it. We only hope that when you speak of plunging into the abyss with it, you don't take the rest of us with you.

To which the Jewish students answered:

> We cannot dissociate ourselves from our past in that fashion. To do so would mean betraying our ancestors, all those Jews who for thousands of years have undergone persecution. It would mean, in effect, collaborating with the persecutors, giving victory to Haman and Hitler and their gangs.

At this the Easterners threw up their hands in horror and said:

> That is exactly the argument that was used during the Vietnam war against the proposal to withdraw from Vietnam. It was said that to do so would mean betraying all those thousands of Americans who had already died defending freedom in Vietnam. If everyone whose ancestors have been persecuted feels that they have to stick to their ancestors' beliefs, one can never hope for peace in this world. Moreover, does this bearing of the burden of the past mean that you have to defend Moses' murder of the Egyptian, the Israelites' cruelty in conquering Canaan or David's brigandage and feuding?

At this point I intervened in the debate to suggest that there must be some way in which you can be loyal to your tradition without sanctioning everything that has been done in the past in the name of that tradition. There must be some principle of discrimination, a revision, a seeing anew, which enables one to discern the thread of the true tradition that has been obscured by the vain imaginings of some of its upholders. The need for such a principle of discrimination is vital for those religions which believe in salvation history. To the Jews of our own day, for instance, it is vital to see the central line of their tradition as running through Amos rather than through Micah and Ezra, just as it is vital for Catholics to see their central tradition as running through St Joan of Arc rather than through the establishment organ, the Inquisition, which burned her at the stake. This does not mean cooking the books of history but rather seeing anew, in the light of God's unceasing work in history, that something previously considered peripheral is actually central to the tradition. In this way the '*Fluch der Geschichte*', the 'curse of history', as one Jewish writer has termed it, becomes transformed into a blessing. This revision is none other than the work of the Holy Spirit. Given

confidence by this intervention, the Jewish students said to the Easterners:

> Because you make things so light for yourselves, as Tagore advises,
> you carry no weight in history. It has been said, *'amor meus pondus
> meum'*, my love is my weight. Smiling away in the face of human
> tragedy, you do not have sufficient gravity to draw close in love –
> you escape from all created things into renunciation and irresponsi-
> bility. Buber pointed the contrast very effectively when he wrote,
> of the comparison between Hasidic masters and the masters of
> other spiritual traditions, that in none of these other movements
> do we find such an enduring power of vitality and an enhancing
> of the every day as here. To this must be added, however, that here
> (in Hasidism) and only here it is not the life of monks that is
> reported but the life of spiritual leaders who are married and
> produce children and who stand at the head of communities com-
> posed of families. Here, as there, prevails devotion to the divine
> and the hallowing of lived life through this devotion; but there it
> is borne by an ascetic limitation of existence even where a helping
> and teaching contact with people is preserved, while in Hasidism
> the hallowing extends fundamentally to the natural and social life.
> Here alone the whole man, as God has created him, enters into
> the hallowing.[12]
>
> Our task in this life is not to go beyond this world by renunci-
> ation but to hallow it, not to cast off this world of signs into
> oblivion but to carry them with us, not losing our remembrances
> of them but, through the sacred gift of memory, keeping them in
> our memory.

To which the Easterners replied:

> What you call history is an illusion. It is a product of your own
> ignorant mind. An example of this is Buber's speaking of the Jew's
> task to carry a heavy sign to the mountain top or plunge into the
> abyss in the attempt. This is a Samson complex. The Jewish illusion.
> Pascal was right when he said of the Jews of old that they were so
> preoccupied with signs that they did not recognise the Real when
> the Real came to them. And nowadays you still get short-sighted
> bending over your books filled with signs from the past instead of

recognising the presence of God, here and now, the Reality beyond all signs. God does not need your burdensome sign; we do not need your sign. Cast it off and you will realise that you yourself are the only signs necessary. In fact you are more than – you are beyond, signs. You are Reality. *Thou art That, Atman is Brahman.* Or do you actually prefer to stick to your aching hunger for God, the sign of God, rather than to recognise his One-ness with you? Because by hugging your hunger, like an adolescent, you can then continue to imagine yourselves to be not as other men but singular, unique?

As will be realised, these exchanges raised many fundamental issues; but the crucial one, as regards any dialogue between Jews and the Indian tradition, is that last point. Traditionally Judaism has always emphasised the fear of God and his remoteness so as to guard against any possible confusion between the infinite Creator and the finite creature. At the same time, is there any strand within the Jewish tradition which allows of a different emphasis, and so brings Judaism closer to Hinduism? According to Leo Schaya there certainly is, and he locates it in the Kabbala, where 'the unveiled spirit' hidden in the 'letter' is intended to lead a being, while still here on earth, 'beyond the symbolism of sacred forms and dualism of thought into knowledge, real identification with the One without a second'.[13] He comments on the Shema that 'affirmation of the One, to the point of union with him, is the essence of monotheism'.

What Schaya says here coincides with what I was once told by an expert on Habad Hasidism who maintained that within the small circles closest to the *tzaddik* a teaching was given that is indistinguishable from the *advaita* (non-dualism) of traditional Hinduism, but that in the past this teaching was purposely confined to a small, esoteric group for fear that the teaching might be misunderstood if it were made more generally available.

In the light of which I would like to suggest that we are witnessing in these extreme times an opening up of the esoteric traditions within the great world religions as a providential response to the extreme confusion and evil of our day – witness the upsurge of mystical teaching within the Christian Church, of Sufism within Islam, of Tibetan mysticism, and the readiness of the elders within Native

American religion to declare openly teachings which they had previously kept secret, but now wish to make more generally available because all the peoples need them if they are not to perish.

Probably no one realised this need so early as the first chief rabbi of Israel, Rabbi Kook, who wrote:

So long as the world moves along accustomed paths, so long as there are no wild catastrophes, man can find sufficient substance for his life by contemplating surface events, theories and movements of society. He can acquire his inner richness from this external kind of 'property'. But this is not the case when life encounters fiery forces of evil and chaos. Then the 'revealed' world begins to totter. Then the man who tries to sustain himself only from the surface aspects of existence will suffer terrible impoverishments, begin to stagger . . . and then feel welling up within himself a burning thirst for that inner substance and vision which transcends the obvious surfaces of existence and remains unaffected by the world's catastrophes. From such inner sources he will seek the waters of joy which can quicken the dry outer skeletons of existence.[14]

Kook went on to warn the rabbis of his day that 'study of the practical aspects of the Talmud by itself is bound to run dry unless we add to it from the vast domain of the Kabbala'.

What Rabbi Kook is urging here amounts to a revision of the Jewish tradition, because until recently mainstream Judaism treated the Kabbala with great suspicion and the word 'mysticism' on Jewish lips could almost be reckoned a swear-word – young Jews were severely warned against it. And what Rabbi Kook proposed as a desirable possibility has been transformed into a reality for Jews by one of the most remarkable feats in the history of scholarship. This has come about through Gershom Scholem, the last representative of that marvellous German Jewish school of learning to which Rosenzweig and Buber also belonged. Scholem, almost single-handed, by the sheer weight of his learning in a whole series of books, has redefined the Jewish tradition so that mysticism is no longer automatically a swear-word on Jewish lips, and the riches of the Kabbala are made available as a source of life to Jews, and especially to the young who are trying to penetrate beyond legalism to the Reality which law has tried to protect. Scholem himself has summed up the situation best in a short article entitled 'Jewish theology today'[15] in which he demonstrates that, in addition to the usually accepted lines for defining the Jewish tradition (that is, the Bible and rabbinical tradition), a further line has now to be recognised in the Kabbala. Of the Kabbala he says that it 'should be regarded as a definitely new beginning on the basis of the other two sources'.

The significance of this for the Jewish students with whom we began is that they can now redefine their tradition by drawing a line through the past of the Jewish people in such a way that the mystical element is no longer seen as peripheral but as central. By the same token they are in a position to offer Judaism's hidden wisdom not only to Jews but to all people, even those who do not fulfil the Talmudic stricture of 'first filling the stomach with *halakhic* or legalistic Judaism'. Hence when they stand at the bar of the world religions they need no longer feel bankrupt, incapable of producing that *theologia religionum* which Werblowsky sees as essential for any worthy religion.

For my Jewish students, therefore, who are wrestling with the question, 'What is it to be a Jew?', and are especially disconcerted when asking themselves the question in the face of Eastern religions, I now feel that I can tell them to look within their own tradition for what they are seeking in Eastern religions. And they do not even need to go beyond their California, not even to the Holy Land, if we may believe the old man who guided me around Safed, the mystical city of northern Galilee. On a brilliantly sunny winter's day he took me into the ancient synagogue where the great Kabbalist Issac Luria used once to teach in the sixteenth century. In the corner of the synagogue was a heap of books. I asked the old man if the Zohar was to be found among them, but he said, 'No'. Up until two years before there had been some old men who came to the synagogue and studied the Zohar, but no longer. 'Can you Kabbala?', he said, 'I can't Kabbala. Kabbala is not for me. But I have heard that in America they can Kabbala.'

15

A Buddhist contribution to peace spirituality

(1985)

There is an intriguing footnote in the *New Catechism*, published by the Dominican friar Herbert McCabe, where he says that we must exercise the virtues of gentleness and compassion towards all God's creatures which are capable of suffering, 'because they are fellow sentient beings'. What makes this footnote so intriguing is the fact that the phrase 'sentient beings' is not, of course, a traditionally Christian phrase, but is Buddhist. Moreover there is something typically Buddhist in the unobtrusive manner in which the phrase has entered into Western consciousness, and has thereby begun slowly to produce an overwhelming change in our hitherto barbaric attitudes towards our fellow creatures. And I use the word 'barbaric' in its literal sense, since those attitudes have been based upon the behaviour-patterns of our barbarian ancestors, the 'badly-baptised' tribes of Dark Age Europe.

It is profoundly encouraging, therefore, to observe this example of how gently and courteously a process of convergence and permeation is taking place in the consciousness of leading thinkers from the different world religions, especially as they address themselves to the two greatest threats ever to the human family: that is, nuclear warfare, and the destruction of the earth that we have inherited, by pollution.

Among these thinkers none has done more to help me, a Catholic, to understand and feel heartened by the above-mentioned process of permeation than the Vietnamese Buddhist, Thich Nhat Hanh.

That, in itself, is quite remarkable when you remember that Thich Nhat Hanh was one of the Buddhist monks persecuted for years by the stridently Catholic movement of Ngo Dinh Diem, which accused him of being a Communist (at the same time, fittingly enough, as the Communists in Hanoi were accusing him of being in the pay of the Pentagon). Far from allowing his shabby treatment at the hands of Catholics to fill him with hatred for them, Thich Nhat Hanh has grown ever closer to them and has even been a formative influence upon the lives of such distinguished Catholic peacemakers as Thomas Merton, Dan Berrigan and Jim Forest.

The clue to Thich Nhat Hanh's capacity for genuinely embracing 'the enemy' is to be found, I believe, in Buddhist teaching on 'interdependent origination'. A recent story of his will illustrate what the term means:

> An American (in the peace movement) told me this: 'Every time I see Mr Reagan on television, I can't bear it. I have to turn the set off or I get mad.' I think I understand him. He thinks that the US government is entirely responsible for the world situation. If only Mr Reagan changes his policy and you have a freeze, there will be peace with the Soviet Union. That is not entirely correct, I tried to tell him. Because Mr Reagan is in yourself. We always *deserve* our government. In Buddhism we speak in terms of interdependent origination: *this* is, because *that* is; this is *not*, because that is *not*. Has our daily life nothing to do with our government?

Such clear awareness of interdependence did not come to Thich Nhat Hanh without tribulation. During the period in the 1960s, when he was working in the war-riven Vietnamese villages as a leader of the School of Youth for Social Service, he found himself under bombardment at different times from both the Vietcong and the American forces. Yet even under those circumstances he had the inner resources to offer a compassionate embrace of understanding to 'the enemy'. Speaking of the shock and anger of Americans in the US when they learnt of atrocities committed in Vietnam by US forces, he wrote:

> People would understand better if they shared the hard life of the soldiers, living all day sometimes in the mud or in the jungle full of mosquitoes and other insects, watched by death. These soldiers tend to regard moral values as unimportant, especially when they think they are not fighting for a right cause but only being forced to do so.

This is, because *that* is.

Against Thich Nhat Hanh no one can level the accusation, so beloved of those who fear to pay the price of peace, that peace-workers are not 'realists' but live in Cloud-cuckoo-land. For many of the years since he was driven from Vietnam by the Vietcong he has spent among the boat people, and witnessed horrors that would have driven many of us mad. Even in the face of the self-drowning by a 12-year-old girl after she had been raped by a sea-pirate in the Gulf of Thailand, he was able to write:

> I was angry, of course. But I could not take sides against the sea-pirate. If I could it would be easier for me; but I did not because I thought that if I had been born in his village and had his history – economic, educational and so on – it is very likely that I would now be that sea-pirate.

This is, because *that* is.

But of all the arresting observations made by this wise teacher, none has lodged itself in my mind more securely than what he said in New York in 1982:

> In the oriental way of therapy, sometimes in order to treat the lung they will take care of the kidney. Our daily life has to do very much with the existence of nuclear weapons. If we think of nuclear weapons as something separate from our daily life we are misled. My brother told me that if only people in the western countries would eat less meat and drink less alcohol then it would be enough to change the situation of the world. I did not believe him. Now I believe him. Smaller things like blocking the weapons industry and stopping the export of weapons to poor countries [would then follow].

This is not, because *that* is not.

Thich Nhat Hanh has been much in my thoughts of recent weeks as a result of my following the story of the privatisation of the Trustee Savings Bank. The hired cheerleaders of Mammon in the media have greeted that event by congratulating the British nation on having five million people in their midst who have applied for shares in TSB in the expectation that their shares may double in price overnight.

What gives the cheerleaders cause for such self-congratulation is

214

known to Buddhists as *lobha* – greed. It gives rise to envy, violence and, ultimately, warfare. To rejoice in it is a sign of insanity. *This* is because *that* is.

16

Abhishiktananda

(1989)

The request to write a Foreword to James Stuart's life of Swami Abhishiktananda came as a surprise. After all, I never met Abhishiktananda in the flesh, as did so many people who have written about him. Moreover, I am a lay person, whereas he spent almost all his life as a monk and hermit amidst monks and hermits.

On reflection, however, I am less surprised by the request, because the time has now come to show that Abhishiktananda's message is a message for all human beings, not just for monks and nuns. Moreover we need to emphasise that in order to receive the message of a spiritual master it is not essential to have met him in the flesh. Indeed as Abhishiktananda often points out, the disciples on the road to Emmaus did not recognise the presence even of Jesus until he had passed beyond the reach of their senses. It has also to be said that the trading of anecdotes about a spiritual master's habits and quirks by his disciples, while sometimes bringing him closer, may easily degenerate into gossip and pander to curiosity.

The very last motive that could make it worthwhile to read the present book is curiosity – curiosity, for instance, about Abhishiktananda's difficulties with Abbé Monchanin, and similar intriguing episodes. Nor would there be much reward in studying the book if one's dominant motive were the desire to test his theology against the yardstick of one's own theological formulations. Because, although Abhishiktananda was, in fact, a much better theologian than he generally made out, and though he did anticipate and wrestle with the major dilemmas that he raised, nevertheless he was passionately aware of the great harm that has been inflicted over the centuries by theologians who, quite literally, did not know what – or whom – they were talking about. And without experience of the reality, the formulations are of no more use than a shaky compass in an unknown land.

This is especially true when the reality in question is the age-old experience of the land and peoples of India. For India is more than a geographical location; it is a dimension of the spirit where all who enter in are changed, and where Western-drawn maps and Western compasses are of little value.

So the way to approach this life of Abhishiktananda, I suspect, is to see in it the traces of the pilgrimage made by a spiritual adventurer who was unusually pure in heart, and upon whose very flesh was branded the truth of Jesus' admonition to Peter: 'I tell you most solemnly, when you were young you put on your own belt and walked where you liked; but when you grow old you will stretch out your hands, and somebody else will put a belt round you and take you where you would rather not go'. As it turned out, the young Breton Henri Le Saux was to be led into places where he found himself torn apart. Had he foreseen what was in store for him, he would scarcely have been transformed into that Abhishiktananda (Joy of the Anointed) who has since become a sign of joy and illumination for many seekers throughout the earth.

Accordingly, for those of us who wish to accompany him on his earthly pilgrimage, and even beyond, the indispensable precondition is that we do so through the medium of the Spirit. And the only preparation for the coming of the Spirit – or, rather, our awakening to him – is to empty our minds of all preconceptions, man-made decisions and reason-based desires. Because what we are faced with is a journey into the 'deep things of God' – a favourite phrase of Abhishiktananda's taken from the letter in which Paul tells the Corinthians that God has prepared for those who love him things beyond what any human being can see or hear or imagine. Yet the Spirit permeates everything, even the deep things of God, even God's own nature, for only the Spirit of God knows what God is.

How to live out in one's everyday life this truth enunciated by St Paul was often illustrated by Abhishiktananda with the aid of a Sanskrit term, *ākāsha*. The term *ākāsha* means both the 'exterior' space and the infinite 'interior' space which are really but one, both spheres being permeated by that same Spirit which fills not only the whole cosmos but equally the human heart. This is possible because the Spirit, being God, is beyond all forms, and so is able to make his presence felt in any form; and being beyond all times, he yet fills all moments of time and is present to every event of history. Thus he is at the core of the universe and of the heart of humanity. He *is* that core.

For Abhishiktananda the great awakening to the Spirit came when he met the Indian holy man Sri Ramana Maharshi. That moment was determinative for the rest of his life. At that moment he *knew,* beyond a shadow of doubt, that he was in the presence of a human being who had been drawn so deep into the cave of the heart (Sanskrit, *guhā*) as to have touched the heart of the cosmos. This holy man, in consequence, had been blessed by a peace that is beyond human comprehension. And he radiated that peace.

For Abhishiktananda that first-hand experience, that knowledge, was to prove both bliss and agony – bliss, because he *knew* that the pearl of great price is not an illusion; yet agony also, because it compelled him to acknowledge that the pearl of great price is not the exclusive property of the Roman Catholic Church, as he had previously assumed.

Later on, towards the end of his life, the agony somewhat abated. Abhishiktananda was able to describe how certain Christians are called to plunge into those very depths that had been plumbed over the centuries by Hindu holy men. He spoke of how such Christians, when they surface again, will find that their faith has been strengthened and enriched by a previously unknown depth of experience. A kind of osmosis will have taken place in their souls between the Hindu experience and the Christian experience of the depths of the heart of Christ. Those Christians will then be able to instruct their brethren in the royal way of the interior life, teaching them how to place themselves entirely at the disposal of the Spirit.

However, for any seeker to imagine that Abhishiktananda provides one with a ready-made formula for such Hindu–Christian osmosis would not merely be an unfortunate mistake; it would be a betrayal of Abhishiktananda's intentions and his agony. For while no one else need now undergo the same excruciating agony as he did, yet all of us, with our intellects and compassion stretched to the utmost, are obliged to read very slowly his anguished cries (especially in the pages of his Diary), his ceaseless self-questioning as to whether he was any longer a Christian and whether he would have to abandon the Church which had mothered and shaped him. Only a very arrogant person would claim to skip lightly over such an abyss on to the safe ground at the other side.

In the end Abhishiktananda did not lose his balance. The fact that he did not do so can be traced – so far as human reason can discern – to his grasp upon two strands of his own tradition. The first ensured that he never ceased to celebrate the Eucharist, even at the most unlikely times and in the most unlikely places. The second made sure that his ardent devotion to the person of Jesus was never dimmed. In later years he came to see more vividly that in the Eucharist the entire cosmos is integrated, where both matter and human consciousness are brought together in union through the Spirit of God and the action of Jesus, who manifests God in his fullness.

And yet that statement could prove misleading if it were not accompanied by an explanation that the fullness spoken of cannot be identified exclusively with the image of Jesus coined by the culture first of the Mediterranean world and later of the European world. For the experience of Jesus was beyond all expression – even by Jesus himself – in the conceptual and verbal possibilities of his own culture or that of the European centuries. Fortunately for Abhishiktananda he found to hand a Hindu term, *pūrnam*, which not only proved far richer in connotation than the Western term 'fullness', but also provided him with a most valuable gift to share with the Church.

In the light of *pūrnam* Abhishiktananda was able to see how limited until now has been the human family's understanding of Jesus' experience of God. He came to see also that the Spirit, who alone can reveal to us the depth of Jesus' experience, had long been at work in the lives of Hindus and in their sacred Scriptures. In Hinduism, therefore, are to be found potentialities of the human spirit which go far beyond what has so far been considered possible within the limits of Western culture. Hence the encounter with Hinduism is an occasion to liberate the Spirit within Christians, and thereby enable them to realise more fully the riches contained in the revealed words of their own Scriptures and to share more intimately in the experience of Jesus as Son of the Father and yet one with him. Also the encounter with Hinduism – as well as with Buddhism, Islam and other great religious traditions of humankind – will usher in a radically new stage in the awareness and development of the Church. As a result, the Mediterranean-based form of Christianity, which is still predominant, will soon be seen as only one of the historical possibilities of living the Christian faith.

It is clear from the present book that by the last years of his life Abhishiktananda himself had largely passed beyond the limits of culturally-conditioned Christianity – or, indeed, beyond the bounds of culturally-conditioned Hinduism – and was behaving with a freedom which is only possible at the level of the spirit. Thus he felt free laughingly to disappoint the expectations of a Sister who was looking to him for some holy words: he told her that God is as much in the making of a good soup or the careful handling of a railway train as he is in our most beautiful meditations. Similarly, with a humorous eye upon himself, he remarks that there is as much true prayer when one's attention is concentrated on an ache, as there is in the marvellous silence when we think we are in ecstasy. In like vein he tells a correspondent not to pay much attention to those who love the esoteric, who run around to ashrams and 'saints'. 'The discovery of the mystery', he writes, 'is so much simpler than that. It is right beside you, in the opening of a flower, the song of a bird, the smile of a child.'

Admittedly his warning against the esoteric is likely to raise a smile in anyone who tries to accompany Abhishiktananda through the thickets of Hindu metaphysics. But even in those thickets he never lost sight of his goal, which was the same as that indicated by the far from esoteric St Seraphim of Sarov, who used to say, 'The whole aim of Christian life is to acquire the Holy Spirit'. And it is surely a sign of how faithful Abhishiktananda remained to the call of the Holy Spirit that some words of his should chime in so perfectly with a remarkable statement of Seraphim, who said, 'I tell you that when God visits us in his ineffable goodness we must be still even from prayer. In prayer the soul utters words of speech, but when the Holy Spirit has come you must be in complete silence.' The corresponding statement by Abhishiktananda runs:

At the end there is no place for prayer, for praise, but the silence which is the origin and completion of all words, when all the manifestations of God have to be left behind, and with all his strength man must aim at the Silence in which alone God is in himself.

17

Inter-faith

(1995)

'It is not a particular form of word that guarantees the truth of our faith but the Reality towards which the words are pointing.' With that one sentence a great Christian thinker clears away much of the confusion which bedevils what is called 'inter-faith discussion'.

I place inverted commas around 'inter-faith discussion' because the term 'inter-faith' can itself be misleading. It suggests that there may be several faiths that are called upon to engage in discussions with one another in order to work out how to understand each other and live together in peace. Yet if faith is true faith it can only be one, since truth is one. There can only be one true faith.

But, of course, the forms of words, pointing to the Reality which alone guarantees the truth of our faith, are numerous – at least as numerous as the languages by means of which we try to point towards that one Reality.

Fortunately, nowadays, since the world's religions have been brought into closer contact with one another, there have emerged thinkers in each of the religions who are skilled at discussing the meaning of such difficult terms as the Trinity used by Christians or *advaita* by Hindus, *anatta* by Buddhists, Torah by Jews or *Dar al ʿAhd* by Muslims. All these thinkers agree that while no such terms are completely adequate for the Reality to which they point, nevertheless they do throw some light on the path; whereas the words of those who do not have faith lead only into darkness.

But the vocation of comparing forms of words is confined to a very small minority of the human family. For most of us, the vocation to live at peace with people of other religions springs out of our everyday life. We meet people of other religions in their gestures and their rituals, in friendship or in conflict with them, as we struggle with them for peace and justice.

And if we refuse to go out towards them in order to learn from the way they live their faith, we impoverish ourselves and lose an opportunity of enriching our own faith. Because even the simplest gesture may reveal a whole world of faith. For, as one Christian has said, 'You can tell the quality of a man's faith by the way he makes the sign of the cross'. Or, as a Muslim has said, 'The truth of a man is not in what he possesses. And it isn't in words, either. His truth is in the gesture of spontaneous welcome he shows to any of his brothers. That gesture is his key to heaven.'

Similarly, one cannot help wondering how many Hindus – or even Muslims or Sikhs and others – have had their faith strengthened by the beautiful, prayerful manner in which Mother Teresa makes the traditional Hindu gesture of greeting, *namaste*.

These examples show that we do not have to be learned theologians in order to pursue our common vocation of working for peace between the world religions. In fact, if you call to mind those places where such peace has been achieved in the past, you will be bound to notice that it was in northern India, in Cyprus, in Jerusalem, in Sarajevo, and other places in previous centuries, that peace was achieved through the ordinary people of different religions sharing in each other's joys and fears, celebrations and sorrows, by being present at those moments when faith is most important to us – at the birth of our children, at our marriages, at our death-beds and funerals.

It is by way of such occasions that hostility towards people of a different religion may be transformed into sympathy for one another in a spontaneous, natural way, without anyone setting out deliberately to change attitudes – indeed such unplanned occasions are often the best and most lasting way for transformation to take place.

We have been told, for instance, by the Anglican bishop, David Brown, how he changed from regarding Islam as an evil religion into realising that Islam is a means of grace for many. This happened when he was a Christian missionary in Khartoum. His frequent journeys northwards out of Khartoum used to take him past a Muslim cemetery where he would regularly observe Muslim women praying at the graves of their beloved dead. It was not long before David was moved to recognise an expression of genuine faith in the women's faithful devotion. He thereby ceased to think of Islam as a source of evil.

Moreover the presence of someone from another religion at one's own rituals may not only open that person's eyes but through his response one's own eyes may be opened to the depths of one's own faith.

On one occasion, for instance, a Christian was accompanied to Mass by a Jewish rabbi. When the priest celebrating Mass came to the words of consecration, the Christian noticed the rabbi breathing hard and trembling. The explanation for the trembling was given to his Christian friend by the rabbi as they walked away from the Church. He said that for a Jew, with a Jew's sense of the awesomeness of God, it was not only wonderful but also terrifying to think that the Creator of the universe might be personally present in the bread and wine on the altar.

The rabbi's explanation made the Christian aware, as never before, of how awesome is the central gesture of faith in the Christian tradition, and of how carelessly many Christians perform that gesture. Perhaps the rabbi had more true faith than such Christians?

But probably the most obvious example of how a person brought up in one religion may learn from another religion, and then make those from whom he has learned aware of riches in their own tradition, which they themselves had virtually lost, is to be found in the story of Mahatma Gandhi.

Gandhi himself tells us how during 1893 in South Africa he read the New Testament and it 'really opened' his eyes, especially to the beauty and truth of the Sermon on the Mount, and there particularly to the teaching on non-violence expressed in the command, 'Resist not evil', but 'if one strike thee on thy right cheek, turn to him also the other'. As a result of that moment when a Hindu's eyes were opened by his reading the Christian Gospel, a current of peace has flowed throughout the violent world. Christians such as Gandhi's friend, the missionary C. F. Andrews, and his correspondent, the great Russian writer, Tolstoy, themselves had their eyes opened to the truth of peace through non-violence. Through their witness and that of others, the whole Christian world has subsequently been stirred by that current released through Gandhi, and has been awakened as never before to the practical application of the Sermon on the Mount.

No wonder that Pope John Paul II, on 1 February 1986, went to the site of Mahatma Gandhi's *samadhi* and laid a wreath there, saying, 'today as a pilgrim of peace I have come here to pay homage to Mahatma Gandhi, hero of humanity'.

How, then, could we possibly doubt that the moment when Gandhi's eyes were opened to the truth of the Sermon was the work of that Holy Spirit which inspired every moment of Jesus' life and which he promised he would send to all who follow him in doing the will of God? For Jesus makes it clear that it is not sufficient to cry 'Lord, Lord', and assume that your own tradition has a monopoly on the Holy Spirit. Indeed some who cried, 'Lord, Lord', at first in Nazareth, were ready to throw him over the cliff because he reminded them that in the days of famine it was not to Israel that the Lord showed favour but to a woman of Sidon, and in the days of leprosy the only leper cleansed was Naaman the Syrian. And later the ones he praises for their great faith include the Canaanite woman and the Roman centurion, while it was through a Samaritan woman that many were brought to faith.

But the climax of Jesus' teaching that the Spirit is not under the control of anyone but blows where it wills, is to be found in St Matthew Chapter 25. There Jesus assures us that many people will inherit the Kingdom (even though they did not think themselves entitled to do so) because they fed the hungry, gave drink to the thirsty, took in strangers, visited the sick and those in prison. Each of them has been proved to have true faith and is beyond the need to recite any particular form of words.

If such a person is a Christian, he or she has reached the climax of Christian life. As a result of which, some Muslims may say of him/her, 'He/she is a true Muslim'; and Hindus, 'He/she is faithful to the *dharma*'; while Buddhists say 'He/she is a *bodhisattva*'; and Jews 'He/she surely belongs to the House of Israel'. Because such a person, no matter what form of words he or she may use about his or her faith, is a living embodiment of faith for all believers.

References

Chapter 1: The beatitude of truth

A University sermon preached at Leeds on 25 October 1987. First published in the *University of Leeds Review,* 1988.

1   John 21:18 (Jerusalem Bible).

Chapter 2: St Bede

First published in *The Month*, November 1959.

1   Jaager, W. (ed.) (1935), *Vita sancti Cuthberti*, 57.
2   Plummer, C. (ed.) (1896), *Opera Historica*, lxxvii. The eye-witness was Cuthbert, afterwards Abbot of Wearmouth and Jarrow.
3   *Opera 12* (ed. Giles), 271.
4   *Opera 7*, 244.
5   *Opera 12*, 267.
6   *Opera 9*, 247.
7   Jones C. W. (ed.) (1943), *Opera de Temporibus*, 132–5. Jones points out that Bede is here criticising St Wilfrid, also, in whose presence the accusation was made without rebuff.
8   St Benedict himself is scarcely ever referred to by Bede.
9   *Opera 11*, 380.
10 *Opera 12*, 212.
11 *Opera 8*, 326.
12 *Opera 8*, 27.
13 *Opera 11*, 68–9, and *Opera 9*, 254.
14 For the sake of brevity I might say quite baldly that I do not think that one can *literally* maintain that Bede was consistent in his use of the terms, mystical, allegorical, anagogical, etc.; but the *spirit* of the distinctions is clear enough.
15 *Opera 7*, 108.
16 *Opera 8*, 360.
17 *Opera 8*, 153.
18 *Opera 9*, 13.

19   *Opera homiletica et rhythmica* (1955), 247–8.

20   *Opera 9*, 283.

21   In addition to the references already given, cf. *Opera 9*, 242 and 365.

22   *Opera 11*, 81–9.

23   cf. *Opera 11*, 186.

24   Laistner (ed.) (1939), *Retractatio in Actus Apostolorum*, 125.

25   Plummer in *Opera Historica*, lvi–lvii.

26   *Opera 8*, 49.

27   *Opera 8*, 262–9.

28   *Opera 7*, 324–5. From his commentary on the tabernacle.

29   *Opera 9*, 50–1.

30   *Opera 11*, 21.

31   *Opera de Temporibus*, 286–90. This chapter is described by Levison [in Thompson, Hamilton (ed.) (1935), *Bede, His Life, Times and Writings*, 22] as 'sublime devotion'. It should certainly be studied by all who wish to understand why the Easter controversy raised such strong passions in the seventh century.

32   The translation is Plummer's (*Opera Historica*, lxi).

33   cf. *Opera 7*, 13, 'It is clear from these words of God that it was in springtime that the adornment of the world was perfected'.

34   *Opera 7*, 419–20.

35   *Opera 8*, 289.

36   *Opera 8*, 379.

37   *Opera 11*, 66–7. In the same commentary (p. 257) he cites Job as the type of married goodness.

38   *Opera 7*, 229. From the context it seems that Bede considers this grace to be limited to certain prophets and patriarchs.

39   Except, of course, in his hagiographical writings where he is simply following his authorities.

40   *Opera 7*, 365–6; *Opera 10*, 37.

41   *Opera homiletica et rhythmica*, 49.

42   *Opera 7*, 273. It may intrigue the reader to learn that this exhortation occurs in Bede's comment upon Exodus 26:5: 'Every curtain shall have fifty loops on both sides, so set on, that one loop may be set against another loop, and one may be fitted to the other'.

43   *Opera homiletica et rhythmica*, 45.

44   *Ibid.*, 266.

45   *Opera 10*, 141; *Opera 11*, 188.

46   *Opera 8*, 51–2.

47   *Opera 7*, 195.

48   *Opera 9*, 1.

49   *Ibid.*, 144. I should point out that these last five notes represent a sharp telescoping of Bede's observations.

50   An instructive comparison may be found in the commentaries upon

the Song of Songs which Bede and St Bernard composed. St Bernard's is 'mystical' in a later sense of the word than that familiar to Bede: he delves into the recesses of the individual's psychology with truly poetic intuition. Bede's commentary is 'mystical' in his own sense, as signifying interior but it is the interiority of moral behaviour rather than of psychological experience.

51 Cf. *Opera 9*, 83–4, on the grave crimes of sowing discord by which 'unity and fraternity, which is welded together by the grace of the Holy Spirit, is dissipated'.

52 *Opera 9*, 146.

53 *Opera 12*, 326.

54 *Opera 12*, 182–3.

55 *Opera 7*, 358.

56 *Opera 10*, 341.

57 *Opera 11*, 239.

58 cf. note 7 above.

59 *Opera 11*, 30–1.

60 The commentary was written between 725 and 730, a period when Bede's discontent at the condition of Northumbria was mounting.

61 *Opera 9*, 22.

62 *Opera 9*, 29.

63 How reminiscent are Bede's words of the advice on this very subject given by Gerard Hopkins to Robert Bridges in his letter of 19 January 1879: 'It changes the whole man, if anything can; not his mind only but the will and everything'.

64 *Opera 11*, 7.

65 cf. Plummer (*Opera Historica*) lxi.

66 *Opera 10*, 83–4.

Chapter 3: The Catholic Church and the Nazis

Inaugural lecture as professor of history and religious studies, University of California, Santa Cruz, 19 February 1975. First published in *Christian*, November 1978.

1 Trevor-Roper, H. R. (1947), *The Last Days of Hitler*, 251.

2 Rausching, Hermann (1941), *The Beast from the Abyss*.

3 1 Corinthians 2:14.

4 Donat, Alexander (1965), *The Holocaust Kingdom*, 168–9.

5 'It was an undramatic decision. Then and ever afterwards I scarcely felt myself to be a member of a political party. I was not choosing the NSDP, but becoming a follower of Hitler, whose magnetic force had reached out to me the first time I saw him and had not, thereafter, released me. His persuasiveness, the peculiar magic of his by no means pleasant voice, the oddity of his rather banal manner, the seductive

simplicity with which he attacked the complexity of our problems – all that bewildered and fascinated me. I knew virtually nothing about his program. He had taken hold of me before I grasped what was happening.' Albert Speer (1970), *Inside the Third Reich*, 48.

6 Wiskemann, Elizabeth, *Europe of the Dictators 1919–1945*.

7 *The Listener*, October 1971.

8 Stern, K. (1951), *The Pillar of Fire*. 125–32.

9 Deuerlein, E. (1963), *Der deutsche Katholizismus, 1933*, 80.

10 Best described in M. Daphne Hampson's unpublished D Phil thesis (1973), *The British Response to the German Church Struggle, 1933–39*.

11 Dibelius, Otto (1964), *In the Service of the Lord*, 129.

12 Schmidt, Dietmar (1959), *Pastor Niemöller*, 108 ff.

13 'The Jews. As I write in Vienna (1938) they are all about me, watching with non-committal, veiled, appraising eyes the comedy that is going on in Insanity Fair. They know that when Hitlerism has passed away they will still be trading in the Kurntnerstrasse.' Douglas Reed (1938), *Insanity Fair; A European Cavalcade*, 159: also p. 416. Also Schleunes, K. A. (1971), *The Twisted Road to Auschwitz*.

14 Granzow, B. (1964), *A Mirror to Nazism*.

15 The most notable ones were the physicist J. Stark, a Nobel Prize winner, and the distinguished legal philosopher, Carlo Schmitt.

16 Deuerlein, E., op. cit., 51.

17 Adolph, W. (1965), *Hirtenamt und Hitler-Diktatur*, 119.

18 Müller, H. (1963), *Katholische Kirche und Nationalsozialismus*, 13–15.

19 Deuerlein, E., op. cit., 49–51.

20 Müller, H., op. cit., 63.

21 Müller, H., op. cit., 78.

22 Deuerlein, E., op. cit., 150 ff; Müller, H., op. cit., 56, n 34.

23 Deurlein, E., op. cit., 158–9.

24 Adolph, W., op. cit., *passim*.

25 Letter of Pope Pius XII to von Preysing, 12 June 1940, *Die Briefe Pius XII an die deutsche Bischöfe*, 74.

26 Adolph, W., op. cit., 119; for *Der gerade Weg*, see Donohoe, J. (1961), *Hitler's Conservative Opponents in Bavaria*, 35 ff.

27 For Bertram's biography, see Hermann, Josef, *Adolf Kardinal Bertram, Ein Lebensbild*, and Adolph, op. cit.

28 Adolph, W., op. cit., 102.

29 Adolph, W., op. cit., 158.

30 Buchheim, Karl (1963), *Ultramontanismus und Demokratie*, 238 ff.

31 Maier, H. (1964), *Deutsche Katholizismus seit 1945*, 169.

32 Lutz, Heinrich (1963), *Demokratie im Zwielicht*, 49.

33 Altmayer, K. A. (1962), *Katholische Presse und N-S Diktatur*, 24.

34 Carsteu, F. L. (1967), *The Rise of Fascism*, 145; also Pridham, G. (1973), *Hitler's Rise to Power*, *passim*.

35   Altmayer, K. A., op. cit., 79; 94–98.
36   Müller, H., op. cit., 56 n 37; 237, n 10.
37   Spael, W. (1964), *Das Katholische Deutschland*, 276–82; 337.
38   Ackermann, K. (1965), *Der Widerstand der Monatsschrift Hochland gegen den Nationalsozialismus*, 92.
39   Spael, W., op. cit., 343; Nicholl, D. (1951), 'Catholic worker tradition in Germany', *New Life*, June 1951.
40   Lewy, G. (1964), *The Catholic Church and Nazi Germany*, 129.
41   cf. his striking speech at the University of Merburg in June 1934, in von Papen (1952), *Memoirs*, 307 ff.
42   Spael, W., op. cit., 390.
43   Frings, 1 May 1942 (*Der Spiegel*, 11 December 1963); Faulhaber, 22 March 1942, (Müller, 327).
44   Mendelssohn-Bartholdy, A. (1971), *The War and German Society: The Testament of a Liberal*, 161.
45   Karl Barth later recognised that he should have made the Jewish question primary at the 1934 Barmen Synod, but also said that to have done so would have been unacceptable at the time even to the Confessing Church (*Evangelische Theologie XXVIII*, October 1968, 555. cf. also the socialist leader, Julius Leber (1952), *Ein Mann geht seinen Weg*; and Prittie, J. (1964), *Germans Against Hitler*).
46   *Die Briefe Pius XII*, 235.
47   Neuhäusler, J. (1964), *Saat des Bösen; Kirchenkampf im Dritten Reich*, 41.
48   *Herder Korrespondenz*, vol. 17, 13.

Chapter 4: Is there a *locus classicus* for theology?

A lecture given at the Ecumenical Institute, Tantur, Jerusalem, 29 March 1982. First published in the Institute's *Yearbook 1981–2*.

1   *New Blackfriars*, October 1981, 408.
2   Jaeger D. M. A. (ed.) (1981), *Christianity in the Holy Land*, 19.
3   Donovan, Vincent (1978), *Christianity Rediscovered: An Epistle from the Masai*, 42.
4   Sinyavsky, Andrei (1976), *A Voice from the Chorus*, 276.
5   Légasse, Simon (1969), *Jésus et l'enfant*, 341.

Chapter 5: The Karamazov brothers as teachers of religion

A lecture given in the University of Aberdeen, 4 December 1979. First published in *Katallegete*, Fall 1989.

1   The tag of *yurodstvo* also attaches to stinking Lizaveta and the late Varsonofy, but here also *yurodstvo* is misbegotten.

Chapter 6: Spirit: a force for survival

The inaugural John M. Todd Memorial Lecture, given in the University of Bristol, 17 November 1994.

1 Mounier, Emmanuel (1903–50), the chief expositor of *Personalism*, was the founder of the journal *Esprit*.
2 cf. his poem, *The Tribunes' Visitation*, in *The Sleeping Lord* (1974).
3 Eliot, T. S. (1944), 'Burnt Norton', *Four Quartets*, 13.
4 *The Sermons of John Donne*, vol. III, 359–60, G. R. Potter and F. Simpson (eds) (1957).
5 Mme Hautval spoke these powerful words when she bore witness, soon after the second world war, at the trial of a Polish doctor accused of complicity in selecting Auschwitz prisoners for the gas-chambers.
6 Dawkins, Richard 'God in a Test Tube', *The Guardian*, 8 August 1994.
7 *There is a Spirit: The Nayler Sonnets*, Kenneth Boulding (ed.) (1979).
8 Guitton, Jean (1989), *Portraits et circonstances*, 293.
9 von Hartmann, Eduard (1890), *Philosophy of the Unconscious*, vol. III, 135. The recent emergence of the Aum Shinrikyo sect in Japan suggests that von Hartmann's proposal has now become part of the *Noosphere*.
10 Kundera, Milan (1992), *The Book of Laughter and Forgetting*, 3.
11 Mandelstam, Osip (1991), *Selected Poems*, 65.
12 Published in 1950.
13 Aitchison, Jean (1994), *Language Joy-riding*, 1.
14 Hague, Rene (ed.) (1980), *Dai Great Coat*, 226.
15 The one who 'stumbled on behind the Four Horsemen', the South African photographer, Kevin Carter, later took his own life. The other journalist was Richard Dowden, *The Guardian*, 22 August 1994.
16 Micah 4: 6–7 (Revised English Bible).
17 *Tablet*, 7 May 1994.

Chapter 7: Good Friday, 1950

First published in *The Life of the Spirit*, March 1951.

Chapter 8: Stalinensis/*yurodivi*

First published in *New Blackfriars*, October 1969.
1 Berdyayev, Nikolai Alexandrovich (1950), *Dream and Reality*, p. 237.

Chapter 9: The eternal child

First published in the *Tablet*, 19 December 1987.
1 Sinyavsky, Andrei (1976), *A Voice from the Chorus*, pp. 275–60

Chapter 10: Hitting the buffers

First published in the *Tablet*, 13 June 1992.
1   Gollwitzer, Helmut; Kühn, Kathe; Schneider, Reinhold (eds) (1956), *Dying We Live*, Harvill.

Chapter 11: The ascent of love

First published in the *Tablet*, 3 July 1993.
1   Romans 8:18–21 (Revised English Bible).

Chapter 12: A wandering scholar

First published in the *Tablet*, 8 January 1994.

Chapter 13: Scientia cordis

First published by the William James Society, Santa Cruz, California, 1975.
1   Arberry, A. J. (ed.) (1969), *Religion in the Middle East*, vol. 2, 636.
2   Rosenzweig, F. and Rosenstock-Huessy, E. (1969), *Judaism Despite Christianity*, 113.
3   *The Times*, 29 January 1973.
4   Stein, K., *Pillar of Fire*, 163.
5   del Vasto, Lanzo (1956), *Gandhi to Vinoba*, Rider, 180; also *Clergy Review*, March 1969, 181–2
6   Woodcock, G. (1971), *Gandhi* (Fontana Modern Masters), *passim*.
7   Shibayama, Z. (1971), *A Flower Does not Talk*.
8   Fyodorov, N., *Obshevo dela*, 138, 683.
9   Maybaum, I. (1966), 'Jew, Christian and Muslim in the secular age', in R. Loewe, and K. P. Loewe, *Studies in Rationalism and Universalism*, 162; and Maybaum, I. (1965), *The Face of God after Auschwitz*, 38.
10 Lewis, C. S. (1966), *Letters*.
11 *Informations Catholiques Internationales*, 15 July 1970.
12 Tenko-San (1969), *A New Road to Ancient Truth*.
13 I.C.T. (Institute of Catholic Theology), 15 May 1971; Minoru Kasai in *Asia Focus*, 14/2 Pramman Road, Bangkok, Thailand (I.C.T. August 1971).
14 Moffitt, J. (ed.) (1970), *A New Charter for Monasticism*, 221–34.
15 Clément, O. (1969), *Dialogues avec le patriarche Athénagore*, 339.
16 Panikkar, R. (1964), *The Unknown Christ of Hinduism*.
17 Matthew 25: 26–7.
18 John 6: 12.
19 Klostermaier, K. (1969), *Hindu and Christian in Vrindaban*, 98–9.
20 Dournes, Jacques (1966), *God in Vietnam*.
21 Saint-Exupéry, Antoine de, *The Little Prince*.

22 Graham, A. (1971), *The End of Religion*, 40. When Aelred Graham refers to belief in an unseen 'without any real knowledge of it', he is using the term 'knowledge' in a narrow, positivist Western sense – more or less what a Hindu means by 'illusion'!

23 Ross, N. W. (1968), *Hinduism, Buddhism, Zen*, 32.

24 Johnston, W. (1970), *The Still Point*, 51.

25 The Song of Songs 5:2.

26 '*Ce serait une erreur de penser que l'Inde a dû attendre d'entrer en contact avec l'Occident pour réaliser le caractère insuffisant d'une attitude de vie purement fataliste. La littérature populaire ancienne, indifférente aux discussions philosophiques, avait une vue beaucoup plus saine de la vie.*' de Smet & Neuner (eds) (1967), *La Quête de l'Eternel*, 134.

27 del Vasto, Lanza, op. cit., 90.

28 Buber, M. (1970), *Tales of the Hasidim*, Introduction.

29 Suzuki, D. T. (1970), *Shin Buddhism*, 90.

30 Yeats actually said, 'We only believe those thoughts which have been conceived not in the brain but in the whole body'.

31 del Vasto, Lanza, op. cit., 37.

32 Tenko-San (1969), op. cit., 61.

33 A collection of letters written by Hakuin (1685–1769) to his disciples.

34 Suzuki D. T. (1970), *The Field of Zen*, 4.

35 Matthew 7:26.

36 Matthew 12:45.

37 Abhishiktananda (1970), *Gnanananda*, 152.

38 Reps, Paul (1971), *Zen Flesh, Zen Bones*, 39.

39 Graham, A. (1968), *Conversations: Christian and Buddhist*, 27.

40 Frankl, Victor (1970), *Psychotherapy and Existentialism*, 50.

41 Buber, Martin (ed.) op. cit., vol. II, 302.

42 Dunlop, J. B. (1972), *Staretz Amvrosy.*

43 Zander, V. (1968), *Saint Seraphim of Sarov.*

44 Fedotov, G. P. (1946), *The Russian Religious Mind*, 340.

45 Reps, Paul, op. cit., 17.

46 Shibayama, Z., op. cit., 43.

47 Tenko-San, op. cit., 176–7. Contrast the remark of the English Benedictine monk, Aelred Graham, in his book, *The End of Religion*, 164: 'The depiction of an almost naked human being nailed to a cross as an object to be revered is unintelligible, with its presentation of barbarous cruelty, to a devout Buddhist, who is predisposed to regard violent death in any form as a result of "bad karma" '.

48 Ross, N. W., op. cit., 94.

49 Kadloubovsky, E. and Palmer, G. E. H., *Early Fathers from the Philokalia*, 185.

50 Clément, O. (1969), op. cit., 254.

51 For Silouan, see Sofrony's *The Monk of Athos* (1973).

52 Shibayama, Z., op. cit., *A Flower does not Talk*, 137.

53 Ross, N. W., op. cit., 140.

54 *Little Flowers of St Francis*, ch. VIII.

55 Tennyson, Hallam, *Saint on the March*, 89.

56 Buber, M., op. cit., vol. I, 245.

57 Kaltenmark, M. (1969), *Lao Tzu and Taoism*, 8.

58 Zaehner, R. C. (1970), *Concordant Discord*, 221, quoting Tao Te Ching, 67.

59 Ross, N. W., op. cit., 142.

60 Tenko-San, op. cit., 67.

61 Suzuki, D. T. (1970), *Shin Buddhism*, 48.

62 *Ibid.*, 75.

63 Shibayama, Z., op. cit., 137 ff.

64 (1960) *The Life of Swami Vivekananda*, 677

65 Suzuki, D. T. (1960), *Shin Buddhism*, 26.

66 Suzuki, D. T. (1970), *Zen and Japanese Culture*, 365.

67 Osborne, A. *The Teachings of Ramana Maharshi*, 99.

68 Meares, A. (1969), *Strange Places and Simple Truths*, 29.

69 Muggeridge, M. (1971), *Something Beautiful for God*, 17–18, 126, 145.

70 Fedotov, G. P. (1950), *A Treasury of Russian Spirituality*, 265–79.

71 Bulgakov, V. F. (1971), *The Last Year of Leo Tolstoy*, 29.

72 Tolstoy, L. (1942), *War and Peace*, 1066–7.

73 Il'im, V. N. (1925), *Prepodobnij Seraphim Sarovskij* (Russian), 70–71, 45, 44.

74 Kaltenmark, M., op. cit., 48.

75 Dobbie-Bateman, A. (1970), *The Return of Saint Seraphim.*

76 Buber, Martin (ed.), op. cit., vol. II. Buber's version is rather different from the one I have given, which I received from oral tradition.

77 Fedotov, G. P. (1946), *The Russian Religious Mind*, 283.

78 *Philosophia obshevo dela*, vol. I, 176.

79 Ross, N. W., op. cit., 176.

80 Scholem, G. C. (1955), *Main Trends in Jewish Mysticism*, 233.

81 Scholem, G. C. (1971), 'The tradition of the thirty-six hidden just men', in *The Messianic Idea in Judaism*, 251–66.

82 See Solzhenitzyn's Story, *Matryona's House*, where he says of Matryona, 'None of us who lived close to her perceived that she was that one righteous person without whom, as the saying goes, no city can stand. Nor the world.'

83 Wiesel, Elie, *Legends of Our Time*, 124 ff; cf. David Jones, *In Parenthesis*, 'In mind of all common and hidden men, and of the secret prince'.

84 de Lubac, Henri (1967), *Images de l'Abbé Monchanin*, 45.

85 Fyodorov, N., *Philosophia obshevo dela*, vol. 1, 46, 95, 131, 133, 139 and 260.

86 Daniel 3.

87   Clément, O. (1969), op. cit., 244, 188.
88   Goullart, P. (1961), *The Monastery of the Jade Mountain*, 139.
89   Bennett, J. G. (1965), *Long Pilgrimage*, 32.
90   de Beausobre, Julia (1946), *Flame in the Snow*, 107.
91   This was told me by a Hasid.
92   Cuttat, J. A. (1961), 'Incarnation and *avatara*', *Frontier*, 267–70.
93   Panikkar, R. (1969), 'Confrontation between Hinduism and Christ', *New Blackfriars*, 200.
94   Tenko-San, op. cit., 174.
95   Buber, M. (1948), *Israel and the World*, 39.
96   Waardenburg, J. and J. (1962), *L'Islam dans le miroir de l'occident*, 166.
97   Cuttat, J. A. (1961), *Frontier*, 267–70.

Chapter 14: Jews and Eastern religions

First published in *Christian*, Epiphany 1980.
1   Goullart, P. (1961), *The Monastery of the Jade Mountain*.
2   Kaifeng seems to have been spelt in two different ways – Kaifeng or Kai Feng!
3   Quoted by André Chouraqui (1971), *Lettre à un ami chrétien*, 167.
4   *Petahim* No. 3, 4.
5   Loewe, Raphael, *Studies in Rationalism, Judaism and Universalism*, 144.
6   Rosenzweig, Franz (1971), *The Star of Redemption*, 36, 37, 38.
7   Maybaum, I. (1966), *Studies in Rationalism, Judaism and Universalism*, 162; (1965) *The Face of God After Auschwitz*, 38.
8   cf. Flohr, P. R., 'The Road to I and Thou', in *Texts and Responses. Studies Presented to Nahum N. Glatzer*, 201–25.
9   Buber, M. (1972), *Briefwechsel*, 326.
10   Buber, M. (1973), *Briefwechsel II*, 78.
11   Hodes, A. (1972), *Encounter with Martin Buber*, 189.
12   Schlipp and Friedman (eds), *The Philosophy of Martin Buber*, 732.
13   Schaya, Leo (1973), *The Universal Meaning of the Kabbalah*, 137.
14   Judaica yearbook 1974, 206.
15   Scholem, Gershom (1974), 'Jewish theology today', *Center Magazine*, 58–72.

Chapter 15: A Buddhist contribution to peace spirituality

First published in Sri Lanka, in *Dialogue*, December–January 1985–6.

Chapter 16: Abhishiktananda

First published as a foreword to James Stewart's book *Abhishiktananda: His Life Told through Letters*, 1989, ISPCK.

Chapter 17: Inter-faith

First published in *Shabda Shakti Sangam*, edited by Vandana Mataji, 1995.